THE TROUBLE
THEY SEEN

THE TROUBLE
THEY SEEN

Black People Tell the
Story of Reconstruction

edited by

DOROTHY STERLING

Doubleday & Company, Inc.
GARDEN CITY, NEW YORK

LIBRARY OF CONGRESS CATALOGING IN PUBLICATION DATA
Main entry under title:
The Trouble They Seen
Includes index.
1. Negroes—History—1863–1877—Sources. 2. Reconstruction—Sources.
I. Sterling, Dorothy, 1913–
E185.3.S65   973'.04'96073
ISBN: 0-385-00476-1 Trade
        0-385-08007-7 Prebound   Oct. 18, 1976
Library of Congress Catalog Card Number 75–19218   75- 192188

All pictures not otherwise credited are from Dorothy Sterling's files.

FOREWORD

In the writing and teaching of American history, Reconstruction, until recently, has been treated as a disreputable episode. To most people it still conjures up a picture of impoverished but proud white Southerners, ennobled by defeat, patiently enduring a decade of misrule. Arrayed against them were the forces of darkness: vindictive congressional leaders, rapscallion carpetbaggers, renegade scalawags, and their ignorant and brutalized Negro tools. But Reconstruction, cleansed of its political connotations, simply means "to build anew." A period of reconstruction has followed all wars from the days of Genghis Khan to the present. Somebody has to govern, to make life livable again in the conquered land. The question, always, is how to restore or change its social order and at whose expense.

During the reconstruction of Germany after its defeat in World War II, Allied armies occupied the country, dismantled its military machine and brought its leaders to trial as war criminals. Because the Nazis believed they were a "master race" ordained to rule over the inferior peoples of the world, the Allied command, under the guidance of its Psychological Warfare Division, carried out an elaborate program of de-Nazification. Nazi editors, writers and teachers were silenced and all the informational and educational media were mobilized to indoctrinate the German people with a belief in democracy.

Germany's defeat meant freedom for millions of surviving slave laborers and concentration camp inmates. International relief organizations took over the immediate task of housing and feeding them and reuniting them with their families. Later, the German government was required to pay more than a billion dollars in reparations to the survivors of the camps, the relatives of those who had been killed, and to the new state of Israel where the majority of the refugees went to build a new life.

Germany in 1945 was very different from the American South eighty years earlier, but there are illuminating parallels. The Civil War was a "brothers' war." The army of occupation that remained in the South was engaged in restoring the economy and returning the region to home rule as rapidly as possible. No Confederate leaders—with the exception of Jefferson Davis who spent two years in prison—were punished for their rebellion against the United States. Their lands and their citizenship were quickly restored.

Like the Third Reich, the Confederacy rested on a racist foundation. It was founded, said Alexander Stephens, its vice-president, "upon the great truth that the Negro is not equal to the white man. That slavery—subordination to the superior race—is his natural and normal condition." No effort was made to stop the dissemination of these racist ideas.

Within weeks after the peace treaty was signed, southern spokesmen were again expounding them in the press and public forums. Less than two years later, Confederate generals were leading a battle for white supremacy with the whips and guns of the Ku Klux Klan.

The defeat of the Confederacy meant freedom for four million slaves. Although they were not broken in body and spirit as were the inmates of the Nazi concentration camps, they were nevertheless homeless, disoriented and in need of protection against their former masters. The Freedmen's Bureau and private freedmen's aid societies stepped in, as UNRRA did in 1945, to supply their immediate needs, but a plan to give them land which would make them self-supporting was quickly abandoned. Reparations for two hundred years of forced labor? When the subject came up at all, it was in terms of compensation to the slaveowners for the loss of their human property. And the possibility of a return to their African homeland was scarcely considered.

In the frontier tradition of the nineteenth century, the freed slaves were told to "root, hog, or die!" Even black leaders saw little wrong with this philosophy. Speaking in April 1865, Frederick Douglass said, "Everybody has asked, 'What shall we do with the Negro?' I have but one answer. Do nothing with us! If the apples will not remain on the tree of their own strength, let them fall! I am not for tying them on the tree in any way. And if the Negro cannot stand on his own legs, let him fall also. All I ask is, give him a chance. If you see him on his way to school, let him alone. If you see him going to the dinner-table at a hotel, let him go! If you see him going to the ballot-box, don't disturb him. If you see him going into a workshop, just let him alone. If you will only untie his hands and give him a chance, I think he will live. He will work as readily for himself as the white man."

Douglass soon realized that his optimism was misplaced. The freedmen *were* let alone—by everyone but their enemies.

For a brief period they were permitted to vote and to participate in governing themselves. But the ballot and the outward forms of democracy were not sufficient armor against oppression. Black people did not own the plantations, the cotton gins, the stores where they traded. Without land, stock, tools—and repeating rifles—they were at the mercy of their former owners, economically and physically. They stood against a withering fire until their friends deserted them.

For a short time, the promise of an integrated society seemed real and immediate. "We are all together now," Frederick Douglass said when the Fifteenth Amendment was passed. "We are made up of a variety of nations—Chinese, Jews, Africans, Europeans." But the promise vanished in 1877.

This was Reconstruction, the period that John W. Burgess, professor of history at Columbia University described, in 1902, as "the most soul-sickening spectacle that Americans had ever been called upon to behold." His colleague, William A. Dunning, added, "All the forces that made for civilization were dominated by a mass of barbarous freedmen." Their viewpoint was unchallenged for more than thirty years, until W. E. B. Du Bois published his *Black Reconstruction in America*. In it he wrote:

"The chief witness in Reconstruction, the emancipated slave himself, has been almost barred from court. His written Reconstruction record has been largely destroyed and nearly always neglected. The Negro is refused a hearing because he was poor and ignorant. It is therefore assumed that all Negroes in Reconstruction were ignorant and that therefore a history of Reconstruction can quite ignore him. The result is that unfair caricatures of Negroes have been carefully preserved; but serious speeches, successful administration and upright character are almost universally ignored. Wherever a black head rises to historic view, it is promptly slain by an adjective—'shrewd,' 'notorious,' 'cunning'—or pilloried by a sneer, or put out of view by some quite unproven charge of bad moral character. In other words, every effort has been made to treat the Negro's part in Reconstruction with silence and contempt."

Since the publication of Du Bois's book, scholars have begun to re-evaluate the period and many of the old stereotypes have fallen by the wayside. There have been several thoughtful studies of the role of black people in Reconstruction. However, with the exception of Lerone Bennett's *Black Power U.S.A.*, even the best of these depend largely on white sources—on letters and newspaper articles written by men who believed in black inferiority.

In this book, black people tell their own story. The speeches and letters of black leaders have been taken from black newspapers and manuscript collections, national and state archives. For "the chief witness in Reconstruction, the emancipated slave," I have turned to an extensive collection of oral history. A new tool for historians, oral history is being used increasingly to capture the experiences of the poor and illiterate who, because they left no written records of their lives have been omitted from most historical accounts or have been presented inaccurately. This is particularly true of black people whose past, until recently, has been largely recorded by whites. To correct for this bias, a new oral history program at Duke University, for instance, is training students to "go to the folk"—to interview ordinary black people about their lives. Obviously it is no longer possible to tape-record the recollections of black Reconstructionists, but their oral history exists and can be found in libraries across the country.

For fifteen years after the Civil War, teams of congressmen and senators visited the South to investigate conditions, find the causes of riots, evaluate disputed elections and, in 1880, to learn the reasons for a mass exodus of black people from the region. The congressmen "went to the folk," interviewing blacks as well as whites. While the witnesses talked frankly, government stenographers took down their words. Historians have used these House and Senate reports—which total more than two dozen volumes—for studies of the Ku Klux Klan or the exodus from the South, but no one has gone through them systematically to study black actions and reactions during Reconstruction. Without attempting to read every word of the twelve thousand-plus pages of these documents, I have found them a source of incomparable riches, filled with human drama and emotion as well as eyewitness reporting of significant events. Here is material for the novelist and playwright, the folklorist and sociologist, as well as the historian.

As I read through the interviews, selecting and editing those which appear in the pages that follow, I came to a totally new perception of Reconstruction. Formerly I had thought of it as a "tragic era," a time of might-have-been when the problems which still divide this country could have been solved had there been enough men of foresight and good will to grapple with them. The tragedy is still there, but along with it there is evidence of a remarkable flowering—a triumph of the human spirit. For two centuries, the slaves were hemmed in, brutalized, forced to believe in their inferiority. Overnight, when emancipation gave them the chance to control their destinies, they seemed transformed. They became students, teachers, preachers, lawmakers, soldiers, each with his own particular brand of eloquence and mother wit. In no other period of our history—not at Valley Forge or in the forests of the frontier—have Americans demonstrated more raw courage in the face of adversity or a greater dignity than the black people of the South in the years after the Civil War. Do I exaggerate? Read the story of Miles Prior who defended his village single-handed against midnight marauders. Or of Charles Caldwell who stood erect, pulling the sides of his coat together just so, as his enemies riddled him with bullets. Or of Henry Adams, the ex-slave who traveled from plantation to plantation to tell farm laborers how to organize to fight for their rights.

In no other period of our history have so many ordinary people become heroes overnight—until "the second Reconstruction" of our own time when the black children of the South hammered on the doors of white schools and their parents chose to walk rather than ride any longer in the back of the bus. Once again the Klan swarmed along the back roads and byways of the South. Once again people braved death in a struggle for their rights.

Resemblance between the two eras is so striking that the span of time between them often seems illusory. Did the children of New Orleans integrate their schools in 1871 or 1960? Was it Charles Caldwell who was gunned down— or Medgar Evers? Was it a preacher of the 1870s or Martin Luther King, Jr., who predicted that historians would some day say, "There lived a great people, a black people, who injected new meaning and dignity into the veins of civilization"?

The Trouble They Seen is not a comprehensive history of Reconstruction. The struggle between Congress and President Johnson, the role of sympathetic white men like Thaddeus Stevens and Charles Sumner, the activities of blacks in the North and West, the passage of the Fourteenth and Fifteenth Amendments are scarcely mentioned. And even within the limits of my chosen theme, I have been obliged to omit many stories and abridge others.

I regretfully discarded letters and speeches by Henry M. Turner, who was writing some of the most trenchant prose of the nineteenth century. I had hoped to include more from Tunis G. Campbell, who has been written off by Georgia historians as a mountebank and scoundrel, but who was in fact one of the first men of his time to understand the strength of black unity and power. Had there been no Civil War and Reconstruction, Campbell might have remained a hotel waiter all his life. But the times transformed him into a teacher, preacher, state senator, justice of the peace and the capable political boss of a Georgia county where blacks outnumbered whites by four to one. I would have liked to investigate further the activities of Thomas W. Cardozo, Mississippi's superintendent of education from 1874 to 1876. Vernon Wharton, in his excellent and sympathetic study of *The Negro in Mississippi, 1865–1890*, dismisses Cardozo as a corruptionist. Perhaps he was. Or perhaps Wharton, who failed to read the black press to which Cardozo was a frequent contributor, accepted the charges of Cardozo's enemies without verifying them.

My favorite figure, in the pages that follow, is Henry Adams. Historians have written about Adams as a leader of the exodus from the South, but he has never been mentioned before in accounts of Reconstruction. Yet he spent fourteen years in rural Louisiana, Arkansas and Texas organizing laborers, shunning "the politicianers" and keeping written records of what he saw. A one-man investigating committee, his observations and penciled notes of "Affairs and Outrages" cover more than one hundred pages of a Senate report. I was able to reprint only a small segment of them.

There are a dozen other themes that suggest themselves for further study. No one has gone through the voluminous records of the Freedmen's Bureau to report on its black officers and agents. There has been no detailed study of the role of black men in the constitutional conventions of 1867–68 or of the multifold activities of black women throughout the period. Some records were destroyed when Reconstruction came to a close, but a systematic investigation of the state archives might still turn up illuminating correspondence from black legislators and cabinet officers. Although several books about the black congressmen have been recently published, there is need for a critical study of the black elite whose goals did not always coincide with those of their constituents.

A word about the documents themselves. In order to avoid a book twice the length of this one, I have made extensive cuts without, however, altering the original meaning of the writer and speaker. Spelling and punctuation have been modernized and, occasionally, tenses or sequences changed for greater clarity. When a word has been added to make the writer's meaning clear, the addition is in brackets. The source is given after each selection except, as indicated, when a number of selections come from the same government document. Perhaps a dozen times in the course of the book, white writers are quoted to round out the story. With the exception of these and my introductory notes, this book is the product of the black people of the South, the main actors and chief witnesses in the drama that we call Reconstruction.

Dorothy Sterling

ACKNOWLEDGMENTS

I am deeply indebted to the staffs of the libraries and historical societies whose manuscript collections were consulted. Dr. Dorothy Porter, former curator of the Moorland-Spingarn Research Center at Howard University, helped me to locate documents, loaned me pictures from her own files as well as from the collection and responded promptly and generously to all my inquiries. Mrs. Jean Hutson and her staff at the Schomburg Collection were, as always, knowledgeable and helpful. Clifton H. Johnson, executive director of the Amistad Research Center, spent many hours going through the files of the American Missionary Association to select significant letters from black teachers and students. I would also like to thank the staffs of the National Archives, the Manuscript Division of the Library of Congress, the

South Carolina Department of Archives and History, and the South Caroliniana Library for their assistance.

I am grateful to a number of historians and writers who made available the products of their own research for use in the pages which follow. Peggy Lamson, author of *The Glorious Failure, Black Congressman Robert B. Elliott and the Reconstruction in South Carolina* (Norton, 1973), a perceptive biography and one of the very few modern accounts of the life of a black congressman, sent me copies of Elliott's letters and speeches as well as pictures that she had collected. Edward K. Graham, author of a soon-to-be published study of Hampton Institute, *A Tender Violence: General Armstrong and the Hampton Heritage,* has loaned me innumerable letters from students and teachers at Hampton and has given me a broad overview of the black colleges of the Reconstruction era. William W. Rogers, author with Robert D. Ward, of *August Reckoning, Jack Turner and Racism in Post-Civil War Alabama* (Louisiana State University Press, 1973), an excellent study of a "plantation orator" of the Reconstruction period and the first of its kind, sent me Jack Turner's letter to the governor of Alabama which appears in Part VI. Joe M. Richardson, author of *The Negro in the Reconstruction of Florida* (Florida State University, 1965) gave me some difficult-to-locate writings of Jonathan Gibbs's. Dr. Pauli Murray was kind enough to transcribe the pages from her grandfather, Robert Fitzgerald's diary which appear in Part II. Victor and Louise Ullman turned over to me their voluminous research on Reconstruction in South Carolina, which they collected while writing *Martin R. Delany, The Beginnings of Black Nationalism* (Beacon, 1971).

My greatest debt is to my husband, Philip Sterling, who helped immeasurably in selecting and editing documents and whose final critical reading of the manuscript was invaluable.

CONTENTS

You say you have emancipated us. You have; and I thank you for it. But what is your emancipation?

When the Israelites were emancipated they were told to go and borrow of their neighbors—borrow their coin, borrow their jewels, load themselves down with the means of subsistence; after, they should go free in the land which the Lord God gave them. When the Russian serfs had their chains broken and were given their liberty, the government of Russia—aye, the despotic government of Russia—gave to those poor emancipated serfs a few acres of land on which they could live and earn their bread.

But when you turned us loose, you gave us no acres. You turned us loose to the sky, to the storm, to the whirlwind, and, worst of all, you turned us loose to the wrath of our infuriated masters.

—*Frederick Douglass, 1876*

I· YEAR ONE

No more is heard the driver's whip and horn
Resounding thru the cotton and the corn;
The slave-hounds in the swamp no longer bark,
The slave no longer travels in the dark,
But in great freedom's light, of recent birth,
He walks erect, a sovereign of the earth!

J. Willis Menard, July 4, 1867

1. Sweet Freedom's Song

When Charleston, South Carolina, was captured by Union forces in February 1865, the Twenty-first Regiment U. S. Colored Troops was the first to enter the city. A black soldier on muleback with a banner that proclaimed LIBERTY led the regiment through the narrow streets. An old woman who tried to embrace the soldier hugged his mule instead as she cried, "Thank God!" Another woman danced for joy.

"I am sixty-nine years old," she said, "but I feel as if I wan't but sixteen!" She broke into a chant:

Ye's long been a-comin'
Ye's long been a-comin'
Ye's long been a-comin'
For to take the land.

The National Freedman, April 1, 1865

A month later, the city's black men and women organized a parade:

It was a jubilee of freedom, a hosannah to their deliverers. First came the marshals and their aids, followed by a band of music; then the Twenty-first Regiment; then the clergymen of the different churches, carrying open Bibles; then an open car drawn by four white horses. In this car there were 15 colored ladies dressed in white—to represent the 15 recent Slave States. A long procession of women followed the car. Then the children—1,800 in line, at least. They sang:

John Brown's body lies a moulding in the grave,
We go marching on!

This verse, however, was not nearly so popular as one which rapidly supplanted all the others, until along the mile or more of children, marching two abreast, no other sound could be heard than

We'll hang Jeff Davis on a sour apple tree!
As we go marching on!

After the children came the various trades. The fishermen, with a banner bearing an emblematical device and the words, "The Fishermen welcome you, General Saxton." Carpenters, masons, teamsters, drovers, coopers, bakers, paper-carriers, barbers, blacksmiths, wood-sawyers, painters, wheelwrights and the fire companies. The carpenters carried their planes, the masons their trowels, the teamsters their whips; the coopers their adzes. The bakers' crackers hung around their necks; the paper-carriers [had] a banner, and each a copy of the Charleston *Courier;* the wheelwrights a large wheel; and the fire companies, ten in number, their foremen with their trumpets.

A large cart, drawn by two dilapidated horses, followed the trades. On this cart was an auctioneer's block and a

Oh, Freedom! (*Boston Public Library*)

black man with a bell represented a Negro trader. This man had himself been sold several times and two women and a child who sat on the block had also been knocked down at auction in Charleston.

As the cart moved along, the mock-auctioneer rang his bell and cried out: "How much am I offered for this good cook? She is an excellent cook, gentlemen. She can make four kinds of mock turtle soup—from beef, fish or fowl. Who bids?"

"Two hundred's bid! Two-fifty. Three hundred."

"Who bids? Who bids?"

Women burst into tears as they saw this tableau and forgetting that it was a mimic scene, shouted wildly:

"Give me back my children! Give me back my children!"

New York *Daily Tribune*, April 4, 1865

There were parades everywhere that summer. A reporter for The New Orleans *Tribune*, the first black daily newspaper, described events in Mobile on the Fourth of July. James H. Ingraham was an officer in the Louisiana Native Guards.

The Fourth was celebrated here by the colored population in fine style. The procession formed as follows: Two regiments of colored troops—Mechanics' and Draymen's Association—Steamboatmen's Association—Firemen's Association, consisting of eight companies—Benevolent Society—Daughters of Zion—Sons of Zion—Missionary Society—Young Men's Association—Sisters of Charity and many others whose names I did not learn. A large number of enfranchised citizens turned out to witness the demonstration. Capt. J. H. Ingraham addressed the vast assembly in the public square. Upon the very spot where, a few years ago, the apostle of slavery (W. L. Yancey) declared that slavery was a divine institution, Ingraham and others declared that slavery was dead and will be buried so deep that the judgment will not find it! Everything passed off quietly and with satisfaction.

The Liberator, July 21, 1865

Celebration in Washington, D.C. (*Boston Public Library*)

Slavery's death and burial were certified by the Thirteenth Amendment to the Constitution, adopted at the end of the year. Four million people—almost a third of the population of the South—had been freed. Until then, they had been forbidden to read and write, to marry, to engage in even the simplest business transactions. But that was yesterday—the past. What of the future? For most freedmen, the vision was a simple one:

Free workmen in the cotton field
And in the sugar cane;
Free children in the common school
With nevermore a chain.

The Black Republican, April 29, 1865

But the question of how free these "free workmen" were to be was not that simple. Henry Adams, who was twenty-two at the end of the war, told about the first months of liberty on a plantation in Louisiana:

The white men read a paper to all of us colored people telling us that we were free and could go where we pleased and work for who we pleased. The man I belonged to told me it was best to stay with him. He said, "The bad white men was mad with the Negroes because they were free and they would kill you all for fun." He said, stay where we are living and we could get protection from our old masters.

I told him I thought that every man, when he was free, could have his rights and protect themselves. He said, "The colored people could never protect themselves among the white people. So you had all better stay with the white people who raised you and make contracts with them to work by the year for one-fifth of all you make. And next year you can get one-third, and the next you maybe work for one-half you make. We have contracts for you all to sign, to work for one-twentieth you make from now until the crop is ended, and then next year you all can make another crop and get more of it."

I told him I would not sign anything. I said, "I might sign to be killed. I believe the white people is trying to fool us." But he said again, "Sign this contract so I can take it to the Yankees and have it recorded." All our colored people signed it but myself and a boy named Samuel Jefferson. All who lived on the place was about sixty, young and old.

On the day after all had signed the contracts, we went to cutting oats. I asked the boss, "Could we get any of the oats?" He said, "No; the oats were made before you were free." After that he told us to get timber to build a sugar-mill to make molasses. We did so. On the 13th day of July 1865 we started to pull fodder. I asked the boss would he make a bargain to give us half of all the fodder we would pull. He said we may pull two or three stacks and then we could have all the other. I told him we wanted half, so if we only pulled two or three stacks we would get half of that. He said, "All right." We got that and part of the corn we made. We made five bales of cotton but we did not get a pound of that. We made two or three hundred gallons of molasses and only got what we could eat. We made about eight-hundred bushel of potatoes; we got a few to eat. We split rails three or four weeks and got not a cent for that.

In September I asked the boss to let me go to Shreveport. He said, "All right, when will you come back?" I told him "next week." He said, "You had better carry a pass." I said, "I will see whether I am free by going without a pass."

I met four white men about six miles south of Keachie, De Soto Parish. One of them asked me who I belonged to. I told him no one. So him and two others struck me with a stick and told me they were going to kill me and every other Negro who told them that they did not belong to anyone. One of them who knew me told the others, "Let Henry alone for he is a hard-working nigger and a good nigger." They left me and I then went on to Shreveport. I seen over twelve colored men and women, beat, shot and hung between there and Shreveport.

Sunday I went back home. The boss was not at home. I asked the madame where was the boss? She says, "Now, the boss; now, the boss! You should say 'master' and 'mistress'— and shall or leave. We will not have no nigger here on our place who cannot say 'mistress' and 'master.' You all are not free yet and will not be until Congress sits, and you shall call every white lady 'missus' and every white man 'master.'"

During the same week the madame taken a stick and beat

one of the young colored girls, who was about fifteen years of age and who is my sister, and split her back. The boss came next day and take this same girl (my sister) and whipped her nearly to death, but in the contracts he was to hit no one any more. After the whipping a large number of young colored people taken a notion to leave. On the 18th of September I and eleven men and boys left that place and started for Shreveport. I had my horse along. My brother was riding him, and all of our things was packed on him. Out come about forty armed men (white) and shot at us and taken my horse. Said they were going to kill every nigger they found leaving their masters; and taking all of our clothes and bed-clothing and money. I had to work away to get a white man to get my horse.

Then I got a wagon and went to peddling, and had to get a pass, according to the laws of the parishes, to do so. In October I was searched for pistols and robbed of $250 by a large crowd of white men and the law would do nothing about it. The same crowd of white men broke up five churches (colored). When any of us would leave the white people, they would take everything we had, all the money that we made on their places. They killed many hundreds of my race when they were running away to get freedom.

After they told us we were free—even then they would not let us live as man and wife together. And when we would run away to be free, the white people would not let us come on their places to see our mothers, wives, sisters, or fathers. We was made to leave or go back and live as slaves. To my own knowledge there was over two thousand colored people killed trying to get away after the white people told us we were free in 1865. This was between Shreveport and Logansport.

Senate Report 693, 46th Congress, 2nd Session

T. Thomas Fortune

T. Thomas Fortune, a prominent newspaper editor in the 1880s–90s, was eight years old when freedom found his village, Marianna, in Jackson County, Florida. He later recalled:

The county of Jackson was upset by the close of the war and the emancipation of the slaves. Nobody had his bearings. The freed people [had] no homes and no names except such as they inherited from their owners. They were in such a frame of mind as not to know whether to rejoice because they were free or to be cast down at their new condition of freedom, responsibility and homelessness.

And then something happened which had never before happened in Jackson county. A former Confederate soldier shot to death young John Gilbert, a popular Negro. Gilbert had a load of wood, drawn by a stout team, coming to town when he was confronted by Sergeant Barnes who commanded him to turn out of the road. This he did as far as possible, but it did not satisfy the sergeant who drew his service revolver and shot the young man. Negro men and women swarmed into the village, fighting mad and determined to be avenged. The village and nearby swamps and forests were thoroughly searched for the bloody miscreant but he eluded capture.

The changed attitude of the white people, the hostility which was everywhere evident gave [the Negroes] a great deal of concern. They were in the midst of their troubles when a detachment of Union soldiers was quartered among them. This was a very great event. They made friends with the Negro people and with the few white loyalists. They represented the Union government in preserving law and order and in the adjustment of the labor relations of the former masters and slaves. They furnished Bibles to all the Negro people who wished them and they remarried all of the Negro men and women who had contracted slave unions and desired to have them legalized. Few, indeed, failed to avail themselves of the chance to do this.

Another important event was the opening of a Freedmen's school in the Negro church. Sergeant Smith and Private Davenport were detailed to the work of teaching the little black children their first lessons. The school was crowded with eager pupils from the beginning and the teachers had very smooth sailing as all were anxious to master Webster's blue-back speller.

Free Children

The soldiers had dress parade twice a day and all of the urchins of the village were on hand to watch it. They thought it was the grandest thing ever. They were transported by the drumbeating and bugle blowing. The bugle call for afternoon drill and parade was heard for miles around and was the first and sweetest music the freed people had ever heard. Have they heard any sweeter since? I doubt it.

Norfolk *Journal and Guide,* July 30, 1927

2. Ambrose, You Must Be Dreaming

What did the freedmen want? What was to be done with them? All during "the year of jubilee" observers from the North traveled South seeking answers to these questions. An early report came from James T. Lynch, a black minister who had left his home in Baltimore to work as a missionary and teacher. Two weeks after General W. T. Sherman's army took Savannah, Lynch wrote to the New York Freedmen's Relief Association:

Savannah, January 4, 1865

My Dear Sir:

I have been here for some days. The colored people did not seem to realize that they were free, as their status was not announced by any proclamation. The scarcity of provisions, the unsettled state of things, no employment—all these had the effect of causing our people to stand on the threshold of freedom like the rescued passengers of a ship on a barren sea-shore, wet and shivering with the cold blast of the tempest. They wanted encouragement, advice, and strength to go forward and assume the responsibilities of free men.

I am happy to say they have been growing every day and seem to lose that dread which slavery had made a second nature. There are a great many very intelligent colored persons in Savannah. We have been holding large meetings of the colored citizens. The interest evoked has been great, and the promise of good being done is bright.

We have secured from the Government the use of three large buildings:

1. "A. Bryant's Negro Mart" (thus reads the sign over the door). It is a large three-story brick building. In this place slaves had been bought and sold for many years. We have found many "gems" such as handcuffs, whips and staples for tying, etc. Bills of sales of slaves by hundreds all giving a faithful description of the hellish business. This we are going to use for school purposes.

2. The Stiles house on Farm Street, formerly used as a rebel hospital, we have also secured for school purposes.

3. A large three-story brick building on the lot adjoining for a hospital for freedmen.

We have organized an Association called the Savannah Educational Association, composed of the pastors and members of the colored churches. There are five very large colored churches in this city, four of them will seat one thousand persons each. Three have fine organs. That the colored people built such churches is astonishing. Hundreds of the colored people are joining the Association as *honorary members.*

We have examined some of the most intelligent of the colored young men and women to ascertain their qualifications for teaching and selected nine. This makes use of the ability and intelligence possessed by the colored people themselves, and gives them confidence and encouragement.

Refugees are continually coming in and filling up the city. I trust that your Association will soon have teachers here. Oh, how much books are needed! We could use right away a thousand spelling-books, if we had them.

James Lynch

The National Freedman, February 1, 1865

Before the Rebellion there had been no public school systems in the southern states. The children of well-to-do whites went to private academies or were tutored at home. Poor whites and slaves received no education. During the war, schools for freedmen were organized in Union-held territory in the South. Set up in abandoned buildings or in crude makeshift structures, these schools were financed by freedmen's aid societies and religious groups in the North. Later the Freedmen's Bureau provided some buildings and supplies.

As a slave carpenter, Ambrose Headen had cut the timbers and sawed the beams for a Baptist Academy in Talladega, Alabama. After the war, when the building was purchased for a freedmen's school, Headen said:

Baptist Academy which Ambrose Headen helped build later became Talladega College (*American Missionary Association Archives, Amistad Research Center*)

It was a hard thing having to build that school for the white boys when I had no right to educate my son. Then when the war was over and they bought that building for our children, I could hardly believe my eyes—looking at my own little ones carrying their books under their arms, coming from the same school the Lord really raised up for them. I rubbed my eyes and said, "Ambrose, you must be dreaming."

The Saga of Talladega College
mimeographed (n.p.n.d.)

Black men and women from all walks of life went South to teach their newly freed brothers. Tunis G. Campbell had been a waiter in a New York hotel, a part-time minister, and the author of a book, *Hotel Keepers, Head Waiters and Housekeepers' Guide.* Turned down by the Army—he was fifty-three in 1865—he persisted in offering his services to the government until Secretary of War Stanton sent him south in March 1865. He organized schools on the Sea Islands off the coast of Georgia. After spending thousands of dollars of his own, he appealed to the American Missionary Association for help:

Saint Catherines Island, Georgia, April 11, 1866
To the Secretaries of the American Missionary Association
Gentlemen:

You will please excuse the liberty I have taken in thus addressing you. I was ordered to Sapelo & Saint Catherines Islands & since Ossabaw & Colonel's Islands have been added. In August last my son T. J. Campbell jr. came down as a Teacher & has since been joined by his wife as a Teacher, also Edward E. Howard, my adopted son. We organized 2 schools on Saint Catherines with an attendance of 250 scholars. We have kept these schools all through the winter from October last with the above number of scholars.

Brother Mobly gave me a few pamphlets & I bought a few Primers & Slates from him. He gave me a set of large cards

Tunis G. Campbell and title page of his book (*Moorland-Spingarn Research Center, Howard University*)

for Primary Scholars. Mr. E. A. Cooly gave me a few books of different kinds, but with these exceptions I have bought all I have had.

There are 2 schools wanted on Ossabaw, 3 on Sapelo and 2 on Colonel's Island. We have 2 on Saint Catherines with good Teachers but want Proper Buildings. I have supported

HOTEL KEEPERS,

HEAD WAITERS,

AND

HOUSEKEEPERS' GUIDE.

BY TUNIS G. CAMPBELL.

BOSTON:
PRINTED BY COOLIDGE AND WILEY,
12 WATER STREET.
1848.

the Three Teachers & Paid their way down. I find it a very severe task. I hope that you will consider our case. There are many calls upon you for the Freedmen but none that merit your attention more than this.

Tunis G. Campbell

American Missionary Association Archives,
Amistad Research Center

The American Missionary Association was the first northern-based organization to send teachers to the South. Even before the war was over, AMA secretary George Whipple was receiving letters of application like the following:

Binghamton, New York, January 18, 1864

Rev. George Whipple

Dear Sir:

I write to make an application to go South or Southwest as missionary. I have been engaged as teacher for two years and a half among my own people. I am about twenty years of age and strong and healthy. I know just what self-denial, self-discipline and domestic qualifications are needed for the work and modestly trust that with God's help I could labor advantageously in that field for my newly-freed brethren. I am engaged at present as a teacher here but I will resign as soon as an opportunity to go South presents itself.

Yours for Christ's poor,
Edmonia G. Highgate

American Missionary Association Archives,
Amistad Research Center

After teaching in Virginia, Edmonia Highgate wrote to the AMA from her post in Louisiana:

Lafayette Parish, Louisiana, December 17, 1866

Dear Friend:

I have a very interesting and constantly growing day school, a night school and a glorious Sabbath School of near one hundred scholars. The majority of my pupils come from plantations, three, four and even eight miles distant. So anxious are they to learn that they walk these distances so

Georgia schoolgirl teaching her grandfather to read (*Boston Public Library*)

early in the morning as never to be tardy. Every scholar buys his own book and slate &c. They, with but few exceptions, are French Creoles. My little knowledge of French is put in constant use in order to instruct them in our language. They do learn rapidly. A class who did not understand any English came to school last Monday morning and at the close of the week they were reading "easy lessons."

There is but little actual want among these freed people. The corn, cotton and sugar crops have been abundant. Most of the men, women and large children are hired by the year upon the plantations of their former so-called masters. Most all of them are trying to buy a home of their own. Many of them own a little land on which they work nights in favorable weather and Sabbaths for themselves. They own cows and horses, besides raising poultry.

The great sin of Sabbath breaking I am trying to make them see in its proper light. But they urge so strongly its absolute necessity in order to keep from suffering that I am almost discouraged of convincing them. They are given greatly to the sin of adultery. Out of three hundred I found but three couple legally married. This fault was largely the masters and it has grown upon the people till they cease to see the wickedness of it.

My three schools take most of my time and strength. I am trying to carry on an Industrial School on Saturday. There are some aged ones here to whom I read the bible. But the distances are so great I must always hire conveyances and I can seldom get a horse.

There has been much opposition to the School. Twice I have been shot at in my room. My night school scholars have been shot but none killed. A week ago an aged freedman just across the way was shot so badly as to break his arm and leg. The rebels here threatened to burn down the school and house in which I board yet they have not materially harmed us. The nearest military protection is two hundred miles distant at New Orleans. But I trust fearlessly in God and am safe.

Edmonia G. Highgate

American Missionary Association Archives,
Amistad Research Center

Other teachers were less fortunate, as The New Orleans *Tribune* reported:

The citizens have opposed by all means in their power the continuance of the great work of education in the country parishes. They have refused to rent buildings for school purposes and to board the teachers. They have whipped Mr. LeBlanc at Point Coupee; dangerously stabbed in the back Mr. Burnham at Monroe; and beaten almost to death Mr. Ruby at Jackson. The record of the teachers of the first colored schools in Louisiana will be one of honor and blood.

The New Orleans *Tribune*, September 5, 1866

George T. Ruby who was "beaten almost to death" was a young New Yorker who taught school in Louisiana from 1864–66. Afterward he went to Texas where he became a newspaper editor and a member of the legislature. Of his experiences in rural Louisiana he said:

I was a traveling educational agent and organized schools in the early part of 1866. I went up into East Feliciana Parish and organized a school at the town of Clinton and also in the town of Jackson. I succeeded in getting a teacher for Clinton, but not for Jackson. The opposition to a school there was so sharp that no teacher could be obtained. I reported the result of my visit to the directors at New Orleans—to the Superintendent of Public Instruction there, and he asked me if I would not go back to Jackson and stay until a school was established and teachers were obtained for it.

I went back and they commenced making threats before I could get a suitable place for a schoolroom. Finally a school was established in the house where I boarded. When we opened the school a party of armed men came to my house, seized me, carried me out and threw me in Thompson's Creek after they had belabored me with the muzzles of their revolvers. Their plea was that they "did not want to have any damned nigger school in that town and were not going to have it."

Senate Report 693, 46th Congress, 2nd Session

In some rural areas even the children were harassed. T. Thomas Fortune recalled a battle in Marianna, Florida:

The white academy opened about the same time the church opened for school for the Negro children. As the colored children had to pass the academy to reach the church it was easy for the white children to annoy them with taunts and jeers. The war passed from words to stones which the white children began to hurl at the colored. Several colored children were hurt and, as they had not resented the rock-throwing in kind because they were timid about going that far, the white children became more aggressive and abusive.

One morning the colored children armed themselves with stones and determined to fight their way past the academy to their school. [They] approached the academy in formation whereas in the past they had been going in pairs or small groups. When they reached hailing distance, half

Students on their way to school (*Boston Public Library*)

dozen white boys rushed out and hurled their missiles. Instead of scampering away, the colored children not only stood their ground and hurled their missiles but maintained a solemn silence. The white children, seeing there was no backing down as they expected, came rushing out of the academy and charged the colored children.

During some fifteen minutes it was a real tug of war. In the close fighting the colored children got the advantage gradually and began to shove the white children back. As they pressed the advantage the white children broke away and ran for the academy. The colored fighters did not follow them but made it hot for the laggards until they also took to their heels. There were many bruises on both sides, but it taught the white youngsters to leave the colored ones alone thereafter.

Norfolk *Journal and Guide*, August 20, 1927

Not all of the teachers were Northerners. In cities like Charleston, Savannah and New Orleans, which had always had a substantial population of educated free black people, the freedmen's schools drew on local talent. The author of the following letter to William Lloyd Garrison, the noted abolitionist, was a doctor by profession:

New Orleans, October 14, 1865

Dear Mr. Garrison:

Among the eight large schools just established in this city is a large one named [Lloyd Garrison School]. Of this school I am Principal, assisted by five colored ladies and two white. We have been open two weeks and numbered 373 pupils last night, graded from the Primer to Fifth Reader—Monosyllables to Grammar—Object-counting to Fractions.

We are proud of our pupils and feel that you will rejoice with us. We feel, also that you will not take it amiss if we ask a little assistance from Boston in the shape of apparatus to illustrate astronomy, a gyroscope and microscope, conic sections, cube-root blocks, a magnet and such other instruments as will enable us to fight this battle for our race against ignorance.

Trusting that this appeal will not be in vain, I remain, dear sir, for another year's teaching here,

P. B. Randolph

The Liberator, November 10, 1865

Abraham Lincoln School in New Orleans was largest
freedmen's school in the South (*Boston Public Library*)

Noon recess at freedmen's school in Vicksburg, Mississippi
(*Boston Public Library*)

School in Charleston, South Carolina

Ex-slaves who learned to read and write in the freedmen's schools remained to teach. One of them reported on her first days as a teacher:

Charlottesville, Virginia, October 15, 1866

I began my school on the 3rd of October with 42 scholars. The sphere into which I have been put is so different from slavery, I hardly knew what steps to take. I read a chapter in the Bible. I then told them I wanted they should conduct themselves so as to reflect credit on the school and their race, in education, and by moral improvements.

We had a meeting of the Freedmen's Aid Society on the first of this month. I read the compositions of Celia Woods and my son John. I think it did great good. They seemed as though their eyes had just been opened to see what education would do for them. All that were there joined the society. I hope we may be successful in aiding the schools here. The schools are filled but children still come to see if they can be admitted. I have sixty-three pupils.

Isabella Gibbins

The Freedmen's Record, November 1866

At annual exercises of the schools, pupils were put through their paces for the benefit of parents and northern visitors. A favorite device was the catechism, with an adult asking questions and the children replying in chorus. In a church in Richmond, a thousand pupils responded to the superintendent of schools:

Superintendent: Are you glad you are free?
Scholars: Yes, indeed.
Superintendent: Who gave you freedom?
Scholars: God.

Superintendent: Through whom?
Scholars: Abraham Lincoln.
Superintendent: Do you want these friends here to go North and send you more teachers?
Scholars: Yes, indeed.

The National Freedman, June 1865

Another catechism, conducted by an official of a Freedmen's aid society in Louisville, Kentucky, seemed less well-rehearsed:

Official: Now, children, you don't think white people are any better than you because they have straight hair and white faces?
Children: No, sir.
Official: No, they are no better, but they are different. They possess great power. They control this vast country. Now, what makes them different from you?
Children: MONEY.
Official: Yes, but how did they get money?
Children: Got it off us. Stole it off we all!

American Missionary, June 1866

3. The Promised Land

Looking back on the first months of freedom, an ex-slave wrote:

At the close of the war they were set free without a dollar, without a foot of land and without the wherewithal to get the next meal even. The labor of these people had for two hundred years cleared away the forests and produced crops that brought millions of dollars annually. It does seem to me that a Christian Nation would, at least, have given them one year's support, forty acres of land and a mule each.

Did they get that or any portion of it? Not a cent. Four million people turned loose without a dollar and told to "Root, hog or die!" Now, whose duty was it to feed them? Was it the former masters' or that of the government, which had conquered the masters, and freed their slaves? My opinion is that the government should have done it.

H. C. Bruce, *The New Man* (York, Pennsylvania, 1895)

In 1865 forty acres of land for each ex-slave and his family was not a dream born in the delirium of sudden freedom. Months before the treaty of peace was signed, the government had promised this to the freedmen—only to renege a year later.

The promise had come from an unlikely source. When General William T. Sherman's army marched across Georgia, tens of thousands of slaves left the plantations to follow him. Ragged, hungry, homeless, they clogged the roads, slept under bridges at night, threatened the health and discipline of his men. The stern-visaged general was no philanthropist, but something practical had to be done with the freedmen. When Secretary of War Stanton visited Savannah in January 1865, twenty of the city's black leaders were summoned for a conference. Sixteen of the men who came to Sherman's headquarters had been slaves; only the Reverend James Lynch was a Northerner. The interview was conducted Army-style, with the black men receiving written questions and their spokesman, ex-slave Garrison Frazier, supplying written answers:

Q—State in what manner you think you can take care of yourselves.

A—The way we can best take care of ourselves is to have land, and turn it and till it by our own labor. We can soon maintain ourselves and have something to spare. We want to be placed on land until we are able to buy it and make it our own.

Q—State in what manner you would rather live; whether scattered among the whites or in colonies by yourselves.

A—I would prefer to live by ourselves. There is a prejudice against us in the South that will take years to get over, but I do not know that I can answer for my brethren. (Mr. Lynch says he thinks they should not be separated, but live together. All the other persons present, being questioned one by one, answer that they agree with Bro. Frazier.)

Q—Do you think that there is intelligence enough among the slaves to maintain themselves under the Government and maintain good and peaceable relations among yourselves and with your neighbors?

A—I think there is sufficient intelligence among us to do so.

The National Freedman, April 1, 1865

Four days later, with the assent of Secretary Stanton, Sherman issued a Special Field Order. It set aside the islands and coastal lands from Charleston, South Carolina, to the St. Johns River in Florida for black settlements. The order stated, in part:

Whenever three respectable Negroes, heads of families shall desire to settle on land and shall have selected for that purpose an island or locality, the Inspector of Settlements and Plantations will afford them such assistance as he can. The three parties named will subdivide the land so that each family shall have a plot of not more than forty acres of tillable ground.

In the settlement to be established, no white person whatever, unless soldiers detailed for duty will be permitted to reside and the sole and exclusive management of affairs will be left to the free people themselves, subject only to the United States military authority and the acts of Congress.

National Archives

The promise was clear. Forty acres of land for each freedman and his family and self-governing black communities. The freedmen hastened to take advantage of the order. Early in February, Ulysses L. Houston, one of the men who had met with Sherman and Stanton, led a party of settlers to an island off Georgia's coast. A slave only six weeks earlier, Houston was described by a newspaperman who accompanied him as an example of the "rising brain power" of the South:

Last Friday, a party with Rev. Mr. Houston, pastor of the Third African Baptist Church, went down to Skidaway Island to select their future homes. Mr. Houston is now forty years old. In his early years he was a nurse in the marine hospital. He had an earnest desire to learn to read and by his kind attention to the sailors was enabled to do so.

He hired his time, paying his master fifty dollars a month, and established himself as a butcher. He went all over Eastern Georgia, purchasing cattle, but employing all his spare hours learning to read, studying the Bible and theology. He was ordained to preach by the Baptist Association of white ministers three years ago.

He and his fellow-colonists selected their lots, laid out a village, numbered the lots, put the numbers into a hat, and drew them out. It was Plymouth colony repeating itself.

"We shall build our cabins and organize our town government for the maintenance of order and the settlement of all difficulties," said Mr. Houston. He has four hundred hides, his own property. "I want to turn them into money, and purchase a portable saw-mill to cut out lumber for our houses."

In one day five thousand acres were assigned to the colonists who are eager to till them. A large party went down this morning with what provisions they could carry. They go out to commence life as citizens.

Yesterday there was a meeting of these men at the old slave market. The room was crowded. They came together to hear remarks from Rev. Mr. French and Lieut. Ketchum, to ask questions and consult with each other. They wanted to know what title they would have to their land—what assurances they could have that it would be theirs after they had improved it. Their questions were plain, straightforward, and showed a shrewdness which I had not looked for.

The National Freedman, April 1865

The question of titles to the land seemed to be settled the following month when Congress set up the Bureau of Refugees, Freedmen and Abandoned Lands. The government had charge of hundreds of thousands of acres in the South—plantations abandoned by Rebels during Union occupation of their districts or confiscated from them for non-payment of war taxes. Many of the plantations had been farmed by ex-slaves during the war, under the supervision of the army. Now Congress instructed the Freedmen's Bureau to set aside this land for loyal white refugees and freedmen:

. . . To every male citizen, whether refugee or freedman, there shall be assigned not more than forty acres of such

On a Sea Island plantation

land and the person to whom it was so assigned shall be protected in the use and enjoyment of the land for three years. At the end of said term, or at any time during said term, the occupants of any parcels so assigned may purchase the land and receive such title thereto as the United States can convey.

Congress had not been as generous as General Sherman. The land was no longer an outright gift but freedmen would be permitted to buy it after three years' occupancy. When General Rufus Saxton, long known as a friend to the freedmen, was put in charge of the Freedmen's Bureau in South Carolina, Georgia and Florida, black families flocked to the coast. By June 1865, forty thousand freedmen were cultivating three hundred thousand acres of land in the southeastern United States.

Tunis G. Campbell, the New York hotel waiter who had been sent south by Secretary Stanton, was one of the first black Northerners to aid in this giant resettlement project. Appointed an agent of the Freedmen's Bureau, he organized farming communities on the Georgia Sea Islands. From letters to an official of the New York Freedmen's Relief Association:

Beaufort, South Carolina, April 13, 1865

Dear Friend:

Called on Gen. Saxton; found him very gentlemanly and business like. The general told me to be ready to go with him to Savannah and Charleston and the Islands, but army movements called him off. I was kept until last Tuesday. Then he said I had better go with the boat that was taking the people to the islands and see what I thought was needed there.

We left with rations and a few families and at Hilton Head got more, and Savannah loaded us as deep as we could swim. With these we went to Ossabaw, Delaware, Saint Catherines, Sapelo and St. Simon's Islands, set them ashore with rations and seeds for planting.

As the season is late, I have begun to work on Sapelo Island, Georgia. I want you to get me ten barrels of sweet potatoes, seed. Please send them as soon as you get this.

These people want clothing for they are robbed of everything. We place them on the islands to work, but they must be covered, or the work of raising them morally or socially must fail. I want to open schools on all of the islands, therefore please get all the clothing and books you can. I want one set of single harness and one saddle for myself.

T. G. Campbell

Plowing in South Carolina (*Boston Public Library*)

Savannah, April 19, 1865

Sir:

I am at Savannah. I have been to Charleston at the raising of the old flag over Sumter. It was a great day.

I am on my way to Sapelo Island of which I am Government Superintendent. We are very late, but by a little exertion can get in a good crop of cotton. I have corn and Irish potatoes, watermelons, cucumbers and citron, tomatoes, onions, radishes, salad, beans and squashes. But the rebels have destroyed the sweet potatoes. Do not fail to send them.

I have got some of the finest cotton land in Georgia. Send eight No. 11 plows, six cultivators. Get the improved ones and twenty-four good hoes. Get them that we can put handles in readily, with two double harrows, with sixty fathoms of heaving line. I can cut it up for lines to drive on the farm.

Bringing cotton to gin (*Boston Public Library*)

We will leave here this afternoon with a load of people for the island. The news of the murder of our beloved President has just reached here; everything is in confusion. I was in hopes it was false, but it appears to be official. I shall try to get a New York paper as soon as this is mailed. No more at present.

T. G. Campbell

The National Freedman, June 1, 1865

Late in 1865 when the black soldiers were demobilized, they too tried to collect on the government's promise. Prince Rivers had enlisted in the Union army in 1862, in the first regiment of ex-slaves, and had served with distinction throughout the war. Now he wrote to General Saxton:

Morris Island, South Carolina, November 26, 1865

General:

I have the honor to ask for a understanding. I was told that the Government has given Land to Soldiers. If this land were given will [it] be just for the time being or will [it] hereafter be held by the Soldiers? I would like very much to know if any Part of the Mainland. If so I would like to get a piece on Mr. H. M. Stuart plantation, Oak Point, near Coosaw River.

Prince Rivers, Color and Provost Sergeant

National Archives

But Prince Rivers was too late. All that summer the former owners of the abandoned and confiscated lands had been calling on President Johnson. After the President granted them pardons for their role in the rebellion, they returned to South Carolina to claim their property. The freedmen, with the backing of General Saxton, armed themselves and drove the planters away. When William H. Trescot asked for the return of his plantation on Barnwell Island, South Carolina, Saxton refused him, explaining to General Oliver O. Howard, Commissioner of the Freedmen's Bureau:

The land in question has been, under my direction, divided up into forty acre tracts and settled upon by freedmen who had been promised it in accordance with the provisions of the Sherman Field Orders.

National Archives

Trescot went to Washington as official lobbyist for the planters and soon had President Johnson's ear. In October he wrote to South Carolina's governor:

It is not necessary that I should report the various conversations which I had the honor to have with the President and Gen. Howard. They were confined chiefly to the discussion of the mode in which restoration [of the land] could be effected, with reference both to the obligations which the Government had assumed towards the Freedmen and to the rights which the Government recognized in the original owners. I found Gen. Howard most anxious to do justice to all the interests concerned.

South Carolina Archives

That same month the President sent General Howard to South Carolina to work out a "mutually satisfactory" agreement between the freedmen and the planters. At a meeting on Edisto Island, Howard told the freedmen that they would have to give up their land. He later wrote:

My address met with no apparent favor. They did not hiss, but eyes flashed unpleasantly and with one voice they cried, "No, no!" One very black man, thick set and strong, cried out from the gallery: "Why, General Howard, why do you take away our lands? You take them from us who are true, always true to the Government! You give them to our all-time enemies! That is not right!"

Oliver O. Howard, *Autobiography* (New York, 1908)

When the freedmen refused to leave the island, or to work for their former masters, the Army was called on to keep peace. General James Beecher, member of a prominent abolitionist family and the commander of a regiment of black soldiers, was at first sympathetic to the freedmen:

November 29, 1865

Maj. Gen. R. Saxton
General:

I am to leave for Edisto Island in the morning. It seems that some of the planters whose lands have been restored were driven off by the freed people. Gen. Sickles immediately ordered that a company of white troops be sent there. Gen. Devens agreed with me that my troops were the ones to send if any and so I take a company with me.

I have apprehended trouble ever since the Govt determined to rescind the authority to occupy those lands. It is true that the War Dept. did not, in so many words, approve Gen. Sherman's order, but it certainly did *act* upon it, and there is an apparent bad faith in the matter which I am sure the freed people will feel. I cannot refrain from expressing grave fears of collisions on the island. The same difficulty is affecting the Combahee plantations. I hope to visit that section by Monday next.

James C. Beecher

National Archives

As the freedmen continued to resist, not only on Edisto but all along the coast, Beecher's sympathies waned. Selections from his letters to his superior officers illustrate the growing conflict between the Army and General Saxton who still supported the freedmen:

January 9, 1866

I went yesterday to [Mr. Nat Heyward's] plantation, called the people together and carefully instructed them in their rights and duties. They said they had been assured by certain parties that Mr. Heyward would be obliged to lease his land to them, and that they would not work for him at any price. They were perfectly good natured about it but firm. I then announced Mr. Heyward's offer:

That they were to retain their houses and gardens, with the privilege of raising hogs, poultry, etc. That he would pay for full hands, men $12, women $8 per month. They to find themselves—or he would pay $10 per month to men, $4 to women and ration them.

I am satisfied that no higher wages will be offered this year. Therefore I told the people that they could take it or leave it, and that if they declined to work the plantation the houses must be vacated. I proceeded to call the roll of all the able bodied men and women, each of whom responded "no." I then notified them that every house must be vacated on or before the 18th inst. I propose to remain and see everyone outside the plantation lines on that date.

Today I have pursued the same course on another large plantation, with the same results. Of course I anticipated this. It could not be otherwise considering the instructions which these people have received. I do not blame them in the slightest degree, and so long as they show no violence, shall treat them with all possible kindness. But it is better to stop the error they are laboring under, at once.

January 31, 1866

I am informed that on or about 12th inst a meeting was called on Wadmalaw Island to take measures to prevent white persons from visiting the island—that the Captain Commanding (very properly) forbade the proceeding, and notified the actors that in future no meetings could be held until notice of the same should be given him.

I am further informed that certain parties immediately proceeded to Charleston and returned with a document signed "By order Maj. Gen. Saxton" stating that the military authorities had nothing to do with them and they were at liberty to hold meetings when and where they pleased. This document was brought by three colored men calling themselves Commissioners from Edisto Island, attended by

In this cartoon from *Harper's Weekly,* July 29, 1865, the planter is saying, "My boy, we've toiled and taken care of you long enough. Now you've got to work!" (*Boston Public Library*)

an escort of forty or fifty freedmen, and exhibited to the Officer. They then proceeded to Rockville, and held the meeting.

It is to be regretted that the Bureau should seem to bring the freed people in collision with the Military Police of the islands. Already in two instances the freed people have committed themselves seriously by acts of stupid violence and I have record of hurtful advice given by speakers at the meeting in question. I shall be exceedingly grieved to find myself in collision with the [Bureau] but being responsible for the military police of these islands cannot do otherwise than prevent disorder by any means in my power.

I respectfully request that instruction be sent to the same "Commissioners" to the effect that the order in question must be respected on Wadmalaw and Johns Island. Such instructions will prevent collision between the [freedmen] and the U.S. forces.

National Archives

Meanwhile Congress had convened for its first postwar session. The Radical Republicans, those most responsive to the needs of the freedmen, were fighting mad at the President for his concessions to the South. Yet few were willing to defend the freedmen's rights to land claimed by the planters. After William Trescot appeared before a House committee, he boasted, "I hired one or two of the Radical members of the Committee." In another letter he told of his greatest coup—obtaining a statement from Sherman in which the general backed down on his promise to the freedmen. From Trescot's letter of February 4, 1866 to Governor Orr of South Carolina:

We went to Gen. Grant's headquarters where we found Gens. Grant, Sherman, Meade and Thomas. They all participated in a discussion of the real meaning of Gen. Sherman's order. Gen. Sherman expressed himself decidedly and said he would make his statement official.

This letter of Gen. Sherman's I enclose. You will find it explicit on the point that he intended his Field Order to serve a temporary military purpose and to terminate with the war. The publication of this letter produced considerable effect.

South Carolina Archives

Trescot had one more bit of business to take care of. "I most earnestly appeal for the immediate removal of General Saxton," he wrote to the President. When Saxton was summarily removed from office, the struggle for land was almost over. In March 1866 his successor, Major General Robert K. Scott, issued a new order:

The former owners of the land in the Sea Islands on the coast of South Carolina and the owners of land on the Main embraced in General Sherman's Special Field Orders will be permitted to return and occupy their lands.

National Archives

In the spring of 1866, squads of black soldiers were sent to the Sea Islands to drive away freedmen who refused to sign contracts with the planters. One soldier wrote to a black newspaper:

Edisto Island, March 26, 1866

Mr. Editor:

I hope soon to be called a citizen of the U.S. and have the rights of a citizen. I am opposed myself to working under a contract. I am as much at liberty to hire a white man to work as he to hire me. I expect to stay in the South after I am mustered out of service, but not to hire myself to a planter.

I have seen some men hired who were turned off without being paid. They try to pull us down faster than we can climb up. They have no reason to say that we will not work, for we raised them and sent them to school and bought their land. Now it is as little as they can do to give us some of their land—be it little or much.

Melton R. Linton, Co. H. 35th Regiment,
U. S. Colored Troops

South Carolina *Leader*, March 31, 1866

Some South Carolina freedmen had purchased land at government tax sales during the war. A small number of others who had received titles from General Saxton were allowed to exchange them for government-owned land around Beaufort and Hilton Head. By the end of 1866 only 1,565 of the 40,000 freedmen who had received land under the Sherman Field Order were still in possession.

The promise of land had not been confined to South Carolina and Georgia. In Hampton, Virginia, 4,500 freedmen appealed to the government:

After the burning of Hampton by the rebel inhabitants, the abandoned and confiscated lots within the town and the [Sinclair] farm, containing 600 acres of land, and the farm of Shields, containing about 400 acres, was set apart by the United States Government for the use of the colored refugees. There are now 800 families upon said lands, each with a humble tenement erected by themselves. The value of the property owned by them amounts to $51,006. We have five churches built by ourselves since the Rebellion and pay our pastors $1,050 per annum. We have a store of our own in Hampton, filled with groceries and goods of all sorts, kept and managed by an Association of our own selection, for the benefit of the colored people.

Our settlement on Sinclair's farm is laid out in streets, with order and regularity. The farms of Sinclair and Shields will this year yield better, richer and heavier crops than was ever known under the system of Slavery. More than thirty-seven of us were raised upon these farms and we know whereof we speak, that *free black labor* is altogether more remunerative than slave labor.

We are anxious and willing, and believe we are able, to build up a city upon our lands, as orderly, as prosperous, as religious, as patriotic, and as intelligent as could be done by any other people, provided we can secure the fee to the lands.

Freedmen's huts (*Boston Public Library*)

In the midst of our happiness and prosperity, the former owners of the lands we occupy have just returned and are seeking to take from us our happy homes. Our attorney and counsel have offered to pay these men liberal sums of money to obtain the lands without controversy; but we are told by Sinclair and Shields that they will have all that they before possessed. Therefore

Resolved, That we will not leave our happy homes unless compelled to do so by legal authority; that we will purchase or lease, at fair prices, of the United States Government its interests in these lots; that we will oppose, in all legal ways, the opening of the decrees of confiscation.

Resolved, That we have confidence and faith that the United States Government will be just and generous with us in the disposition of these lands and that we hail *the Freedmen's Bureau* as a wise and beneficent institution for the protection of our rights and interests and that we invoke its aid and cooperation in the social and political demonstration we are making; and we promise that nothing shall be wanting on our part to make us worthy of the great boon of *freedom*.

Resolved, That we respectfully request all papers in the United States friendly to our interest to publish these proceedings.

William B. Taylor, President
Peter Pryor, Secretary

The National Freedman, September 15, 1865

In 1865 the South was dotted with colonies of freedmen who had settled on abandoned lands during the war and had begun to build their own independent communities. A year or two later, most of these colonies had been broken up and the freedmen were once again working for white planters.

4. Don't I Know That Ain't Justice?

In the summer of 1865, Lewis Hayden, a black Bostonian, traveled through the South to organize Masonic lodges among the freedmen. On his return home he reported:

In each of the places I visited there is a deep and unalterable purpose in the hearts of the old oppressors to crush out the rising hopes of their late bondsmen. I rejoice to say that there is among our people that abiding faith in the justice of their cause which enables them to look to the future, not only with confidence but with exultation.

This is the feeling of our people in the cities. With the dwellers in the country, it is different. Away from the cities, the condition of the colored man is deplorable. He is still almost completely at the mercy of his old master. If the latter treats him kindly, it is well. But if ill-used, in nine cases out of ten he has no remedy. The United States army can do nothing for him, for it has gone. If an agent of the Freedmen's Bureau happens along, no complaint can reach his ear till it has been forestalled by the story of the master. The power of organized effort which may be available in the city is denied to him. What then can he do? God help him! for Andrew Johnson will not.

Lewis Hayden, *Caste Among Masons. Address before Grand Lodge of Free and Accepted Masons of the State of Massachusetts* (Boston, 1866)

Assaults were so common in the country districts that freedmen appealed to the army for help:

Newberry, South Carolina, August 8, 1866
Major General Sickles, Commandant of South Carolina
Sir:

The undersigned would most respectfully call your attention to the fearful condition of affairs in Newberry, S.C. The colored people are suffering the most fearful wrongs. For the last two months, a band of outlaws—Bushwhackers—and Murderers have been shooting down colored men and women, at will. They have murdered not less than ten persons within the last four weeks; and have driven away hundreds from their homes and families.

We have applied to the agent of the Bureau at this place, but he is powerless to do anything, not having a soldier, or any means of protection for himself or for us. We are murdered with impunity in the streets and the murderers are walking at large and no notice taken of them. We have no law. We appeal to the Government for protection.

We earnestly pray you to send a garrison of Soldiers to protect us—or authorize us to organize and protect ourselves.

G. Franklin, Parris Simpkins

National Archives

Freedmen's Bureau officers were required to file monthly reports of "Outrages Committed by Whites Against Freedmen" and black newspapers carried accounts like the following in almost every issue:

HORRIBLE OUTRAGE

We are informed that a most fiendish outrage was committed near Hamburg, S.C. one night last week by five white men, disguised with masks. They went to the house of Chandler Garrot, a colored man, and each violated the person of his wife. They then went to the shop of Wesley

Girl being whipped by ex-Confederate soldiers (*Boston Public Library*)

Brooks, a poor colored man, and robbed him of $60, nearly all the money he possessed.

Men of Georgia and South Carolina, we appeal to you, will you not help put a stop to these outrages?

The Loyal Georgian, January 27, 1866

Often these "outrages" were senseless attacks on women and children. Captain O. S. B. Wall, a black Ohioan who had served in the army until his appointment to the Freedmen's Bureau, reported:

Charleston, December 20, 1865

Major O. D. Kinsman, Asst. Adjt. Genl.

Major:

A Mr. Henry Sinclair owns two Plantations near Pines-ville. Tuesday last Sinclair becoming intoxicated & without any reason tied up by the wrists a young woman who is heavy with child, or caused a man (white) Elliott to tie her. Elliott also treated this woman brutally while she was tied. Finally Mr. Sinclair ordered away from the plantation all the members of the family to which this young woman belonged. The woman's name is Molsie Rivers. Molsie was tied up for about two hours & was kicked by Elliott while tied up.

O. S. B. Wall

National Archives

In other incidents, whites were angered when their authority was challenged. Complaints filed with the Freedmen's Bureau in Augusta, Georgia:

On the morning of the 8th of September 1865, Mr. William Page, *white,* came into the kitchen where I was sitting and asked me who was it that had meal in the wagon. I told him that I did not know or either did I care a damn, I myself had none in the wagon. He then said he had whipped one nigger that morning, and was going to whip me. Making at me with a stick he struck me several hard blows with it, at the same time cutting me over the eye with a knife, and his Father, David Page shot at me with his gun as I ran off.

his
Daniel × Dunbar
mark

Caroline Rogers, being duly sworn, deposes that Luke Rogers (white) did on or about the 7th of Nov. 1865 while at work in the field with deponent and daughter (Mary) say that if Mary did not run and keep up with him that he would whip her and see if he could not make her mind.

That since she had become free, she would not do anything that he told her. So he got a stick and struck her, at which time Caroline Rogers told her daughter that she should not stay and for her to go and get her clothes and leave. Rogers come up to her and struck her across the face with a board cutting her badly, at the same time telling her to hush her mouth. She left taking her daughter with her, when Rogers said that she should not have her things when she come after them.

her

Caroline X Rogers

mark

National Archives

At the end of the planting season when it was time to give the freedmen their share of the crop, the number of outrages soared. A report from a Freedmen's Bureau officer in Charleston, South Carolina:

December 30, 1865

Laura Perry (col'd) represents as follows:

Her husband Robert Perry and herself were formerly owned by William Turno who lives in the town of Pendleton. They had planted a crop for Turno and worked it till it was ready to "lay by" when, Laura states, Turno proposed to them with others to sign a contract for their lifetime. They with two others, Novel and Richard, refused to sign such contract and Turno drove them away without food or any compensation for their labor.

They proceeded toward Columbia and had reached a place called Rocky Mill when they were overtaken by two white men who had been sent by Turno. They shot at Robert, killing him instantly. They did the same to Novel. Richard ran to a creek, plunged in, was shot at but succeeded in making his escape. They then took Laura, stripped her bare, gave her fifty lashes upon the bare back and compelled her to walk back to Pendleton, some 25 miles. They then put her at the plow by day and confined her in the "dark house" by night for one week, giving her nothing to eat. An officer from Anderson happened at the place. When Laura revealed to him her terrible situation said officer took her and her two children in a cart to where her husband and Novel had been shot, found remnants of their bodies and buried them and then placed Laura and her children on board the cars for Charleston. Soon after reaching this city Laura gave birth to a dead infant.

National Archives

Rather than feed their field hands during the first winter of freedom, some planters shipped them to the cities after the crops were harvested. Hundreds, perhaps thousands, of people who had been turned away by their employers appealed to the Bureau for help. A typical report by Captain O. S. B. Wall:

October 14, 1865

About 4 years ago Mr. James Hopkinson carried away all his servants from Johns and Edisto Islands to a plantation about 18 miles from Abbeville Court House. Eighty-one of these people are now in this city. All have been treated this past summer the same as in former years, there being one overseer and two drivers on this plantation.

On the 2nd of this month Mr. Hopkinson sent away, with two wagons to carry the children and some bedding &c, these eighty-one people, promising to meet his people in this city. His people cannot find him.

The wagons broke down before reaching Orangeburg and the military authorities there sent the people to this city by Railroad. These people are in a destitute condition and are thrown upon the support of the government. Mr. Hopkinson caused these ignorant people to believe that he was *acting* by *authority* and *by orders* of U.S. Officers and that they would be taken care of somehow. Mr. Hopkinson told these people they had no share in the crop.

National Archives

Army officers, the freedmen said, often sided with the planters:

Clarendon County, S.C., February 21, 1866

We were servants and served our owners faithfully until released by the United States authorities. We then contracted with our former owners for a part of the crop last year and at the close of the year we were driven off without anything or any settlement for our year's work because we would not contract with them for the present year.

We immediately looked out for ourselves and made a contract with Mr. E. M. Burkett as laborers for a portion of the crop. If we were left alone by our former owners we could do very well, but we cannot rest day or night for them. They first tried to coax us back. We refused to go. They then tried to scare us back, but we still refused. They are now threatening to send a military guard after us. Lieut. Burns was here yesterday with our former owners. Lieut. Burns ordered us to leave immediately or he would send down a military guard after us. We are unwilling to leave and our employer is unwilling to part with us, therefore do petition for protection and advice.

	his		his		his		his
Sam	×	Alfred	×	Ephram	×	Cato	×
	mark		mark		mark		mark

	her		her		her		her
Amantha	×	Clarissa	×	Susan	×	Betty	×
	mark		mark		mark		mark

National Archives

In the first months of peace, the army was in charge of the South's judicial system. When the courts were turned back to the civil authorities complaints from the freedmen multiplied:

Macon, February 8, 1866

Mr. Editor:

Should anyone think that with the freedom of the black man has come equal justice let him come to Macon and visit the Mayor's court and he will see his mistake. A white may assault a colored gentleman at high noon, pelt him with stones or maul him with a club and the colored man is fined or imprisoned. To attempt to define the outrages and mean acts of our citizens here towards those who have a different complexion would be a task too arduous for a single correspondent.

George Macon

The Loyal Georgian, February 24, 1866

Since the Recorders' Courts have been restored to the civil authorities there seems to exist a determination on the part of the magistrates to inflict punishment upon the colored people not according to law, but at the pleasure and caprices of the judges. Exorbitant fines are generally imposed upon colored delinquents when, on the same day and in the same tribunal, white prisoners who have committed greater offenses escape punishment.

These abuses should be stopped; and it can be done very easily by the formation of an association, whose duty it shall be to employ counsel and see that justice be done to everyone. A trifle from each member would be sum sufficient to attain this aim.

The New Orleans *Tribune*, December 18, 1866

Black men served on Washington jury for the first time in 1869 (*Boston Public Library*)

Yes, we are ignorant. I am ignorant and they say all niggers is. They say we don't know what the word constitution means. But if we don't know what the Constitution is, we know enough to know what justice is. I can see for myself down at my own court-house. If they makes a white man pay five dollars for doing something today, and makes a nigger pay ten dollars for doing that thing tomorrow, don't I know that ain't justice?

They've got a figure of a woman with a sword hung up there, Mr. President. I don't know what you call it—('Justice, Justice')—well, she's got a handkerchief over her eyes and the sword is in one hand and a pair o' scales in the other. When a white man and a nigger gets into the scales, don't I know the nigger is always mighty light? Don't we all see it? Ain't it so at your court-house, Mr. President?"

The Nation, October 19, 1865

5. We Simply Ask That We Be Recognized as Men

The Dred Scott decision, handed down by the U. S. Supreme Court in 1857, declared that blacks "had no rights which a white man was bound to respect." Emancipation struck down that doctrine, but belief in black inferiority was deep-rooted, North as well as South. The freedmen were determined to change the minds as well as the laws of white America. In the final months of the war, a black man wrote:

It is not enough to tell us that we will be respected according as we show ourselves worthy of it. When we have rights that others respect, self-respect, pride and industry will greatly increase. I do not think that to have these rights would exalt us above measure or rob the white man of his glory. We do not flatter ourselves with the idea that we are yet fitted to fill high stations; yet we do think that often white men are put in positions over us that might be better filled by a man of our own race.

Surely the heroic deeds of colored men on the battlefield will enable us to show the world that we are a people worthy to be free, worthy to be respected.

The National Freedman, April 1, 1865)

In Florida an ex-slave told a northern teacher:

I've got a handsome piece [of land] both side of the road. I chose him there purpose to hurt their feelings; to be riding 'long the road and see the nigger crop a flourishing; for they tells me there won't no cotton go to market from the niggers this year. Niggers can't do it on their own responsibility. We'll show 'em how the nigger can work the farm for himself.

The National Freedman, March 15, 1866

On St. Helena Island, South Carolina

On St. Helena Island, South Carolina, the slaves had been freed in 1861, after Union forces captured the Sea Islands. A government plantation superintendent described their reactions when their ex-masters returned four years later. From a report to General Saxton, August 17, 1865:

Very many of the freedmen who three years ago were utterly destitute have been able by their earnings to buy themselves from ten to twenty acres of land, a horse, mule or yoke of oxen, a cow, a cart, even good light vehicles for driving—household utensils—clothing and in several cases they have had houses built for themselves in their own lots.

The thrift and success of the freedmen makes them objects of attention to their former masters who are returning every day to visit their plantations. Two young ladies went from house to house among their father's slaves, pleading their poverty and receiving from one some grits or potatoes, from others plates and spoons—or money. One woman took the shoes from her own feet and gave them to her former mistress.

These donations are made partly from pity and partly to let their former owners see how well they can take care of themselves—an intense satisfaction if a little boastful.

One freedman, Jim Cashman, who had been guide to some of our Commanders here, and a corporal in a regiment for three years met his old master who had come to visit the plantation he used to own.

"You come back again, Sir," said Jim most respectfully. "The Lord has blessed us since you have been gone. It used to be Mr. Fuller No. 1, now it is Jim Cashman No. 1. Would you like to take a drive through the island, Sir? I have a horse and buggy of my own now, Sir, and I would like to take you to see my own little lot of land and my new house on it, and I have as fine a crop of cotton, Sir, as ever you did see—and Jim can let you have $10 if you want them, Sir."

Mr. Fuller *did* want them. He took up quite a collection on his place. Another of the old proprietors came to ask for aid and received from his people over $70. One lady came to Beaufort a week or two ago and sent word that "she thought some of her Ma's niggers might come to wait upon her." None volunteered. Some went to see her, however, and from these she received food, money and clothes. She offered to become a dressmaker for the Negroes and will probably get enough money for a support in that way.

Although to the first who came back the people gave liberally, they are becoming more cautious for they say that two come for every one they send away relieved and that it is a new way "maussa" has of making them work for him.

National Archives

The freedmen quickly learned that to win respect they must secure all the rights of citizens, and the most important of these was the right to vote. When Chief Justice Salmon P. Chase visited Savannah in May 1865, a black delegation called on him. Their interview was recorded by a newspaperman:

Chase: Suppose you *were* permitted to vote, what guarantee would the Government have that you would know how to vote?

Black man: Oh, Mr. Judge, we know who are friends are! We knows our friends.

Chase: Perhaps you in the cities may. But here is a great mass of ignorant field hands from the plantations. What is to prevent them from voting just as their old masters may tell them?

Black: We'll tell them how to vote, sir. We have means of

reaching them; and they'll follow us sooner than they will their old masters or any white man. We know the difference between the Union ticket and the Rebel ticket. We know that much better than you do! Because, sir, some of our people stand behind these men at the table and hear'em talk. We see'em in the house and by the wayside. We *know*'em from skin to core better than you can do till you live among'em and see as much of 'em as we have.

Chase: What your friends at the North are afraid of, is, that your people in the interior will not know how to tell whom to vote for, and that in their bewilderment they will vote just as their old masters tell them they ought.

Black: I tell you, Mr. Judge, we can reach every colored man in the State and they would rather trust intelligent men of their own color than any white man. They'll vote the ticket we tell them is the ticket of our friends; and as fast as they can, they'll learn to read and judge for themselves.

Whitelaw Reid, *After the War* (New York, 1866)

Soon, freedmen all over the South were meeting, informally and in convention, to ask for their rights. For a people only months from slavery these meetings were remarkable affairs. Black soldiers who had learned to read in the army, runaway slaves who had lived in the North and were returning home, free-born blacks from the cities and freedmen fresh from the plantations debated, drew up petitions, chose officers, appointed committees as if they had been following parliamentary procedure all their lives.

In May, a gathering of North Carolina blacks sent a petition to the President:

Some of us are soldiers and have had the privilege of fighting for our country in this war. Since we have become Freemen, we begin to feel that we are men, and are anxious to show our countrymen that we can and will fit ourselves for the creditable discharge of the duties of citizenship. We want the privilege of voting.

New York *Daily Tribune,* May 19, 1865

In June, Georgia freedmen sent two petitions. The first asked for the vote, the second said:

To His Excellency, Andrew Johnson, President of the United States

Should your Excellency grant the Petition now in circulation among the White People, asking for the appointment of a Military Governor, we humbly and most earnestly pray that our interests, as well as theirs, may be regarded in your selection of the proper person for the important office. We ask not for a Black Man's Governor, nor a White Man's Governor, but for a People's Governor, who shall impartially protect the rights of all, and faithfully sustain the Union.

The Liberator, June 30, 1865

The President did not reply. He was hastening to restore civil government in the South before Congress met. The provisional governors he appointed were not "People's Governors" but representatives of the old slaveowning class. They were empowered to call conventions and hold elections for state offices. Everyone could vote who had received a presidential pardon—except black men.

Assembling in Maryland and Virginia, the Carolinas, Mississippi, Tennessee, Florida, Louisiana, and Georgia, freedmen petitioned Congress, sent delegates to Washington and wrote addresses "to the People of the United States." In a long and carefully reasoned appeal to the nation, black Virginians explained why the act of emancipation was not enough:

Cartoonist Thomas Nast mocks Andrew Johnson's claim
to be the black people's Moses

We have no means of legally making or enforcing contracts; we have no right to testify before the courts in any case in which a white man is one of the parties to the suit; we are taxed without representation. In short, so far as legal safeguards of our rights are concerned, we are defenceless before our enemies.

We are still more unfortunately situated as regards our late masters. They have returned to their homes, with all their old pride and contempt for the Negro transformed into bitter hate for the new made freeman. In the greater number of counties of this state meetings have been held *deploring* while accepting the abolition of slavery, but going on to pledge the planters to employ no Negroes save such as were formerly owned by themselves, without a written recommendation from their late employers, thereby keeping us in a state of serfdom. They have also pledged themselves, in no event, to pay their late adult slaves more than $60 per year for their labor, out of which we are to find clothes for ourselves and families, and pay our taxes and doctors' bills. In many of the more remote districts planters are to be found who still refuse to recognize their Negroes as free, forcibly retaining the wives and children of their late escaped slaves. There are a number of cases in which a faithful performance by colored men of the labor contracted for has been met by a contemptuous refusal of the stipulated compensation.

Fellow citizens, the performance of a simple act of justice on your part will reverse all this. We ask for no expensive aid from military forces, stationed throughout the South. Give us the suffrage and you may rely upon us to secure justice for ourselves.

In conclusion, we wish to advise our colored brethren of the State and nation, that the settlement of this question is to a great extent dependent on them. Then be up and active, and everywhere let associations be formed, having for their object the agitation, discussion and enforcement of your claims to equality before the law and equal right of suffrage. Your opponents are active; be prepared and organize to resist their efforts.

The Liberator, September 5, 1865

All during the summer and fall, the state legislatures of the South met. They grudgingly repealed the old slave laws, "under the pressure of federal bayonets," said the governor of Mississippi. But the Black Codes that replaced them were scarcely an improvement. Freedmen had the right to own property, to marry, to sue in the courts—with limitations. In Mississippi a black man could not rent or buy land except in a city. In South Carolina he could not follow a trade or open a store without a special license costing up to $100 a year. He could testify in court only in cases involving other blacks, but could not serve on juries, join the militia, or vote. Most onerous were the laws controlling labor. All freedmen—and often their wives and children—were compelled to work. Unemployment was a crime and the guilty were sentenced to work without pay on white-owned farms.

A week after South Carolina's General Assembly ratified its Black Code a Colored People's Convention met in Charleston. This time there were no parades, yet the atmosphere of the convention was one of quiet optimism. Following six days of deliberations, the delegates issued a series of documents—to Congress, the legislature and to their white fellow citizens. Repeating the demand for full citizenship rights, they summed up the mood of the black South as the year of jubilee drew to an end:

Heretofore we have had no firesides that we could call our own. The measures which have been adopted for the development of white men's children have been denied to ours. The laws which have made white men great, have degraded us, because we were colored. But now that we are

Colored People's Convention in session (*Boston Public Library*)

freemen, now that we have been lifted up by the providence of God to manhood, we have resolved to come forward, and, like MEN, speak and *act* for ourselves.

We have not come together in battle array to assume a boastful attitude and to talk loudly of high-sounding principles or unmeaning platforms. Although we feel keenly our wrongs, still we come together in a spirit of meekness and of patriotic good will to all the people of the state. Thus we would address you, not as enemies, but as friends and fellow countrymen who desire to dwell among you in peace.

We ask for no special privileges or favors. We ask only for *even-handed* Justice. We simply ask that we shall be recognized as men.

> "Proceedings of the Colored People's Convention of the State of South Carolina" (Charleston, 1865)

II · WE ARE LAYING THE FOUNDATIONS OF A NEW STRUCTURE

Despite compromise, war, and struggle, the Negro is not free. In well-nigh the whole rural South the black farmers are peons, bound by law and custom to an economic slavery from which the only escape is death or the penitentiary. In the cities of the South the Negroes are a segregated servile caste, with restricted rights and privileges. That is the large legacy of the Freedmen's Bureau, the work it did not do because it could not.

W. E. B. Du Bois, 1901

1. The Bureau

The Freedmen's Bureau was originally intended to be a one-year "bridge from slavery to freedom." As far as black people were concerned, it was the government in the South from the end of the war until the Rebel states were readmitted to the Union. The Bureau distributed rations to the needy, helped organize schools, churches and medical facilities, and was the only court of appeal for black people. The voluminous Bureau records contain thousands of letters like the following. Unless otherwise noted, all of the documents in this section come from the National Archives.

The old and sick wait for rations outside of Freedmen's Bureau office (*Boston Public Library*)

Newberry, S.C., March 18, 1867

Brevt. Major General R. K. Scott
Sir:

Some months ago I complained to your department that Mrs. Charles Strauss and Mrs. Clinch, her sister, to whom I formerly belonged, detained my son Henry, nine years old. Since I have heard that Mr. Chas. Strauss had received a letter from the Freedmen's Bureau ordering the surrender of the child to me but they still detain the child. From other sources I hear Mrs. S. & C. say they will not give my son up and threaten anyone who goes for him and I am afraid to go near them. The parties detaining who paid me no wages for 14 months after freedom resort to the policy to force me to return to them and one of them told me they acted under the orders of a lawyer.

her
Elizabeth × Stone
mark

Freedmen's Bureau office in Richmond, Virginia (*Boston Public Library*)

Calhoun, Gordon County, Georgia, August 27, 1867
Matilda Frix, Freedwoman, states that on Tuesday night, the 20th of August late in the night, three men came into the house where myself and Cheary Ransom are living, about fifty yards west of the railroad depot. We had the door fastened by putting a shovel under it. They forced the door open, struck a light, walked around the room, pulling the covering from my face, went over to Cheary Ransom's bed, pulled the covering from her face, said they would blow her brains out if she made any noise. Jim Printen and my brother was sleeping in the house. Jim Printen started out of the door. Those men fired at him, started out **after**

him, could not catch him. Before Jim Printen started out some of the party said, "Let us burn them out." Had a light and was trying to catch Cheary's dress on fire when Jim Printen started to run out which frightened them. Think their intention was to drive us away from town. In fact they told Cheary Ransom to get out of here or they would kill her.

On the evening of the 24th we got some men to come and put a fastening on our door so that no person could come in. Some time in the night was awakened by some party throwing large rocks in through the window, firing pistol shots through the house just above our bed. The reason for their doing so was I think because Cheary Ransom had complained to the Bureau Agent about Mrs. Hunt owing her for services. They had a trial over it before Mr. Blacker, the agent, and he ordered Mrs. Hunt to pay Cheary $20. Mrs. Hunt said that same night if she had to pay her that Cheary should not live here to enjoy it.

her
Matilda × Frix
mark

Actually, Bureau officers lacked the authority to settle anything but minor disputes. Although their presence in the South undoubtedly helped to prevent wholesale murders of black people, their chief task was to start the wheels of agriculture and industry turning again. In his first annual report to Bureau Commissioner Oliver O. Howard, General Robert Scott, Bureau chief in South Carolina in 1866–68, described the beginnings of "the free labor system":

All agreed that the only way a Negro could be induced to work would be under a system of forced labor. The planters

Workers were summoned to fields at break of day as they
had been during slavery (*Boston Public Library*)

demanded a system of contracts that would give the owners
as absolute control over the freedmen as though they were
still slaves. Thus a conflict arose between landowner and laborer—the former struggling to retain absolute control and
the latter determined to maintain his newly acquired free-

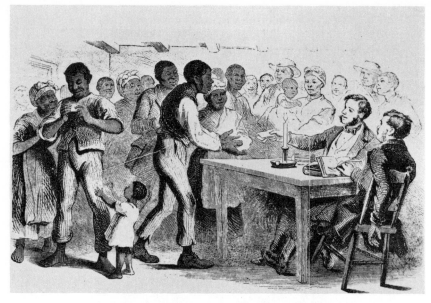

Payday usually came at the end of the year

dom. In view of the facts I issued a form of contract for the guidance of all which, although not in all respects such a contract as my judgment approved, was yet perhaps as fair as the extreme notions of the people would admit of.

"The free labor system" encouraged by the Bureau was not exactly free. Freedmen were required to sign contracts with employers in which they agreed to a year's work. Some contracts called for payment in wages. More often the freedmen were to receive a share of the crop that they planted and harvested. The employer supplied living quarters—usually the old slave cabins—and food and clothing; the cost of the latter was deducted from the worker's share when the crops were in. It was the job of the Freedmen's Bureau to see that both groups carried out the terms of their agreements.

The administration of the Freedmen's Bureau varied from state to state. In Louisiana when the first Bureau chief was accused of being too sympathetic to the freedmen, he was dismissed at the request of President Johnson. His successor did not make the same mistake. Jacob Borgest, an ex-soldier, told of his experiences with Bureau agents:

Soon after being mustered out of the military service, [I] was met by Captain J. G. Colvit, a runner for Gen. Wells, who lives in the Parish of Rapides. On his fair promises I solicited a large number of my comrades to go with me to work on the plantation of Gen. Wells. [We were promised] rations including sugar, coffee, blankets, cooking utensils, two suits of clothing and whisky daily, beside $15 per month, but he has never paid anything and charges all these things to be deducted from their $15.

The boys were greatly dissatisfied so some of them went off to complain to the agent of the Bureau at Alexandria, Lieut. Butler. They were followed by this man Colvit and placed in jail where they are now and have been all summer. Soon after this, a large armed party of persons in Confederate uniform came into the field to arrest some more of the boys. Then all the hands went and got their guns and would not let these boys be taken off unless they went to see what became of them, as it was thought they were to be killed.

This constant dissatisfaction and complaining of the boys for my having induced them to come up here determined me to leave. I gave three days' notice that I was going away. While waiting for a boat I was seized by this man Colvit and dragged to jail where I was confined many weeks, covered with vermin, robbed of my clothes and cheated out of my earnings. A part of the other boys, under the persuasions of Maj. Willaur, agent of the Bureau, signed a contract he prepared for them and returned to the plantation. The laws of Rapides Parish are administered wholly in the interests of the white man and the colored people have no justice. I warn all colored men not to go there.

The New Orleans *Tribune*, September 23, 1866

A year later an editorial in The New Orleans *Tribune* said:

The laborer on the plantations is, to a very great extent, in the clutches of his employer. If he goes to the Bureau's agent, he finds there an officer who rides with his employer, who dines with him and who drinks champagne with him. He is not likely to receive impartial justice at the hands of such a prejudiced officer. Most of the agents think their particular business is to furnish the planters with cheap hands and to retain at any cost the laborers on the plantations. They are in fact the planter's guards.

It is therefore perfectly useless for the poor laborer to look at the Freedmen's Bureau for relief. He knows in advance that the Bureau will send him back to his unjust or exacting employer. He will not be assisted to get his pay or to get redress but will be told to go back to his master and do his work.

The New Orleans *Tribune*, October 31, 1867

Blacks were also critical of the operations of the Bureau in Mississippi, Florida and Georgia. Florida's Bureau chief, in a letter to General Howard, described blacks as of "gross physique, degraded intellect, grovelling pursuits, habitual slothfulness and licentious habits." In Georgia, members of the Civil and Political Rights Association sent Congress a memorial to record their dissatisfactions:

An idealized portrait of Freedmen's Bureau officer (*Boston Public Library*)

The crop of 1865 was most altogether of cereals and the freed people worked for part of the crop. Hence the 1st January, 1866 found very many of them with a year's provision on hand. Encouraged by their success, they were buoyant and hopeful, readily employing themselves as laborers for 1866. But their hopes were soon blighted by the transfer of the powers of the Freedmen's Bureau from military to civil agents.

These civil agents were selected from among the native residents. They were advocates of the doctrine that the "Negro has no right the white man is bound to respect." This induced the late slaveowners to be "themselves again." The same crouching servility required of us as slaves was now exacted of us as free people and a deviation from this requirement subjected them to the overseer's cudgel or the Bureau ball and chain.

After the [second Freedmen's Bureau Act] became law this cruel mode of punishment was discontinued, but the identical civil agents were continued in office and they used their power to the injury instead of to the benefit of the freed people. They pandered to the exacting whim of our employers, conceding to them the right to discharge and drive us away without pay whenever they chose to consider the contract violated, though often no violation had occurred. We have no data by which to estimate the number of murders committed on colored people during this year but from our personal knowledge we believe there were several hundred, for which no one was ever punished.

Thus matters went from bad to worse and the 1st day of January 1867 found the colored people in a condition similar to if not worse than that of slavery. They made contracts and entered upon the work of 1867, but with nothing like the zeal they had the year before.

House Miscellaneous Document No. 52, 40th Congress, 3rd Session

---

Although the contract system was designed to bring stability to agriculture, at least one Georgia agent used it to keep a cook at work in the kitchen. Affidavits from a freedwoman and her husband:

Taliferro County, Georgia, May 25, 1866
Sofia Chapman on oath saith that she asked permission of Mrs. Nancy Reynolds to visit her daughter. Mrs. Reynolds replied that she could not go by her permission but that she could ask Mr. Reynolds. On doing so he replied that he did

not care if I went and never returned. This was on Thursday. On Friday morning the agent of the Bureau came over and read the law concerning our duty and advised me to carry my contract out without further trouble, stating to me if I did not that he would have to punish me. On my return home I was sent to him and he fined me five days imprisonment.

Sofia Chapman

Bunny Chapman, a freedman, on oath says that my wife Sofia who is to work for Mrs. Nancy Reynolds asked Mrs. Reynolds' permission to go down to see her daughter. She said she would start on Friday in the 2 P.M. train and would return Sunday 11 A.M. train. The permission was granted and Sofia returned at the appointed time and went to go into the kitchen. Mrs. Reynolds told her to go out, that she should cook no longer for her. My wife asked me what to do. I told her to go to Mr. Jones, the agent, which she did. He immediately put her into jail.

Bunny Chapman

The leading black men of Beaufort, South Carolina, all of them later active in politics, complained to General Scott about a Bureau officer:

Your honor:

We the undersigned citizens of Beaufort, S.C., believing that the Freedmen's Bureau was established for the purpose of protecting refugees and freedmen, take this opportunity to set forth the facts relative to Lieut. J. S. Powers, officer of the Freedmen's Bureau in Beaufort. In all his dealings with freedmen, he manifests a contempt for them. He compels them to live up to their contracts and allows those they contract with to drive the freedmen off without compensation for their labor. He uses profane language whenever they happen to get before him. He keeps them in such fear that those who have been in his office once fear to enter the second time. He kicks and strikes them whenever he desires and he thinks they will not retaliate. He arrests them, puts them in jail.

He is controlled by persons whose desire it is to make it appear that slavery is a blessing and freedom a curse to the Negro. Instead of being in his office, he is in some shop or out horseback or carriage riding. He is in the habit of going a hunting and staying a week at a time while Freedmen are around his door and lying out in the weather night after night.

We have done all in our power to aid Lieut. J. S. Powers, but our labors have been in vain. We have tried to encourage him to do right but he fails to be moved in that direction. The Freedmen have been enraged, almost to the point of rising up against him. We have caused them to forebear. We therefore respectfully request that Lieut. J. S. Powers be removed from our midst.

> Robert Smalls, Late Capt. of U. S. S. *Planter:*
> Jonathan J. Wright;
> William J. Whipper; R. H. Gleaves;
> Prince Rivers [and others]

However, other Bureau officers in South Carolina seem to have dealt more fairly with the freedmen than those in neighboring states. Although less sympathetic to the ex-slaves than Saxton, Major General Robert K. Scott was one of the few Bureau chiefs to employ black subordinates. No study of the black men in the Freedmen's Bureau has yet been made, but a roster of Bureau employees in South Carolina in 1867 lists five blacks. Almost all were Northerners who had come South with the army; all except one were agents, the lowest-ranking Bureau job.

Benjamin F. Randolph

Benjamin F. Randolph, a graduate of Oberlin, was chaplain of
the Twenty-sixth U. S. Colored Troops. When his regiment was
demobilized, he applied for a Bureau position:

Charleston, S.C., August 31, 1865

General:

I am desirous of obtaining a position among the freedmen where my qualifications and experience will admit of the most usefulness. I don't ask position or money. But I ask a place where I can be most useful to my race. My learning and long experience as a teacher North, and my faithful service as Chaplain demand that I seek such a place. If you should obtain for me some responsible position in the Freedmen's Bureau or if you should obtain for me the position of Principal Teacher or Superintendent of Schools you would never regret it.

B. F. Randolph

Randolph worked in the educational division but he was also assigned to see that laborers fulfilled their contracts:

Charleston, S.C., February 28, 1867

Rev. Mr. B. F. Randolph, Agent, B.R.F. and A.L.

Sir:

The Assistant Commissioner directs that you visit the Freed people on the plantations in the Parishes of St. Thomas, Christ Church and St. James and use your efforts to induce the Freed people to labor faithfully. Exhort them to be prompt and diligent in the discharge of their duties, and whenever you find people who are idle and have not contracted for the present year, you will advise them that they must at once enter into contracts and thus become self-supporting. Say that they will not receive any assistance from the government.

You will also induce them to establish Schools for their children and support them themselves by subscriptions paid monthly. You will report to these Headquarters any localities in which there is a reasonable prospect of the Freed

Martin R. Delany

people being able to support or to contribute to the support of schools. If they can hire a teacher and schoolhouse, the Bureau will supply them with the necessary text books.

Edward L. Deane, Bvt. Major

Except for John Mercer Langston, who worked out of Washington as Inspector of Bureau schools, the highest-ranking black officer of the Freedmen's Bureau was Martin R. Delany. A well-known abolitionist editor, Delany had traveled to Africa before the war to find a place for an Afro-American settlement. After serving as a major in the Union army, he was transferred to the Bureau at war's end. His title was Sub-Assistant Commissioner in charge of the district of Hilton Head, which included half a dozen of South Carolina's Sea Islands. He remained in office until 1868, despite numerous attempts to dislodge him.

Unlike most Bureau officers, Delany cared passionately about what happened to the freedmen. He envisioned for them a future as independent small farmers and preached vigorously the gospel of work as the means of achieving this goal. In his first days on the islands, the black major, as he was called, advised the freedmen not to work for whites:

Before the South depended on you. Now the whole country will depend on you. Get up a community and get all the lands you can. Grow as much vegetables as you want for your families. On the other part of the land cultivate rice and cotton. One acre of land will grow a crop worth $90. Ten acres will bring $900 every year—and carpets will take the place of bare floors in your cabins.

When he found that blacks could not obtain land to farm independently, he accepted "the Shares System" while pointing out its flaws. He could not foresee that this system, slipping from the Bureau's feeble control into the planters' hands, would chain black farmers for a century to come almost as completely as slavery had done. In the face of government apathy, white hostility and, in one case, black cupidity, he tried to correct obvious abuses but was largely unsuccessful. The failure belonged not to him but to the Freedmen's Bureau, to "the work it did not do because it could not," as Dr. Du Bois was to write.

In the first labor contracts, planters offered freedmen from one fifth to as little as one tenth of the crop and listed all sorts of regulations reminiscent of slavery. A typical contract approved by the Bureau included the following:

State of South Carolina }
District of Beaufort }

Articles of agreement made and entered this
twenty Sixth day of March 1866 by, and
between __Wm. Henry Heyward__ and the
Freedmen and women whose names are hereunto
attached.

I. The said Freedmen and Women agree to hire their
time and labor on the plantations of the said Wm.
Henry Heyward. from this date of signing this
agreement to the first day of January 1867. They
agree to conduct themselves honestly and civilly, to
perform diligently and faithfully, all such labor
on said plantation as may be connected with and
necessary for, the raising, harvesting, and protec
-ting of the crop.   The said freedmen further
agree, not to invite visitors upon the premises, or
absent themselves from the same, during working
hours, without the consent of the employer or his
agent.

II. The said freedmen agree to perform reasonable
daily tasks on said plantation, and in all cases
when such tasks cannot be assigned, they agree
to labor diligently, ten hours per day, unless
the weather be such as to actually forbid labor,
or the employer or his agent excuse them from
work. In either case, no deduction for loss
of time shall be made .

III. For every days labor lost by absence.
                              (refusal)

A typical labor contract (*National Archives*)

The said Freedmen and Women agree to conduct themselves honestly and civilly, to perform diligently and faithfully, all such labor [ten hours a day] on said plantation as may be connected with the raising of the crop. The said Freedmen further agree not to invite visitors upon the premises or absent themselves during working hours.

For every day's labor lost by absence, refusal or neglect to perform the daily task, the laborer shall forfeit fifty cents. If absent without leave two dollars a day. If absent three days without leave to be liable to dismissal and forfeiture of wages.

Said freedmen agree to take care of all tools and implements; also to be kind and gentle to all work animals; also to pay for any injury done to either the animals or farming tools while in their hands and by reason of their carelessness or neglect.

It is expressly agreed by the Freedmen that Firearms shall not be used within the boundary of the plantation without permission and that violation of this agreement will subject them to dismissal and forfeiture of wages.

Delany drew up a model contract requiring payment of one third of the crop to the freedmen. His contract made no mention of visitors, fines or firearms, but laid down some rules for the planters:

No labor is to be performed by hand that can better be done by animal labor or machinery. All damage for injury or loss of property by carelessness is to be paid by fair and legal assessments.

All Thanksgiving, Fast Days, "Holidays" and National Celebration Days are to be enjoyed by contractors without being regarded as a neglect of duty or violation of contract.

Good conduct and good behavior of the Freedmen toward the proprietor; good treatment of animals; and good care of tools, utensils, etc; and good and kind treatment of the Proprietor to the Freedmen, will be strictly required by the Authorities.

No stores will be permitted on the place and nothing sold on account except the necessaries of life such as good substantial food and working clothes. Spirituous liquors will not be permitted.

In all cases where an accusation is made against a person, the Proprietor or his Agent, [and] one of the Freedmen selected by themselves, and a third person chosen by the two shall be a council to investigate the accused. In all cases where a decision is to be made to dismiss or forfeit a share of the crop, the officer of the Bureau or some other Officer of the Government must preside in the trial and make the decision. When the Proprietor is prejudiced against an accused person, he must name a person to take his place in the Council.

Delany's earlier suggestions for safeguarding freedmen's rights had met with stony silence. When he submitted his model contract to headquarters, however, the response was prompt:

Charleston, S.C., March 6, 1866

Major:

Brig. Genl. R. K. Scott, Asst. Comm'r, directs me to instruct you that when fair and equitable contracts are entered into between the planters and Freedmen, there will be no interference on the part of the agents of this Bureau. It is entirely impracticable to attempt to establish a uniform contract, therefore all equitable forms of contracts will be approved, when the freed people enter into them willingly.

H. W. Smith, Asst. Adjt. Genl.

During the planting season freedmen bought food, clothing and supplies on credit from the plantation commissary or from stores in Hilton Head, on a street known as "Robbers' Row." At the end of the year, they sold their share of the crop to the storekeepers. Inevitably they were overcharged when they bought and underpaid when they sold. In one of his first reports, Delany wrote:

As a protection to the freedmen I intend to adopt a Pass-book system, making it obligatory on all planters and persons having stores to enter in a pass-book held by the customer, every item charged against him in the grocery or commissary store. This will be more generally satisfactory to the freedmen since he can readily satisfy himself that he is not overcharged.

I intend also to make commissary arrangements whereby the freedmen of the Island may be enabled to obtain their supplies of rice and grits at prices far below those now charged, probably from thirty to fifty per cent less.

I am directing the freedmen to hold their cotton and not dispose of it in the seed to the brokers here at the petty price of ten cents for long staple (Sea Island) but wait for such arrangements as are in contemplation on St. Helena Island. This establishment contemplates the sale of all freedmen's cotton raised on the neighboring Islands to be disposed of at the highest market price.

Bucking the system was slow work. Ten months later he was writing:

A prevailing custom, very disadvantageous to the progress of the freedmen is the taking advantage of his ignorance, making him pay double and treble what an article is worth.

For instance, he is made to pay $10 and $11 dollars a barrel for grits which cost the trader only $5 or $6, and if he gets it on credit he is compelled to give his obligation for $14 or $15. And corn meal which cost the purchaser two cents a pound, the freedman is compelled to pay six and eight cents for. Indeed, whatever of bread stuffs the blacks buy, they are made to pay the most extravagant prices.

The disposal of their cotton is a subject of much importance. Totally ignorant of trade regulations, of prices and rates of exchange, they are incapable at present of disposing of their own staple without protection by the authorities. A deep laid scheme and system are at work to obtain the produce of these uneducated people for little or nothing. Cotton worth from $1 to $1.40 per pound prepared are got from the producers at from twelve cents to twenty cents per lb. in the seed. When I came to the Island they were disposing of it at prices ranging from six cents to ten cents a lb.

To prevent this an Agency under Government auspices should be established to dispose of their cotton to the highest purchaser from New York and Liverpool. Last year an Agency at Lands End, St. Helena sold for the Freedmen $140,000 cotton, the minimum price being $1 a pound; doubtless the highest price which they could have obtained would have been forty cents, or a saving to these poor people of $84,000. This year the interest of the Freedmen call for the same kind of protection under the auspices of the Major General.

When the Major General again failed to act Delany went ahead on his own:

I recommended the establishment of a Freedmen's Cotton Agency, to be attended to by a competent Agent, where all

who desired it could have their cotton deposited on con-
signment, culled, ginned, bagged and sold at the highest
cash market value in Charleston, they realizing the net profits themselves, instead of the speculators. A suitable building
was obtained from the Quarter Master's department (free of
rent, of course) and all or any Freedmen owning foot-gins
were invited to put them up in the establishment. The faithful conductor of the Freedmen's Cotton Agency is Robert L.
Houston, Esqr., (Colored), late Purser on the Steamer
Planter.

The Agency had scarcely begun operations when Delany received a letter from Scott:

Charleston, S.C., October 16, 1866

Major:
It has been represented to these Headquarters, that you
have established a Depot at Hilton Head where you compel
all the Freedmen to store their Cotton. I cannot believe this
Report to be true, and, that the public may be corrected
on this subject, I wish a full and clear report of the manner
and extent to which you exercise control over the Cotton
of Freedmen. I thought I had been sufficiently explicit in
stating that the only object in having a Weigh Master,
was to see justice done, and not to act as a factor, or take
charge of the Cotton. The people must be left free to sell
when they think proper.

Robert K. Scott, Bvt. Maj. Gen.
and Asst. Commissioner

The letter was followed by an official visit from Brigadier-General
B. F. Foust, one of Scott's aides. After interviewing merchants and
freedmen, Foust reported, "Major Delany has been over-zealous,

but his intention has been to benefit the freedmen and not himself."
The Cotton Agency continued, and so did the merchants' efforts to
stop it. Months later a merchant-inspired affidavit from a freedman
was forwarded to Scott:

Major M. R. Delany ordered the people to meet him at
the Church in Mitchelville. Your deponent attended the
meeting, two or three hundred Freedmen being present.
He [Delany] made a speech to the people and told them
they must not sell their cotton to the merchants, that they
would cheat them. He further said they must bring the
cotton to him and that he would sell the same to the best
advantage. Under this order your complainant delivered to
him one Bale Ginned Cotton for which your deponent
has never received any proceeds. Not having any money
or anything to eat for myself & family [I] called on him.
He said "that the cotton was sold and that Mr. R. L. Houston, the person who took the cotton to Charleston would
be back in a few days." I have called on him several times
and have been unable to obtain a settlement.

his
John ✕ Robinson
mark

Delany countered with a second affidavit by John Robinson
denying that he had dictated the first one. Unfortunately, however,
Robert Houston, "the faithful conductor" of the Cotton Agency,
chose this moment to run off with $3,000 of the freedmen's money.
Delany pursued him, reporting:

So soon as the fraud was discovered I repaired to Charleston and had him arrested by a military guard and held in
custody till he executed a Bond to the full amount of his
liabilities to the Freedmen.

Major Delany was mustered out of Freedmen's Bureau in September 1868 (*National Archives*)

The freedmen were repaid eventually, but the black-run Cotton Agency was closed and it would be a long time before a similar enterprise started up again. Reprimanded for "a possible error of judgment," Delany continued to battle against official indifference and planter-merchant hostility. He brought about small reforms in his district but he could not uproot the system of buy-high, sell-low which kept the sharecropper in perpetual debt to the planter.

2. I Saw People Fall Like Flies

In the spring of 1866, President Johnson sent Generals Joseph Fullerton and James B. Steadman to the South to report on the operations of the Freedmen's Bureau. After a four-month tour, the generals recommended—as Johnson had hoped they would— that the Bureau be abandoned because it was no longer needed. They wrote:

At the close of the war the Freedmen's Bureau did good. The people of the South, having at first no faith in the Negroes working under a free labor system, were desirous of getting rid of them and during the summer of 1865 judicious Bureau and military officers did much toward restoring order and harmony. Before the close of 1865 there was an entire revolution in the sentiments of the people of the South with regard to Negro labor. A feeling of kindness sprang up towards the freedman.

American Freedman, September 1866

The quality of the generals' report became clear when whites in Memphis and New Orleans attacked blacks in the two cities, killing almost a hundred men, women and children. The genocidal fury of the two outbreaks shocked the country. They were not spontaneous incidents. A congressional committee investigating the riot in Memphis reported "an organized and bloody massacre of the colored people, inspired by the press and led on by officers of the law, actuated by feelings of the most deadly hatred." And General Philip Sheridan, military commander of the Department of the Gulf, wrote that the outbreak in New Orleans "was an absolute massacre, a murder which the mayor and police perpetrated without the shadow of necessity."

Destruction of a freedmen's school in Memphis in 1866

The black people of Memphis, freed early in the war when the city fell to Union forces, had joined the army or worked for the government at nearby Fort Pickering. They had amassed savings and built homes, churches and schools. More than $100,000 of their property was stolen or burned in the three-day riot which killed forty-six and wounded eighty-five. When it was over a local newspaper said, "Thank heaven the white race are once more rulers in Memphis."

The following selections from the testimony of eyewitnesses were printed in House Report No. 101, 39th Congress, 1st Session. All of the speakers were ex-slaves.

Jane Sneed, wife of a black soldier:

On Wednesday, they came into my house and searched for arms and not finding any, went away. Before they came to my house they went to Adam Lock's, right alongside of mine. With Rachael, my daughter, I went out to help get the things out of his house. The house had been set on fire and was burning. There was a man in the house asleep and some of the people asked me to go and wake him. When I went back, I walked upon the body of Rachael. She was dead and the blood running out of her mouth. Her clothes were all burned off from her.

Q—How old was your daughter?

A—About fourteen years old.

Frances Thompson, a washerwoman, was one of five women raped at gun or knife point:

Tuesday night, seven men, two of whom were policeman, came to my house. They said they must have supper and asked me what I had, and said they must have some eggs and ham and biscuit. They all sat down and ate. A girl lives with me; her name is Lucy Smith; she is about 16 years old. When they had eaten supper they said they wanted some woman to sleep with. I said we were not that sort of women. They said "that didn't make a damned bit of difference." One of them hit me on the side of my face and, holding my throat, choked me. Lucy tried to get out of the window when one of them knocked her down. They drew their pistols and said they would shoot us and fire the house if we did not let them have their way with us. All seven of the men violated us. Four of them had to do with me, and the rest with Lucy.

Primus Lane, a brewery worker:

On Wednesday, they came to my house about midnight. They said "Make a light—make a light damn quick." I lighted a match and they looked around and found a piece of candle. Then they set the house afire. When we came out

I was in my shirt-tail and [my wife] in her chemise. I ran in and got my old pantaloons and a dress for my wife. I lost all I had and I had a good deal for me to lose. I had a couple of hogs that weighed two hundred that they burned up. They burned about twenty chickens and little stuff that was in the cabin. I had right smart of garden stuff there too and all that was destroyed.

Albert Harris, a shoemaker, was robbed of $350:

On Tuesday night I was sitting down just before supper when somebody knocked at the door. I said, "Come in." In walks a man and some other people with him. He said he had orders to search my house for arms; that he was a detective. I told him I had a shotgun and, of course, if he had orders to take it, it was all right. When I brought it to him he said, "This is not all."

They unlocked my trunks and went searching all over the premises. They turned my bed and everything upside down. At length they opened the trunk where my money was. This man says, "What is that you have got?" I said it was money and not to take that. He said he had orders to take every cent for having that gun.

They had a pistol all the time and pointed right at the side of my head. When they started to go I said, "Don't carry my money away. It is all I have and I worked hard for it." They said, "Go to the Freedmen's Bureau in the morning and you will get your money."

The taunt about the Freedmen's Bureau pointed up the Bureau's helplessness in the face of serious trouble. Freedmen came to Bureau headquarters to ask for protection, but the superintendent could make no reassuring reply:

Office of Freedmen's Bureau in Memphis (*Boston Public Library*)

I told them I had no troops and could not protect them; to go back to their houses, have nothing to do with the riot, and if the government was not able to protect, it would at least redress their wrongs after the riot was over.

New Orleans blacks, many of them free-born, had been working with white Unionists to establish a stable government and a Republican party. A convention had been called for July 30, 1866, at Mechanics' Institute to consider whether to allow some blacks to vote. Rioters, led by police and firemen, shot at people who were marching to the Institute, then broke into the convention hall and attacked the delegates. Thirty-four blacks and three white Unionists were killed and hundreds of others wounded.

The following testimony from black witnesses was printed in House Report No. 16, 39th Congress, 2nd Session.

Charles W. Gibbons, a house painter and former captain in the Louisiana Native Guards:

Men marching to convention in New Orleans were shot
by police and firemen (*Boston Public Library*)

At half past eleven I went to the convention. A friend
went with me. As we were going along he said, "Captain,
there is a procession coming up." There were perhaps
forty or fifty persons in the procession. They had an American flag which belonged to the First Native Guards. A man
stepped out and ordered the procession to halt. Then he
fired.

There was a policeman about ten feet from me who said,
"There goes one damned nigger captain, the son of a bitch.
Kill him." He fired at me. I ran with the friend who was
with me. I said to him, "Let us turn round and we may have
a chance to dodge the balls." I had done that when I was
in the army. We retreated about ten steps backwards when
my friend said, "I am shot." I turned and ran. Two men
grabbed me and said, "You God damned black son of a
bitch, go 'way."

Edward Campenel, a woodworker:

I was in the hall waiting for the convention when I heard pistol-shots outside. They commenced firing through the windows, throwing brickbats &c. They tried to break in the doors but parties inside had taken chairs, tables &c and barricaded the door. After a while the policemen succeeded in opening the door and firing through the chairs and over the barricade. I rushed out and two police officers took hold of me. While they were holding me, I was beaten over the head and stabbed. The mob rushed at me crying, "Kill him, kill him."

L. J. P. Capla, a merchant:

I was standing on the west side of the Mechanics' Institute when they began to shoot. I saw policemen shooting poor laboring men, men with their tin buckets in their hands and even old men walking with sticks. They tramped upon them and mashed their heads with their boots after they were down.

I was in the Institute and heard Doctor Dostie say, "Keep quiet. We have here the emblem of the United States. They cannot fire upon us when we have this emblem." But they came in and fired upon us, although he took up the flag. I saw people fall like flies. When the policemen broke into the hall they did not respect the United States flag but cried, "Damn that dirty rag." I heard a woman call out, "Those dirty Yankees that were sent down here to destroy us, and those niggers—kill them; don't let one of them get away." There is not one inch of ground in Louisiana that is loyal to the United States. They teach their children to be disloyal in the school-books they use.

Delegates to New Orleans convention were killed when they fled from Mechanics' Institute

The outbreak in New Orleans, three months before the congressional elections of 1866, convinced northern voters of the danger of restoring civil government in the South. Johnson's defense of the rioters in that year's political campaign stiffened popular opposition to his southern policy. The result was a decisive victory for his opponents. When Congress reconvened in December, the Radical Republicans had a two-thirds majority in the House.

In March 1867 Congress passed the first Reconstruction Act—"An Act to Provide for the More Efficient Government of the Rebel States." Dividing the South into military districts, the act authorized the military commanders to supervise the election of delegates to

Crowds outside galleries of House of Representatives cheer passage of bill favorable to freedmen (*Boston Public Library*)

state constitutional conventions. After new constitutions were written, ratified by the electorate, and approved by Congress, and after the states had ratified the Fourteenth Amendment, they could be readmitted to the Union.

What distinguished these elections and conventions from any earlier ones in U.S. history was the phrase in the Act which said that "male citizens . . . of whatever race, color or previous condition" could vote and serve as delegates. Twelve northern and western states still limited or prohibited Negro suffrage but a new era was about to begin in the South. Sitting in the gallery of the House of Representatives the day the Reconstruction Act was passed, Beverly Nash, a freedman from South Carolina, said, "The clock of civilization has been put forward a hundred years."

3. We Are Entering a New Era

In the spring and summer of 1867, the officers of the Freedmen's Bureau had a new assignment—to register voters. Everywhere in the South, the new citizens were studying politics. Their teachers were men of their own color—preachers and teachers who had come from the North, educated black Southerners, ex-soldiers and ex-slaves. Together with white Unionists, they organized state and local Republican parties. A Republican newspaper described a political meeting in Alabama:

A meeting of colored people held at Montgomery was a remarkable one. A large room was filled with men from different parts of the state. One very intelligent, educated Negro said "I don't want the colored people to vote for five years. Here, and for twenty miles away they'll vote right, but farther off they will vote for 'Mass William' and 'Mass John' to get their good will."

Whereupon an old Negro called out, "Every creature has got an instinct—the calf goes to the cow to suck, the bee to the hive. We's a poor humble degraded people but we know our friends. We'd walk fifteen miles in wartime to find out about the battle. We can walk fifteen miles and more to find out how to vote."

The Loyal Georgian, April 10, 1867

Those were heady days. Men traveled long distances to attend mass meetings and barbecues and to take part in parades. "We are entering a new era." The New Orleans *Tribune* rejoiced:

The people of New Orleans witnessed last night one of the noblest scenes of which an American city can boast—a phalanx of freemen walking the streets with national colors flying and transparencies enunciating the principles of a free government. This marks a new and glorious era in our history.

The signal was given at 8 o'clock and in a moment the clubs which had formed on the cross-streets poured into the wide avenue and Rampart street was suddenly illuminated with fifteen thousand Chinese lanterns, transparents and torches. The banners and flag were flying to the breeze; the drums were beating and the fifes playing; men in the ranks were joining their vigorous shouts to the joyful hurrahs of the immense crowd gathered on the sidewalks.

Riding behind a squad of torch bearers [was] the Grand Marshal, escorted by a splendid staff of assistant marshals. They were followed by the First Ward Club, with transparents among which was "Free School Open to All," the Third Ward Club with transparents bearing "Eight Hours a Legal Day's Work," "No Contract System," the Fourth Ward—"Free Press," "We Know Our Friends."

The procession marched the whole route, coming down to Lafayette Square where the meeting took place. It was then a few minutes past midnight. Drums, fifes and brass bands were heard from all sides. Beautiful sky-rockets were now and then rising up in the sky and would elicit from the crowd volleys of deafening hurrahs.

The New Orleans Tribune, May 30, 1867

In a more somber mood, Dr. R. I. Cromwell, a black Northerner, published "An Address to the Colored People of Louisiana," which he delivered at church and club meetings. He began by warning against "wolves in sheep's clothing," then explained the electoral process:

Everywhere in the South, the new citizens were talking politics (*Boston Public Library*)

The overseer of plantations who once dared prowl around your cabins to destroy your families, the old master (so-called) now comes to tell you he is your best friend, vote for a Southerner whom you know! Yes, you know him. You know that when you were his slave you, your wife, your children were treated like dumb beasts, half-fed, half-clothed. These men now come to you and ask you to trust them, elevate them into office and they will do you good.

Will you be deceived by these old foxy fellows? Believe them not, trust them not, for if you do, we are shipwrecked. When any of that class comes to you to ask you to vote for him tell him *no*. Don't be afraid of his not giving you employment for he is compelled to have your labor. Fulfill your contracts to the letter and vote right and we will be sure to win.

In order to vote on election day, we must comply with the laws of our country. What are these laws? Everyone must go to the register, give his name, number of his house, his ward, and street, get his certificate, put it away until election day, then take it out, go to the polls and vote for some good man. This certificate is to show you are a citizen of Louisiana and entitled to vote FOR WHOM YOU PLEASE.

Now, the persons for whom you vote have to meet in a convention to make a constitution for this State. If we do not vote in good and true men we will have slavery in another form, and qualified suffrage, excluding colored men. We want every man to vote, hold office, sit on juries, travel on steamboats, eat in any restaurant, drink in any saloon, dine at any hotel, or educate our children at any school we choose. We demand equal privileges with the whites in all things. We must elect as many of our own race as we can, join with our Southern loyalists, choose good men from among them. But be sure to vote for no rebel or secessionist, for if you do, you are pulling the hemp to hang yourself with.

Reader, I hope you will cut this out and keep it until after the election. If you know of any that cannot read, read it to them. Remember, it is from one of your race who is an old abolitionist of the North who has been here in New Orleans the last four years fighting against conservatism and prejudice and traitors and shall continue to fight on till this State is reconstructed on the true basis of liberty—political, social and religious.

The New Orleans *Tribune,* April 25, 1867

In every community, would-be voters sent their leading men to state conventions where the candidates for the forthcoming election were to be chosen. Young Robert G. Fitzgerald, a Pennsylvanian, who had been teaching in a small Virginia town was asked to be a delegate to the Republican convention in Richmond. Excerpts from his diary show him hesitant to accept for fear of incurring the enmity of his white neighbors:

July 10th, 1867—Received my mail and a request signed by 30 persons begging that I accept the nomination as delegate to the coming Convention:

July 8, 1867

Sir:

We the undersigned members of Republican Party and citizens of Amelia Co. Va. do hereby nominate and request you to attend the coming State Convention; as we believe you are the most reliable we can send to represent our interests in that important Body. We therefore beg that you accept the nomination.

Thos: B. Pollard
Wooster Miller   }   & 27 others
Grandison Harris

A startling announcement to me, and I feel that it is almost unkind to request me to fill that very important post which will incur the utmost hatred of the whole white population and then too I am so unprepared, but still how willingly would I serve were I qualified for so important a trust.

July 20th—Weekly mass meeting today at Chapel. The citizens of Amelia County held a meeting at F[reedmen's] Chapel to elect Delegates to the Convention of August 1st. Had a very animating time speaking etc.

July 31st—Getting ready to go to Richmond. The Road issued half-price tickets to Delegates, so delegates are not sorry by a great deal. At 5 we were safely landed in R[ichmond]. Tonight attended a meeting at the "Montecello" house. Also attended a caucus meeting at which the County delegates spoke. Stopped tonight at Mr. Stewart. 62 cents. Pd. Mr. Harris $1.20 on board.

August 1st—The great day of trial has at last come; and with it hopes and fears for the success of the Republican Cause. Went to the "Old African Church" where there was a very large number of Republicans awaiting the opening of the Church, to gain admission. ½ past 11 a cry was raised, "Make way for the Committee" and a dense rush made for the doors. The Republicans succeed in gaining and crowding out the Conservatives and effectually organizing. The Reps were the only successful party, working so rapidly that the Conservatives stood aghast, not knowing how to take hold of the matter. There were about 5,000 Delegates and others present.

A political meeting (*Boston Public Library*)

August 2nd—Meeting convened at 10 A.M. After finishing
up the business of the convention, Gov. Pierpont and others,
made excellent addresses and at 4, the meeting adjourned.
August 10th—At a great Mass Meeting at Amelia C. H.
speakers advocated a unanimity of feeling between races
and a quiet acquiescence on the part of the white to the
Black holding office, etc.

> From Robert G. Fitzgerald's unpublished diary, quoted
> by permission of his granddaughter, Pauli Murray

Not all of the new spokesmen were Northerners like Cromwell
and Fitzgerald. At a mass meeting in Savannah attended by seven
thousand people, the man of the hour was James Sims, an ex-slave.
Formerly a waiter in a Savannah hotel, Sims had educated himself
by listening to the diners' conversations, studying a dictionary to
master the words they had used. After emancipation he became
a teacher and minister. His brother, Thomas, had made newspaper
headlines sixteen years earlier when, as a runaway slave, he had
been captured in Boston and returned to Georgia. From a report of
the meeting:

Col. Fitch who made the *white* speech of the day gave
the colored people a great deal of advice. He said, "Politics
is not the study of a day, but of years of toil and a perfect
knowledge of human nature. Take your politics from your
homesteads and firesides; learn to suspect those whites who
tell you that you are their equals. Politicians will be your
bane if you fail to act wisely in your new relations to the
race which always has and always will be the predominant
race."

James Sims, a colored man, said that [whites] knew
nothing of his race. Under the old system Negroes were

compelled to use dissimulation towards their masters. Now, for the first time, he could tell them the truth.

"Colored men are not fools. They knew enough to fight right and they will vote right. I wish the white people to understand distinctly that we will not elect a Rebel Mayor or have any more *brutal policemen.*

"Offices should be filled by both white and colored men who are capable of serving with honor. I would have white and colored aldermen and white and colored policemen and the sooner people know it the better. Some people might be surprised to see white and colored men working shoulder to shoulder in the political field—I am not. I have children at school in Massachusetts and expect to see them in Congress some day."

It is impossible to describe the intense enthusiasm exhibited by the speaker and the proud look of triumph with which he alluded to the great change within a few years —to the difference between his brother, the great fugitive, brought from Boston and dragged through the streets of Savannah to jail—and him, James Sims, introduced by a Southern gentleman to address a political gathering. The crowd caught his enthusiasm and applauded him to the echo. Sims will undoubtedly be elected one of the City Council, or go to the Georgia Legislature next summer. His clear musical voice, distinct enunciation and elegant style of delivery impressed everyone and greatly astonished those who had never heard him speak before. He was followed by T. G. Campbell, a colored man, and an excellent speaker.

The New Orleans Tribune, April 13, 1867

Sims's insistence on black as well as white candidates for office was echoed in other states. When the Republicans of South Carolina met in July, Richard H. Gleaves, a black Pennsylvanian, was elected convention president. At a meeting in Louisiana, P. B. S. Pinch-back, formerly a captain in the Louisiana Native Guards, proposed:

That the Radical Republican Party of the State of Louisiana will support no man for office who will not openly and boldly pledge himself to make an equal distribution among white and colored alike, of all offices to which he may have the power of appointment. The resolution was put to a vote and adopted.

The New Orleans Tribune, June 14, 1867

In an article headed "Has the Time Come to Drop the Words 'White' and 'Black'?" the editors of the New Orleans *Tribune* wrote:

Some of our friends, through good motives are indignant at the words "white" and "black" being found still in the proceedings of a Radical Convention. They argue, and not without some show of reason, that men who aspire to eradicate all distinctions on account of race should not take into consideration these very distinctions. But to this we must answer that in order to suppress a wrong it is not sufficient to omit mentioning it. We have to see that no such wrong shall be committed in the future.

It is said fitness should be the only qualification for office. We agree. But fitness should be as readily recognized in a black man as in a white; and this has not been the fact since the Reconstruction bill has been passed. Eleven ward clubs have been organized in the city of New Orleans and only ONE [black] President was chosen. Was it that only ONE man from among our 17,000 colored citizens was fit to occupy the chair of a political assembly? No one will assume that position. It was, therefore, because their fitness was disregarded.

Registering to vote (*Boston Public Library*)

Nearly 200 registrars were appointed for the State of Louisiana. NOT A SINGLE CITIZEN of African descent was selected. Was it because none was fit?

Fitness is, at the present time, but another word for color. It reminds one of the celebrated inscription that the Spaniard Menendez affixed, two centuries ago, to the gallows where he suspended the companions of the Frenchman Rigaud, in the Carolinas. As Spain and France were at peace, as the white and colored Republicans are today, the Spaniard did not dare to hang the Frenchmen as such and therefore he inscribed upon the gallows: "Hanged—not as Frenchmen, but as heretics." The modern Menendez will say to colored applicants: "Rejected—not as Africans, but as incapable."

The New Orleans *Tribune*, June 18, 1867

Before summer's end, the pressures exerted by the new electorate resulted in a trickle of black registrars, policemen and magistrates. A black mayor took office in St. Martin, Louisiana, and P. B. S. Pinchback became an Inspector of Customs in New Orleans.

Black official supervises voting in Washington (*Boston Public Library*)

In some areas, freedmen sought alliances with their old masters, only to be rebuffed. T. Thomas Fortune told of his father's efforts to work with the whites in Florida:

It was natural for [Emanuel Fortune] to take the leadership in any independent movement of Negroes. During and before the Civil War he had commanded his time as a tanner and expert shoe and bootmaker. In such social life as the slaves were allowed and in church work, he took the leader's part. When the matter of the Constitutional Convention was decided upon his people in Jackson County naturally looked to him to shape up matters for them. He visited the leading white people and invited them to join in selecting a proper delegation, but they took the position that it was the business of the Negro and the carpetbaggers, "the Yankee strangers," as they styled them, and they would have nothing to do with it. Mr. Fortune strove to prove to them that it was their business and to their best interests to help in making a new constitution and government on the Reconstruction plan provided by Congress, but they would not be convinced. The southern whites very generally took this position.

Norfolk Journal and Guide, September 3, 1927

John R. Lynch, an ex-slave who became active in Mississippi politics, explained the policy of "masterly inactivity" adopted by most white Southerners:

The Democratic party took the position that no respectable white Democrat could afford to participate in an election in which colored men were allowed to vote. To do so, they held, would not only be humiliating, but the contamination would be unwise, if not dangerous. Besides they were firm in the belief that the country would ultimately repudiate the congressional plan of reconstruction and that in the meantime it would be wise for them to give expression to their abhorrence of it by pursuing a course of "masterly inactivity."

The Autobiography of John Roy Lynch,
John Hope Franklin, ed. (Chicago, 1970)

Some whites, however, attempted to control the elections by intimidating blacks. From complaints received by the commander of the Third Military District, which included Georgia, Alabama and Florida:

Calhoun, Georgia, August 25, 1867

General:

We the Colored people of the town of Calhoun and County of Gordon desire to call your attention to the State of Affairs that now exist in our midst.

On the 16th day of the month, the Union Republican Party held a Meeting which the Colored people of the County attended en masse. Since that time we seem to have the particular hatred and spite of that class who were opposed to the principles set forth in that meeting.

Their first act was to deprive us of the privilege to worship any longer in their Church. Since we have procured one of our own, they threaten us if we hold meetings in it.

There has been houses broken open, windows smashed and doors broken down in the dead hours of the night, men rushing in, cursing and swearing and discharging their Pistols inside the house. Men have been knocked down and unmercifully beaten and yet the authorities do not notice it at all. We would open a school here, but are almost afraid to do so, not knowing that we have any protection for life or limb.

We wish to do right, obey the Laws and live in peace and quietude but when we are assailed at the midnight hour, our lives threatened and the Laws fail to protect or assist us we can but defend ourselves, let the consequences be what they may. Yet we wish to avoid all such collisions.

We would respectfully ask that a few soldiers be sent here, believing it is the only way we can live in peace until after the Elections this fall.

[Twenty-four signatures]

The first vote

Forsyth, Georgia, October 31, 1867

Dear Sir:

To inform you of some things going on here in this county and other counties joining, the white people won't let the colored people register their names nor vote. Last Saturday there was 250 colored people went up to the county seat to register their names and the Rebels run them off from the place and not let them register their names.

George H. Clower

Pompey Daniel being duly sworn, Deposeth and Saith that his employer, Mr. Abraham Gammil did on the 30th day of October 1867 discharge the said Pompey Daniel from his employ for voting at the present Election and has refused to pay the said Pompey Daniel what he owes him. The said Abraham Gammil now owes the said Pompey Daniel from his contract the sum of $150 Dolls.

his
Pompey × Daniel
mark

National Archives

By the fall of 1867 seven hundred thousand black men and six hundred and sixty thousand whites had registered to vote. During the winter and spring of 1868 the delegates they elected met to draw up new constitutions for the states of the old Confederacy. For the first time in history black men sat alongside whites in the legislative halls of the South.

Southern newspapers labeled the conventions "The Menagerie," "Ring-Streaked and Striped Negro Convention," the "Black and Tans" and wrote of the delegates as "baboons" and "monkeys." Readers shuddered at reports of "unshaven, uncombed, unwashed" field hands making laws for aristocratic whites. "No such hideous bodies of men had ever been assembled before upon the soil of the United States" a historian wrote three decades later.

These descriptions bore little relation to reality. Most of the blacks who assumed leadership in the conventions were ministers, teachers, lawyers, and doctors who prepared themselves carefully for their new duties. Francis L. Cardozo who had been born free in Charleston, South Carolina, was a graduate of the University of Glasgow in Scotland. At the end of the war he returned to his birthplace to organize freedmen's schools. He was principal of

Francis L. Cardozo (*Boston Public Library*)

Avery Institute, a school supported by the American Missionary Association, when he wrote the following to the secretary of the Association:

Charleston, South Carolina, November 4, 1867

Dear Brother:

My friends here have requested me to become a Candidate for the Constitutional Convention, and I have consented to do so, more, however, from a sense of duty, than from choice, for I have no desire for the turbulent political scene, but being the *only educated colored* man here my friends thought it my duty to go if elected, and I consented to do so.

Black Members of Louisiana's Constitutional Convention and first Reconstruction Legislature (*Walter Brainerd Spencer Collection, Special Collection Division, Tulane University*)

It is not yet certain whether there will be a Convention or not, and if there be one, whether the Republican Ticket, on which I am, will be elected. But it is probable both these things will happen and I should like therefore to commence preparing myself now. I wish you would send me for that purpose a copy of the Book containing the Constitution of *all the States*. I am told that work can be obtained in New York only. I wish you would send it down as soon as possible. If you think of anything else that would be suitable for me in such a position I would be obliged to you to send it. I can't think of any other work except the one mentioned, but *you* will know of others.

I have taken it for granted you will have no objections to my going if elected. I presume it will meet sometime in December. I shall take care that the School does not suffer.

F. L. Cardozo

American Missionary Association Archives,
Amistad Research Center

Educated men were found in every state convention. James T. Rapier, another graduate of the University of Glasgow, was prominent in Alabama's assembly. Florida's roster included Jonathan C. Gibbs, a graduate of Dartmouth and Princeton Theological Seminary. The Rev. James T. Lynch was a leader in the Mississippi convention and Henry McNeal Turner, later a bishop of the A.M.E. (African Methodist Episcopal) Church, spoke for black Georgians.

Although a majority of the delegates were former slaves, some illiterate, others lacking in formal schooling, they could not be dismissed as witless Republican puppets. They came untrained to the art of politics, but what they lacked in experience they made up in their understanding of the uses of political power. Most were skilled workers—shoemakers, blacksmiths, carpenters—men of natural ability who, like Emanuel Fortune, had been leaders in their localities before emancipation. Many had proven themselves in battle. Prince Rivers' commanding officer had said of him, "If there

Robert Smalls

should ever be a black monarchy in South Carolina, he will be its king." Robert Smalls had liberated the Confederate gunboat *Planter* and served the Union as its captain until 1866. Others were runaways who had obtained an education and some knowledge of the political process during their years in the North.

One of these runaways, George Teamoh, described his first foray into politics. Formerly a brickyard-worker he had lived in the North for twelve years. After his return to Virginia he was elected to the constitutional convention and then to the state senate.

The colored members of the convention displayed remarkable good sense in not allowing themselves to be captured by sophisticated arguments. We did not have a

George Teamoh (*Library of Congress*)

colored member who could offset a speech of any great length coming from the other side, but we invariably voted right. Nor was it to be expected that we could at that time have had knowledge of constitutional reconstruction as many of us could neither read or write, having gone there from the farm yards &c. For my part I went there a "graduate" from Capt. John Thompson's brickyard. Hence if there had been anything to perform in that direction I was on hand to assist. But in spite of their disqualifications, my people seems to have been possessed of a natural itching to meet, in open debate, every question which came up

Virginia's Constitutional Convention was labeled the "Black Crook Convention" because a quarter of the delegates were black (*Boston Public Library*)

for discussion. Under all the circumstances, the colored members bore themselves well.

For ourself, we had a turn at the wheel of fire, and in about forty minutes it burnt all the education out of us which we had gathered within that number of (40) years. Agricultural degrees and brickyard diplomas, I found, passed for but very little. After delivering our speech we had but little to say during the entire session, beyond that of voting and rising to questions of privilege.

"George Teamoh's Autobiography," manuscript,
Carter Woodson Papers, Library of Congress

Beverly Nash, who as a slave had been a hotel waiter, was equally modest when he told the South Carolina convention:

Beverly Nash (*Boston Public Library*)

We are not prepared for this suffrage. But we can learn. Give a man tools and let him commence to use them and in time he will earn a trade. So it is with voting. We may not understand it at the start, but in time we shall learn to do our duty.

Nash learned quickly. His shrewdness soon made him one of the most listened-to members of the convention. When it was proposed to invite South Carolina's governor to address the gathering, he objected:

We are here to provide a Constitution for South Carolina, not for the purpose of making converts. We didn't come here to see Governor Orr make a flight like a squirrel from one tree to another. I remember he said to me last spring, "Better wait and find out whether this is going to be a failure or not; don't jine the Republican party yet; don't jine the Democratic party." He wanted me to sit on the fence with him and when he got ready to make one of his flights, I suppose he wanted me to follow him. No, gentlemen, I don't propose that Governor Orr shall come here to teach us ground and lofty tumbling.

I come from a part of the country where the people are Republican; from a District where they would rather hear Governor Perry because we know he is going to cuss us and abuse us, but Governor Orr! Why he tumbles so fast that it makes a man's head dizzle to look at him.

Now, Governor Orr is in a position which reminds me of what an old woman once told me about John Tyler. He's hanging upside down between two parties. The Conservatives are trying to kick him off; the Republicans don't want him, and I reckon he'll hang there until the blood runs down into his brains and then we shall get rid of his body.

Proceedings of the Constitutional Convention of
South Carolina (Charleston, 1868)

Only one fourth of all of the delegates to the constitutional conventions were black and in only one state were the blacks in a majority. The eyes of the country focused on Charleston where seventy-six black men and forty-eight whites met to write new laws for South Carolina. Their convention was called "the maddest, most unscrupulous and infamous revolution in history" and its black members were described as "African savages" and "gibbering, louse-eaten, devil-worshipping barbarians." Yet the minutes of their convention show them working with dignity, intelligence and restraint. Better than any other contemporary document, the nine-hundred-

Robert C. De Large who later became a congressman
(*Library of Congress*)

page "Proceedings of the Constitutional Convention of South Carolina" (Charleston, 1868) from which the following selections are
taken illustrates the thinking of black men in the fateful year of 1868.

When the convention began there was a motion to employ
messengers and pages. Among the black delegates who opposed
it were:

Robert C. De Large [a former slave]: I am opposed to having so many hangers on and digging unnecessarily into the State Treasury. If we keep on we will soon have as many officers as delegates.

Jonathan J. Wright [a lawyer from Pennsylvania]: Most of us have been used to waiting on ourselves and I think we can do it yet.

Francis L. Cardozo: The Convention does not need them and it is desirable to avoid all unnecessary expense, especially in the present empty condition of the State Treasury.

As the volume of committee work increased, the delegates considered shortening the daily meeting hours of the convention as a whole. Black members spoke against the proposal:

Jonathan J. Wright: We are here to work and the people are paying our expenses. We have most of us been in the habit of working. There are but few persons in this assemblage who have not been in the habit of getting up in the morning at six o'clock, while we do not get to work here before nine or ten and work until three.

Henry E. Hayne [a free-born Charlestonian who had fought for the Union]: We have been since half-past ten o'clock and it is now twenty minutes to one, discussing whether we shall have two sessions a day or one. The best remedy would be to do less talking and more real working.

The Charleston *Mercury,* owned by R. B. Rhett, a Confederate strategist, took the lead in attacking the convention and mocking the delegates. When a motion to ban the *Mercury* reporter from the convention was introduced, black delegates spoke against it. (The reporter was ultimately excluded, but after a fist fight with a white delegate.):

Henry Hayne (*Boston Public Library*)

Francis L. Cardozo: The *Mercury* has burlesqued us but to attempt to exclude its reporter would be only to exhibit a smallness, a pettiness of spite, unworthy of our character. Let it come and pursue what course it may please; let us pursue our straightforward course and the world will judge between us.

Alonzo J. Ransier [a free-born Charlestonian]: It is dangerous to turn away any reporter on account of his political opinions. It is a stab at the liberty of the press.

William J. Whipper [a lawyer from the North]: Its editors have a right to burlesque if they choose to use it. We have come here for a great purpose and we should not be swerved from it.

When a proposed bill of rights for the state was under discussion, a white delegate objected to the phrase: "all men are born free and equal." A black delegate replied:

Benjamin F. Randolph: It always seemed strange to me that any intelligent person should question the meaning of the phrase. We know that some men are born tall, some short, some with good sense, some with little sense, some with big and some with little feet. But this phrase was not intended to refer to men in a physiological sense. It refers to the rights of men politically speaking and in that sense I understand and defend it. All men are born with certain inalienable rights which it is their privilege to enjoy.

Randolph proposed a clause which was sharply debated, then included, in the bill of rights as adopted:

Benjamin F. Randolph offered the following amendment: Distinction on account of race or color shall be prohibited and all classes of citizens, irrespective of race or color, shall enjoy all common, equal and political privileges.

After two white delegates spoke against the amendment, blacks defended it:

Francis L. Cardozo: As colored men we have been cheated out of our rights for two centuries and now that we have the opportunity I want to fix them in the Constitution in such a way that no lawyer, however cunning, can possibly misinterpret the meaning. Nearly all of the white inhabitants of the State are ready at any moment to deprive us of these rights and not a loophole should be left that would permit them to do it. By all means insert the words "without distinction of race or color" wherever necessary to give force and clearness to our purpose.

The Committee on Education, chaired by Cardozo, proposed a statewide system of free public schools, institutions for the insane, blind, deaf and dumb, and the maintenance of a state university. This was radical enough, for South Carolina had never had a public school system or made provisions for its handicapped. But it was Section 11 of the proposed law that provoked the greatest discussion:

All the public schools, colleges and universities supported by the public funds shall be free and open to all the children of the state without regard to race or color.

After the final reading of the education report, there was a motion to recommit Section 11 to the committee:

Benjamin F. Randolph: The object of this motion is to get rid of those two little words "race or color." I ask the house not to allow it. There is no use in our backing down from these questions. We are laying the foundation of a new structure here and the time has come when we shall have to meet things squarely, now or never. The day is coming when we must decide whether the two races shall live together or not.

When the committee brought back Section 11, unchanged, a white delegate said that its passage would endanger the "peace and harmony" of the state.

Jonathan J. Wright: This provision leaves it so that white and colored children can attend school together, if they desire to do so, but I do not believe the colored children will want to go to the white schools or vice versa. The colored people do not want to force what is called social equality; that is a matter which will regulate itself. No law we can pass can compel associations that are distasteful. When the idea is held up before you, it is only a bugbear with which some persons would frighten you.

All you have to do is to stand up, face the music for a while and every man, white and black, in South Carolina will come to time. This prejudice will be broken down. We are not framing a Constitution for today but for years. Let us so enact laws that all children will have the benefit of all schools for which the public pay. We must not falter or shrink one inch, or pause in the work of doing all classes justice. Time will prove our work.

Francis L. Cardozo: To remove prejudices the most natural method would be to allow children five or six years of age to mingle in schools together. Under such training, prejudice must eventually die out; but if we postpone it until they become men and women, prejudice will be so established that no mortal can obliterate it.

We have not said there shall be no separate schools. On the contrary I have no doubt there will be such in most districts. In Charleston I am sure the colored pupils in my school would not like to go to a white school. Without flattery I may say I have not seen as good a public school in Charleston as my own. In sparsely-settled country districts where perhaps there are not more than twenty-five or thirty children for ten or fifteen white children to demand a separation would be absurd. I hope the Convention will give its assent to no such proposition.

Section 11 finally passed on the convention's next-to-last day, with four white delegates voting against it.

In Congress, Thaddeus Stevens had been advocating confiscation of the plantations of leading Confederates so that their lands could be given to the freedmen. South Carolina's black spokesmen were more conservative. Richard H. Cain, Methodist minister from the North, proposed to petition Congress for funds to buy land which would be sold to the freedmen.

Richard H. Cain: Over three thousand men, women and children are homeless, landless. How are they to live? The New York *Tribune* says "root, hog or die" but we ought to have some place to root. As long as people are working on shares and at the end of every year are in debt, so long will they and the country suffer.

I do not desire to have a foot of land confiscated. I want every man to stand upon his own character. I want these lands purchased by the government and the people afforded an opportunity to buy from the government. If the same amount of money that has been employed by the Bureau in feeding lazy, worthless men and women had been expended in purchasing lands we would today have no need of the Bureau.

If this measure is carried out we will see all along our lines of roads, little farms, log cabins filled with happy families. There will spring up depots for the reception of cotton, corn and other cereals. Prosperity will return to the state. I want to see the state alive, to hear the hum of the spindle and the mills. I want to see cattle and horses and fowls and everything that makes up a happy home. The white man and black man may then work in harmony and secure prosperity to all coming generations.

Robert C. De Large: There are over a thousand freedmen in this state who have, within the last year, purchased lands from the whites. We propose that the Government should aid us in the purchase of more lands, to be divided into small tracts and given on credit to homeless families. In every district freedmen are roaming because the large land-holders will not sell their lands unless the freedmen have the money to pay cash for them. We propose to give them lands and to place them in a position by which they will be enabled to sustain themselves.

After extended discussion, the petition passed, although three black men voted against it. There was a similar lack of unanimity when the convention debated whether or not to have a moratorium on debts contracted before June 30, 1865—debts contracted largely for the purchase of slaves. Cardozo opposed the moratorium because he hoped that the planters' indebtedness would force them to sell their big plantations:

Francis L. Cardozo: Let the lands of the South be divided. I would not say for one moment they should be confiscated, but if sold, let the plantation system go. We will never have true freedom until we abolish the system of agriculture which existed in the Southern States.

About a hundred poor colored men of Charleston formed themselves into a Charleston Land Company. They subscribed for a number of shares at $10 a share, one dollar payable monthly. They have been meeting for a year. Yesterday they purchased 600 acres of land for $6,600 that would have sold for $25,000 or $50,000 in better times. They would not have been able to buy had not the owner through necessity been compelled to sell. I look upon it as the natural result of the war that this system of large plantations should be abolished.

Several black delegates favored forgiving the indebtedness. Among them:

William J. Whipper: I spent two years of the morning of my life in the war carried on for the purpose of crushing the rebellion. These things should be forgotten now. Assembled as we are, representing the people of South Carolina, our sole object should be to pass laws that will benefit the whole people. And if we see any class of people suffering, it is our duty to relieve them. I care not whether they are people crying "ring-streaked-and-striped" or not. Here we should forget all prejudices and not be swerved from our purposes for anything.

Whatever you do, above all I hope it will not be done for the purpose of revenge. When I left the army at the close of the war, I was zealous to see the leaders of the rebellion hung and every man engaged in it disfranchised and their lands confiscated. The government has thought proper to pursue a different course. For us to suffer anything to be done that savors of vengeance is wrong, cruel and unjust.

The debate concluded with a compromise resolution asking for a three-month moratorium on debts. Another issue of major importance was voting. In the opening days of the convention, B. F. Randolph proposed:

That all persons coming of age after the first of January 1875 shall possess the qualifications of reading and writing intelligently in order to vote.

When the proposal was adopted by the Committee on Franchise, other black men opposed it:

Robert B. Elliott: For nearly two hundred and fifty years we have been deprived of the rights of education. This Convention has met for the purpose of laying down a basis of universal suffrage. How would you face your constituents? Would you say to them, you sent us to lay the foundations of liberty deep and broad for your children and your children's children but after getting to Charleston we found out you were not fit for it; neither do we believe your children would be fit for it; consequently we have taken it away from you? Will you face your constituents and tell them this is the case? I for one will not do it.

A. J. Ransier: The right to vote belongs alike to the wise and the ignorant, to the virtuous and the vicious, and I cannot consent to any qualification. I do not like to use the words "colored" or "white" in discussing this case, but necessity compels me to do so. So long as the question of suffrage to the white man was concerned I never heard of an educational qualification. So soon, however, as the colored man applies for this privilege, you at once hear the demand that he must be surrounded with restrictions which would deprive a large portion of our race of this privilege. It is our chief means for self-defense.

Richard H. Cain: I would not deprive any being, rich or poor, of that franchise by which alone he can protect himself as a citizen. Whether learned or ignorant he has an inalienable right to say who shall govern him. He may not understand a great deal of the knowledge that is derived from books but he can judge between right and wrong. For two hundred years it has been the curse of the slave states that a certain class of men have deprived the majority of their right to express their will. In remodeling the institutions of this country we propose to establish them on a broad basis so that the halo of liberty may overshadow every class of men. The present condition has opened up to us an age of progress in which mankind will take a forward bound toward humanity. In this Constitution we do not wish to leave a jot or tittle to remind our children of their former state of slavery. I would have this instrument hold up to every man an inducement to become, in mind and estate, an honest, educated and efficient citizen of this country.

After the educational qualification was defeated, William Whipper moved to strike out the word "male" from the new election law. The convention had passed a divorce law and a law giving married women the right to retain their own property, two "firsts" for South Carolina, but no one seconded Whipper's motion for women's suffrage. At that time he was courting Frances Rollin, a brainy and beautiful woman who later became his wife. Perhaps he was thinking of her and her four equally talented sisters when he persevered in calling for support for his motion:

William J. Whipper: However frivolous you may think it, I know the time will come when every man and woman in this country will have the right to vote. I acknowledge the superiority of woman. There are large numbers of the sex who have an intelligence more than equal to our own. Is it right or just to deprive these intelligent beings of the privileges which we enjoy? The time will come when you will have to meet this question. It will continue to be agitated until it must ultimately triumph. However derisively we may treat these noble women who are struggling for their sex, we shall yet see them successful in the assertion of their rights.

There were no speeches in reply, but the minutes recorded:

The question was taken on the motion to strike out the word "male" and decided in the negative.

During its fifty-three days of deliberation, the convention took care of other essential business. It passed a homestead law; re-organized the courts with a requirement for elected instead of appointed judges; abolished imprisonment for debt; outlawed duel-ing; and petitioned Congress to restore full citizenship to leaders of the Confederacy.

The convention was far from being a "sure thing" contest between a black majority and a white minority. Many, perhaps most, of its decisions were made by members of one race joining those of the other, on the merits of the issue. Together, these one hundred and twenty-four delegates gave South Carolina its first democratic con-stitution, the most progressive one the state would see for a hundred years.

Two eloquent men, one a former slave, the other a free black, looked hopefully to the future:

Beverly Nash: We must unite with our white fellow-citi-zens. Can we afford to lose from the councils of state, our best men? Can we spare judges from the bench? Can we put fools or strangers in their positions? No, fellow-citizens, no! gloomy indeed would be that day. We want in charge of our interest only our best and ablest men. And then with a strong pull, and a long pull, and a pull together, up goes South Carolina.

Richard H. Cain: I want to see a change in this country. Instead of the colored people being always penniless, I want to see them coming in with their mule teams and ox teams. I want to see them come with their corn and potatoes and exchange for silks and satins. I want to see children coming to enjoy life as it ought to be enjoyed.

III· THE SPOKESMEN

At the North, the Negro is "a man and
a brother" but at the South he is a man
and a power.

The New National Era, August 3, 1871

1. The Grass-roots Politicians

On November 24, 1868, a black man became lieutenant governor
of Louisiana:

Shortly before noon, yesterday, H. C. Warmoth, white,
and Oscar J. Dunn, colored, proceeded to the Governor's office in the Mechanics' Institute and qualified for holding office according to Reconstruction Acts by taking the test

oath. At noon the lieutenant governor entered the senate chamber and took possession of the chair as presiding officer. His presence was greeted by the colored persons present with cheers and loud clapping of hands.

New Orleans *Picayune,* November 25, 1868

Twenty-seven years earlier the *Picayune* had published an advertisement:

$5 REWARD.
RUNAWAY from the subscribers, on the 23d Nov. last, the negro boy OSCAR DUNN, an apprentice to the plastering trade. He is of a griffe color, between 20 and 21 years of age, and about 5 feet 10 or 11 inches high. All persons are cautioned not to harbor the said boy, under penalty of the law.
WILSON & PATTERSON,
47 tf   Corner of St. John and Common sts.

Now Oscar Dunn, fugitive slave, Union veteran, Republican party leader and second in command of the state's government addressed the senate:

The fact that the senate of Louisiana is presided over by a man of my race shows the progress which has taken place in the southern states. I hope that progress will continue until everywhere throughout this land intelligence will be respected, whatever the color of the skin. Not that I claim intelligence for myself, but that I hope by your assistance and kindness toward me and my race to prove worthy of every advantage bestowed upon us. There is no one present more anxious than I am to see that the State of Louisiana is restored to the Union—not as it was, but as it is. Previously she was said to be a free government; but her freedom was confined to one class. Now she is going in under a republican form of government granting civil and political rights to all men.

As to myself and my people we are not seeking social equality; that is a thing no law can govern. We all have our preferences. We all wish to select our associates and no legislation can select them for us. We simply ask an equal opportunity of supporting our families, of educating our children, and of becoming worthy citizens of this government.

I am truly happy that we are about to return into the Union, for I as much as any of you object to military rule. There is ability enough in the State to govern our own affairs and I believe that harmony will exist among us, to such an extent that no interference of military power will be necessary.

Gentlemen, I thank you for the kind courtesies you have extended toward me. I shall use my utmost endeavors to preside impartially over this honorable body and to promote harmony and dignity in its deliberations.

Louisiana Senate Journal (New Orleans, 1868)

Oscar J. Dunn, gavel in hand, symbolized the beginning of Radical Reconstruction when, for a brief period, there was a movement toward genuine democracy in the South. By the summer of 1868, eight Rebel states had been readmitted to the Union. That fall black men cast their first ballots in a presidential election, assuring victory for Ulysses S. Grant, nominee of the Republican party.

All over the South men who had been chattel a few years earlier sat in the legislatures and state cabinets. Ex-slaves and black Northerners served as superintendents of public education, sheriffs, justices of the peace and judges. In South Carolina, Mississippi and Louisiana, black voters were in the majority. Yet even in these states, black leaders never urged "Negro domination." At a meeting in Charleston, Jonathan J. Wright, associate justice of South Carolina's supreme court, explained:

It has been represented that the colored people of this State desired to hold all or a great majority of offices. I here

Oscar J. Dunn (*Boston Public Library*)

Black policeman in Charleston, South Carolina (*Boston Public Library*)

Jonathan J. Wright (*Boston Public Library*)

assert (and I can show that my assertion is true) that the colored people were never, or are they at this time, desirous of holding even one half of the offices of the State, though we have thirty thousand majority of the voting population.

[In] 1868, a State Convention was held to choose State officers. There were in that Convention about two colored persons to one white, yet all the State officers chosen were white, save one, the Secretary of State (F. L. Cardozo). As Governor we selected R. K. Scott, as Lieutenant Governor L. Boozer, a native South Carolinian, one who had been a slaveholder but had cheerfully accepted the situation of affairs. The General Assembly met on the sixth day of July of the same year. Of the thirty-two State Senators chosen, nine were colored. In the House of Representatives there was a majority of colored. The United States Senators were chosen both white. Of the eleven Judges all were white; of the thirty-one County Treasurers appointed all were white; of the thirty-two Auditors appointed all were white but one; of the Magistrates appointed about three-fifths were white; of the thirty-one School Commissioners elected ten were colored.

Now I ask, does this plain statement of facts warrant the report that is heralded abroad that the colored people in South Carolina, because they have the power, have set up a black man's government? No, no; but it shows that such a report was gotten up to influence the American people against the colored people, and make political capital for those who, if they had it in their power, would not give one of us a situation in the General Assembly higher than a spittoon-cleaner or an office-sweeper.

"Speech Delivered by Hon. J. J. Wright, Charleston,
South Carolina, May 31, 1872" (Columbia, 1872)

The situation was different in Louisiana where blacks were quickly disenchanted with their white allies. Before a state convention, Lieutenant Governor Dunn sent the following to leading black men:

New Orleans, July 26, 1871

My dear Sir:

Being very much interested in the success, politically and otherwise, of our race, I write to ask your support in behalf of the colored people. An effort is being made to sell us out to the Democrats, by the Governor, and we must nip it in the bud. Just look at his recent appointments of Democratic Judges, Constables, Justices of the Peace, Tax Collectors,

Police Jurors and other Officers. It is said that he declares that if he is elected in 1872, no colored man shall hold any office. Now he seeks to force us to elect such delegates to the coming State Convention as will endorse and support him. I ask you to use your influence to elect good, honest men that will look out for the interests of the colored man, and not be duped by the money or the promises of Governor Warmoth. Above all, do not elect as delegate any of his office-holders, who being under obligations to him for position will be compelled to support his policy. Let me hear from you immediately.

Oscar J. Dunn

Henry Clay Warmoth, War, Politics and Reconstruction (New York, 1930)

Dunn's efforts to control the convention were so successful that Warmoth called a rump convention and Louisiana had two Republican parties. When Horace Greeley, editor of the New York *Tribune*, supported Warmoth, Dunn sent him an open letter:

New Orleans, August 31, 1871

Sir:

We believe that Governor H. C. Warmoth is officially derelict and politically untrustworthy. He has shown an itching desire to secure the personal support of the Democracy at the expense of his own party and a craving to obtain a cheap white respectability by the sacrifice of the colored Representatives. He is much more concerned to have entree into good Southern society than he is to do the arduous work of elevating the masses of that race who elected him and to perfect harmony between the races by an impartial and honest enforcement of the law. We cannot support him, even though the New York *Tribune* should remain his champion, for such support would inevitably involve the disastrous defeat of the Republican party in the State of Louisiana.

Oscar J. Dunn

The New National Era, September 14, 1871

Dunn and his followers prepared to impeach Warmoth, but a month before the legislature met Dunn died suddenly, his last words, "Tell the boys to hold together." Although his death certificate gave the cause of death as "congestion of the brain" there are still Louisianans today who believe he was poisoned.

During the first years of Reconstruction in Mississippi prominent white men, some of them former slaveowners, led the Republican party and James D. Lynch was the only black in the first state cabinet. Five years later, when the number of black office holders had increased, they too found it necessary to defend themselves against the charge that they were "negroizing" the state:

September 5, 1873

Dear Sirs:

The state convention met at Jackson and nominated a ticket which for political as well as moral strength and the personal worth and ability of each member can compare favorably with any of the reconstructed states. Yet the political vultures are flapping their wings and cawing their dismal howls, asseverating that the colored men are trying to monopolize all the offices. There are seven state officers. We have only claimed three when we might have demanded five and our white brothers would still have been represented in proportion to their numbers.

The sheriff's and chancery clerk's offices are the only ones in the counties that pay; yet out of twenty-seven Republican counties we have only six sheriffs and one chancery clerk. Still we are "negroizing" the state. There is Lowndes county with four thousand five hundred colored and one thousand five hundred white voters who have but one colored officer, a constable, exclusive of the representatives. However, they are endeavoring to shake off their political incubus by electing as sheriff the Hon. Robert Gleeds who has been appropriately called the "Toussaint" of eastern Mississippi. The day is not far distant when public patronage will be equally distributed throughout Mississippi and "equality" no longer a shadowy phantom.

DAISY

The New National Era and Citizen, September 11, 1873

Thousands of blacks were politically active during Radical Reconstruction. They organized Union Leagues and Grant Clubs, held "speakings" in rural areas and escorted voters to the polls on election day. Seldom more than footnotes in the history books, these grass-roots politicians were a transforming force felt long after Reconstruction ended and they were out of power—or dead.

Many of the first men who came to the fore were ministers or teachers from the North. James D. Lynch, who became presiding elder of the Methodist Episcopal Church in Mississippi, was the most influential black man in the state until his untimely death in 1872. A white contemporary not otherwise sympathetic to blacks described Lynch in action:

He was a great orator; fluent and graceful, he stirred his audiences as no other man could do. He was the idol of the Negroes who would come for miles, on foot, to hear him speak. He rarely spoke to less than a thousand, and often two to five thousand. He swayed them with as much ease as a man would sway a peacock feather with his right hand. They yelled and howled, and laughed and cried, as he willed. Imagine one or two thousand Negroes standing in a semi-circle facing the speaker; not a sound to be heard except the sonorous voice of the speaker, whose tones were as clear and resonant as a silver bell; and of a sudden, every throat would be wide open, and a spontaneous shout in perfect unison would arise and swell and subside as the voice of one man. Then for a moment a deadly silence would follow and every eye would be fixed on the speaker as he resumed, until all of a sudden the mighty shout would rise again, and again.

Lynch always spoke outdoors as no house could hold his audiences, and always spoke in daylight. He was elected to the office of Secretary of State. He died before his term of office expired and before reaching the full meridian of his manhood. The mongrel legislature appropriated $2,500 for a monument to his memory.

W. H. Hardy, "Recollections of Reconstruction in East
and Southeast Mississippi," *Publications of the
Mississippi Historical Society* (1901)

Born free in South Carolina in 1834, Henry M. Turner studied in the North and was pastor of a church in Washington until the war. Returning to the South as chaplain of a black regiment, he organized the African Methodist Episcopal Church in Georgia and became its presiding elder. A member of Georgia's constitutional convention and its first Reconstruction legislature, he described his political work in a speech in Savannah in 1871:

I first organized the Republican party in this State and have worked for its maintenance and perpetuity as no other man has. I have put more men in the field, made more speeches, organized more Union Leagues, Political Associations, Clubs and have written more campaign documents that received larger circulation than any other man in the state. And as you are well aware these labors have not been performed amid sunshine and prosperity. I have been the constant target of Democratic abuse and venom, and white Republican jealousy. The newspapers have teemed with all kinds of slander, accusing me of every crime in the catalogue of villainy. I have been arrested and tried on some of the wildest charges ever distilled from the laboratory of hell. Witnesses have sworn that I tried to get up insurrection, a crime punishable with death. All such deviltry has been resorted to for the purpose of breaking me down. I neither replied to their slanders nor sought revenge. I let them say their say, and do their do. While they were studying against me, I was studying for the interest of the Church and working for the success of my party.

The Quarto-Centennial of Bishop Henry M. Turner
(Philadelphia, 1905)

Probably the best-educated man in Florida's Reconstruction government was the Reverend Jonathan C. Gibbs, who became secretary of state and then superintendent of public instruction. His official papers, like those of some other black leaders, disappeared from the state archives many decades ago, but in an interview with a congressional committee in 1871 he gave a brief autobiography. When he died three years later, there were rumors that he too had been poisoned.

I am forty-two years of age. I was born in Philadelphia. I was educated in Dartmouth College in New Hampshire and I studied theology at Princeton, New Jersey.

Q—Were you in the theological institute there?

A—Yes, sir, for nearly two years. From there I went to Philadelphia and was a pastor of a Presbyterian church there. Then I was selected to come down here and take charge of the scattered members of the Presbyterian Church and open schools and churches for them. I operated in North and South Carolina until the latter part of 1867 and

Jonathan Gibbs when he was student at Princeton Theological Seminary (*Moorland-Spingarn Research Center, Howard University*)

then I came to Florida. I was elected as a delegate to the constitutional convention. There was a necessity for men to take hold and I became interested in politics. When the organization of the State took place I was chosen as secretary of state and have been acting as such ever since.

Testimony Taken by the Joint Select Committee to Inquire into the Condition of Affairs in the Late Insurrectionary States. (Washington, 1872) (Hereafter cited as *Condition of Affairs*)

Thomas W. Cardozo, who came South as a teacher, became Mississippi's superintendent of public instruction in 1874. Less well known than his brother, Francis, he has been virtually ignored by historians. The Mississippi *Pilot,* a Republican newspaper, sketched his life on the eve of his election:

The Republican nominee was born in Charleston, South Carolina, on the 10th of December, 1838. His mother had been a slave but had obtained her freedom. His father, one of the most aristocratic gentlemen of that intensely aristocratic state, took great pride in educating his colored children. The subject of this sketch attended a private school in Charleston, [then] entered the Newburgh, N.Y., Collegiate Institute where he acquired an academic and normal course of instruction. He then turned his attention to teaching.

From 1861 to 1866 he was employed as an agent for the American Freedmen's Union Commission. In 1868 he was sent to North Carolina to establish a Normal School and to aid in organizing a system of Common Schools. He remained there until the schools were firmly fixed on a substantial basis.

He came to Vicksburg in 1870. He did not apply for any office but organized a large school which soon took rank among the first in the State. In 1871, at the earnest solicitation of members of the Republican party, he was elected to the office of circuit clerk of Warren County. For the manner in which he has discharged the intricate duties of that office, he has elicited the highest compliments. Many lawyers say that the office is today in a better condition than it has been for twenty years.

Mr. Cardozo is no novice. All his early training and subsequent experience with the public school systems in other states, and his methodical habits, not only as a teacher, but as an organizer on a large scale eminently fit him for the position to which he has been nominated. In his intercourse with his fellow-men he is a modest, reserved and dignified gentleman, and as such we commend him to the people of the state of Mississippi.

The New National Era and Citizen, September 18, 1873

Israel D. Shadd, who was elected speaker of Mississippi's house of representatives in 1873 was born in Delaware. In Canada before the war, he published the *Provincial Freeman,* a weekly paper. Coming to Mississippi in 1870, he was employed as bookkeeper by B. T. Montgomery & Sons, ex-slaves who were raising the best cotton in the state on land formerly owned by Jefferson Davis' brother. Shadd's family had long been active in the Negro freedom movement. His brother Abraham, one of the first graduates of Howard University Law School, was also in Mississippi, practicing law. His older sister, Mary Ann Shadd Cary, to whom the following letter was addressed, was a noted journalist and teacher. James J. Spelman, mentioned in the letter, was a member of the Mississippi legislature and editor of the Jackson *Colored Citizen.*

House of Representatives, Jackson, Mississippi,
March 26, 1872

Dear Sister:

I received yesterday a copy of the *Era* and saw in it a letter from you on Trades for Boys. I was glad to see it & regret that you have not been writing more frequently. It is the

James J. Spelman

only way you can regain your former prominence. The shades are advancing so rapidly that without you keep yourself before the public one seems to die out.

We will adjourn the House about the 5th of April. I like the position quite well. I would like it if I could study law. I feel the need of it much. I never was fairly used by my family & now I feel the need of it.

Mrs. I. D. middling well. Self in the best of health but am getting quite grey. I think the change of climate has something to do with the grey hairs for I have the best of health in this state.

J. J. Spelman who sits two seats from me carried off the *Era* before I got to read your letter. He promises to bring it back this afternoon.

I am so out of practice in writing that I have not attempted to write for the *Era*. I wish I had more self esteem. It is a ruinous failing. Again there are many excellent col'd writers & I do not like to appear inferior—hence I remain silent.

I. D. Shadd

Mary Ann Shadd Cary Papers, Moorland-Spingarn Research Center,
Howard University

Ex-slaves also contributed their own quota of leaders. Some were sons of their masters and had received a smattering of education; others were field hands and artisans who were barely literate. But even these men did not come to politics unequipped. From the exclusively black community life of slavery, which had existed out of their masters' sight and hearing, they had developed a considerable fund of experience in group action.

Thomas W. Cardozo described James Hill, who became Mississippi's secretary of state eight years after his emancipation:

Mr. Hill is in appearance very much like Mr. Sumner, tall and aristocratic in his bearing, and with that same fall of the hair over his forehead. He seems also in temper the same as Mr. Sumner—when he takes hold of a subject he contends for it with a lionlike tenacity.

Mr. Hill is a native of this state, about twenty-seven years of age, but never enjoyed any educational advantages as afforded by attending schools. He has, however, made considerable progress through efforts of his own and now enjoys a fair degree of education. He has a good taste for literature and delights to converse upon such literary subjects as he is familiar with.

He was elected assistant sergeant-at-arms in the legislature of 1870 and in 1871 was elected a representative. When he rises in the house he addresses the Speaker in a deep, heavy monotone. If not noticed, his lungs are called upon for action and the same tone is made to ring in the Speaker's ears as if to say, "Why don't you pay attention to me, sir!" He is always direct in his remarks, wears an ugly and grim countenance when speaking and contends for that which he thinks is right. He was the elector for his district and did good service during the campaign for Grant. He was also a delegate to the National Republican Convention at Philadelphia. Mr. Hill is a member of the Methodist church, but enjoys a good dance as much as he does a good prayer meeting.

The New National Era, March 3, 1873

Hill's stentorian voice and political know-how made him a power in Mississippi and in the Republican party nationally until the end of the century. Other ex-slave legislators lacked his self-assurance. George Teamoh was apologetic when he spoke in the Virginia senate yet his plea for the abolition of the whipping post was shrewd and well reasoned:

If we have not been able to strike steel with you on the rugged field of debate, the fault has not been ours, but is to be found with those whose Democratic bible contained no measures for the poor man's education. During a life of fifty years I have not had the advantages of being taught five minutes. I speak this in advance because someone might charge my unscholarly productions to the unclassical genius of our colored teachers down home.

The whipping post and cowhide dooms black or white, poor, but not the rich to a life of shame, written in red colors on the back. Why, sir, we whip one for stealing a chicken and then turn him loose on society, ten-fold more the child of devilish incendiarism than ever he was before. He dives deep into his hell of revenge. Judging from the past, whipping settles nothing but only harrows up and brings out what was really in the man—the evil of his heart.

Make a law that will meet the demands of justice without maiming the body, crippling the intellect, brutalizing the man. The rich man never, or but rarely, steals on a small scale, and when he does so, it is generally decided by our law tribunals to be the effects of *non compos mentis* which means that he had lost his mental balance, in which case he is pitied rather than punished. No danger of his being stretched upon that whipping post; none in the least.

The New National Era, January 26, 1871

Few personal letters from the ex-slave politicians have been found. The following offer an unusual picture of a lonely man more concerned about his family back home than about affairs of state. James M. Alexander bought his freedom before the war. Owner of a dry goods store, he was Arkansas's first black justice of the peace before he was elected to the legislature. He died soon after writing these letters. Sixteen years later, his son John became the second black graduate of the United States Military Academy at West Point.

House of Representatives, Little Rock, February 6, 1871
My Dear Wife:
I am glad to know that you are well and also our dear little children. I am very well tonight. Trigg is well. I had him a Suit of Clothes made, cost $20. I had mine made. My

Suit costs $20. I sent to the City Marshall to [send] me my Tax list. Amount is $97.79. The Sheriff send me my list of State Tax, $101.75. I will send the money in a few days.

My Dear Wife, how much I would like to see [you] today. I am fifty six years old. Today is my birthday. My dear, you must git what you want to eat from Mr. Straub. You may have my dray [fixed] for me if you can git anyone to do so. Have Mr. Stewart paid you $15? If not, you must ask him for the money.

I cannot tell you when I will be at home but I will tell you that I will never again stay away from you if I [can] help. You must [write] soon and let me know how you are giting along. Oh, may the Lord bless you is my prayer.

James M. Alexander

Say to my son John that I Rec'd his letter. I think he has improved very much in his writing. Kiss Family and the Baby.

House of Representatives, Little Rock, February 24, 1871

My Dear Son Johnny:

I am proud that I have a son of seven years old that can write me a letter. Your description of the tornado was so very good. You said in your letter that when the storm came the church commenced shaking. Some of the people commenced shouting and some hollering, some crying, but you did not tell me what you did on that alarming and afraidful occasion.

My dear Johnny, you must tell Coolidge and Fannie and little Buddy that they must be good children and when papa comes home he will bring something nice. You must be a good boy and say your prayers every night before you go to bed. Tell Mama how much I would like to see her.

Dear Johnny, you must kiss Mother and the children for me. My love to grandma and Aunt Maria and cousin Maria.

Tell Hank he must take good care of my horses. Tell Mrs.
Hutton her sister is well and sends love to her. I will now
tell you goodnight. May the good Lord bless my little son
Johnny is the prayer of your devoted father.

J. M. Alexander

John H. Alexander Papers, Henry E. Huntington Library

It took courage and a quick wit to be a black politician in the
deep South during Reconstruction. The men who tell their stories in
the following pages were typical of hundreds of others who
jeopardized their lives in order to exercise their rights. Except where
otherwise noted their accounts come from *Testimony Taken by
the Joint Select Committee to Inquire into the Condition of Affairs in
the Late Insurrectionary States* (Washington, 1872).

A white Republican said of James H. Alston, a member of the
Alabama legislature, "He had a stronger influence over the minds
of the colored men in Macon County than ever I saw exerted by
any man." Alston, a shoemaker and musician, was living in Montgomery when he was interviewed by the congressional committee:

My place of residence is Tuskegee. I was representative
of that county. I had to leave there to keep from being shot.
This is about the first thing that caused it. (The witness ex-
hibits the following paper:)

UNION LEAGUE OF AMERICA

Liberty, Union, Equality

Know ye, that we, the State Grand Council of the Union
League of America, for the State of Alabama, do grant unto
James H. Alston, J. J. Martin and their associates, this charter, constituting them a council to be located in Tuskegee,
county of Macon, State of Alabama . . .

Q—Did you institute such a council?

A—Yes, sir. We changed it to be a Republican club after
the League died out. I was shot somewhere about May or

June, 1870. It was done by a band of men who were against my politics. They fired through the windows. Two hundred and sixty-five shots were counted in the weatherboarding of my house the next day and sixty, as near as we could count, passed through the window—five through the headboard of the bed I was sitting on, two through the pillow that my head would have laid on and two in my body.

I was threatened by a good many white persons. I was president of the lodge or club. I was appointed by Governor Smith to canvas the third district. Mr. Johnson offered me $3,000 to use my influence in favor of the Democrats. I told him that Jesus Christ was betrayed for thirty pieces of silver, only one to the thousand to what he offered me, but that I wouldn't do it for $3,000 or to save my life; that I held my life dear but I wouldn't betray my people.

They posted [a notice] upon the bridge I was compelled to cross going to my house. It said that if ever I attempted to cross the bridge my throat should be cut and that a damned nigger that was a Republican should not live anywhere about them. I told them that on the thirteenth, fourteenth and fifteenth amendments I had a right to cross any place that would lead me to property I had bought and paid for. I crossed the bridge several nights.

Then there was a committee sent to wait on me, to make me sign something that I didn't do. It was to show that I had got up a conspiracy in Macon County and that I was willing to go away to Georgia or some other state. I jumped my fence out of my own house and run. I stayed in the swamp ten days and made my escape by walking fifty miles, all night and day, going to Montgomery.

I have been in this place 16 months, not allowed to go to my own property. My horses, one of them, is killed and the buggy cut up. From the station I took in that county I carried it Republican every time. I was register and then representative. Every black man, woman and child was for me and I was offered $3,000 to change and because I wouldn't take it I was shot. I was one of five men that went up to Washington and I am the only man that is living. Everyone is killed that went there to the inauguration of Grant.

George Houston was also a member of the Alabama legislature:

I was in the first legislature after emancipation. I attended two sessions before I was shot. Men came in August, after the election of our Congressman. They were rapping on my door and calling me. My son looked out and says, "Pa, that's a white man with a gun in his hand." He said the white man had his gun right up to shoot my head off if I opened the door. I stove the axe under my door and got my own gun.

They said, "Houston, ain't you coming?" I never made no answer. They said, "Now if you ain't coming, God damn you, we are going to burn your God-damned house down on top of you and your wife and children." I never said a word yet. I heard one of them say, "Let us break down his God-damned door." They commenced bursting the door and hit ten or twenty licks and the door fell in.

I wheeled back to my other room. I opened the window and saw the crowd. One said, "Shut that window." He fired and hit me. The ball is right here in my thigh. As he said, "Shut the window," I cocked the barrel and shot at his head, but it was only squirrel shot. My wife jumped and fastened the window. They shot the window full of holes and the side of the house beside that. The balls came in the house like rain.

Q—Had you had any trouble with your neighbors?

A—Nothing more than some talk. They looked upon me as

being the prominent Negro of the county. They wanted me to deny the Union League. I was a tailor. My master had learned me this trade on account of my crippleness when I was a slave. I had run a shop for sixteen years there. They said I made my living off of them and not off of the damned niggers and if I turned against them they would turn against me. I said my belonging to the Union League didn't do them any harm. They said, "Yes, it does." I said, "It's only to teach our ignorant colored men."

There was a public meeting. We had some speeches and I told them I was opposed to colored men being shot down like dogs when I knew that the officers of the county could stop it. I told the sheriff that to his face. If they took exception to me on that account that is all I can tell for I was raised there and they never could have put a scratch of a pen against me before.

Q—How long did you stay there after you were shot?

A—Five days, guarded night and day by colored men. One evening my friends brought a buggy to my door and wrapped me in a quilt and took me off. I laid all night in the rain in Sucarnoochee swamp. I laid there bleeding all night. My brother got four men to guard me that night and put me on the train at sunrise next morning. I have not been there since. My wife had to sacrifice my property.

Q—Has anyone been punished for this shooting?

A—No, sir. The sheriff resigned his office and went to Texas to keep from prosecuting big friends in the county. Doctor Moore got the appointment directly he left.

Q—Is he a Radical?

A—He claims so—just to get a position.

Q—You think most of these [white] fellows are just after office?

A—There is a great many, I think, just after office. They come around colored men, talking about getting up an organization to themselves and not trusting any of the white men. Now, if they do that they are a heap bigger fools than I am. The man that helps me, I help him. If he sticks to what he promises to do, I am his man; but to stick to a man that tries to make a traitor of himself with me and tries to get me to be used as a tool, why, he will find my edge is going to break off, and if it breaks off once, he never can grind it any more.

I am a Republican, and will die one. The Republican party freed me and I will die on top of it. I vote every time. I can work in the cotton-patch and at my trade and get along so I will stick to the Republican party.

In Florida, Robert Meacham described his background:

I am thirty-six years old, born in Florida. I am a state senator and also register of the United States land-office. My father was my master. He gave me money and started to send me to school once. Some of the parents sent word to the teacher that if he was going to teach a nigger they would keep their children at home, so I had to quit.

Q—What offices have you held?

A—The first one was register under the Reconstruction acts. I was a member of the constitutional convention. I have been superintendent of schools in Jefferson County, and I was once clerk of the county court.

Q—What was your occupation prior to the war?

A—I drove a carriage and superintended around my old boss—my father. Until I was eighteen I never did anything more than to stay about him and ride in the buggy with him. He was a doctor.

I was elected four years ago. Last year, a few days before the election I stated to all our friends that we hoped they would not bring any guns or pistols with them, but leave them at home. Although I had heard threats, I made this remark to them, that the 8th of November would not be a day of war with cannon and musket, knife and pistol, but a war with the ballots and the tongue. So far as I knew all was quiet up to half past 3 o'clock. We were voting at the courthouse. The ballot-box was sitting right on the window-sill and the people would walk up to the window and hand in their ballots to the managers of the election. A majority of the white people had voted at that ballot-box and they were all through.

Some of the colored men, quite a crowd, a hundred or more, were standing outside waiting to vote. Some hollered out to me, "Mr. Meacham, the sun will be down directly, and then the polls will be closed and the half of us will not vote. What will we do?" I said, "Go up to the polls and vote."

I went up to vote. A man there by the name of William C. Bird stamped and cursed and asked me if I intended to make those "niggers" crowd them out. He said, "No damned nigger shall vote here." I did not answer. I started to go to the window and crowded in as best I could. Said he, "There are three other polls your colored people can vote at. This is our poll. It belongs to the white people."

I then said, "Colonel, I do not think there is any one poll set aside for the white people or the black people. They are set aside for the citizens of the county." I pushed on until I got close to him when he called me "a damned son of a bitch." I said, "Colonel, I have not insulted you. Now you take that back." He said, "I will die first." I said, "Colonel, you will have to take it back," just that way. I looked him right in the face.

He had on a pistol, a large one with a white ivory handle. When he said, "I will die first," he drew his pistol part out. He did not put his other hand on it. I knew he could not cock it with one hand. A great many saw what was going on and the report went out that I had been shot by Colonel Bird. In about ten or fifteen minutes there were about a thousand colored men with arms, but not near so many whites. I suppose there were nearly a thousand shots fired off in the air. Finally the thing was quieted down and no one was hurt at all. Then the polls were opened and they went on voting again.

Q—Where did the colored people get their arms so suddenly?

A—They must have had them somewhere. They were shotguns mostly.

Q—Were you armed?

A—I was not.

Q—How did your difficulty with [Colonel Bird] end?

A—Some of his people carried him off and locked him up in a store. I said, "Well, if Colonel Bird will say that he did not say that, I have nothing more to do with it." I did not want to have any fuss. Colonel Bird sent word that he had not seen me that day and whoever said he had insulted me told a falsehood. I said, "Well, I have nothing more to do with it."

Emanuel Fortune served five terms in the Florida legislature. A sketch written after his death gave a brief biography:

Emanuel Fortune was born at Marianna, Florida, in 1832. He entered actively into Reconstruction politics, was a delegate to the constitutional convention in 1868 and a member of the first five sessions of the Florida legislature in the Reconstruction period. Emanuel Fortune was a remarkably fine shot and practiced target shooting regularly, with pistol and rifle. Everyone in Jackson county not only knew that he was a dead shot, but that he would shoot. When the outrages began, Mr. Fortune promptly fortified his home and drilled his household. The house was of two stories, built up from the ground. The children slept upstairs, Mr. Fortune's bedroom being on the first floor, facing the highway. He dug a pit under the flooring, directly below his bed, and made portholes of the trellis work facing the gate, thus converting his residence into a sort of arsenal. His instructions were that if the place were raided, the children should remain upstairs. He was to descend to the pit. His wife was to open the door and pull it after her and thus shield herself behind it.

Mr. Fortune had many hairbreadth escapes but times at last got too critical for him and he moved to Jacksonville. He was elected five times city marshal of Jacksonville, three times alternate delegate to national Republican conventions, twice county commissioner and three times clerk of the city market. When he died in his sixty-fourth year he left an estate valued at $30,000.

Cyrus Field Adams, "Timothy Thomas Fortune," in *The Colored American Magazine*, January 1902

In 1871, Fortune was interviewed by Congressional investigators:

Q—When did you leave Jackson County?
A—In May 1869. There got to be such a state of lawlessness that my life was in danger at all times. In fact I got information that I would be missing some day and no one would know where I was, on account of my being a leading man in politics.
Q—Did you hear any expression in reference to your people having the right to vote?
A—Yes, sir. They would argue very strong against it. I would talk very liberally with them and they generally

respected me to my face. I have had a great many arguments with them and they always spoke very bitterly against
it.

Q—What language would they use?

A—"The damned Republican party has put niggers to rule
us, and we will not suffer it." Mr. Barnes who ran for Congress said that this was a white man's government and that
colored men had no rights that white men were bound to
respect.

Q—Did he call them colored men?

A—No, sir. He said "niggers."

Q—How much education have you?

A—Only what I have got by my own perseverance. I
learned to read before the war. Since the war I have learned
to write.

Backstopping the officeholders were a host of others—farmers,
field hands, small tradesmen—who did the day-to-day work of organizing in the country districts and took the greatest risks. Mifflin
Gibbs, brother of Jonathan Gibbs, and a municipal judge in Little
Rock, described a campaign tour that he made in rural Arkansas:

The speakers, with teams and literature and other ammunition of political warfare, would start at early morn
from their headquarters on a tour of one or two hundred
miles, filling ten or twenty appointments. The meetings,
often in the woods adjoining church or schoolhouse, were
generally at a late hour, the men having to care for their
stock, get supper and come several miles; hence it was not
unusual for proceedings to be at their height at midnight.
I was at such a gathering where Jack Agery, a noted plantation orator, was holding forth, denouncing the Democracy and rallying the faithful. He was a man of great

Mifflin Gibbs

natural ability and bristling with pithy anecdote. From a rude platform half a dozen candles flickered a weird and unsteady glare. Agery as a spellbinder was at his best when a hushed whisper announced that members of the Ku Klux were coming.

Agery, in commanding tones, told the meeting to be seated and do as he bid them. The Ku Klux very soon appeared, but not before Agery had given out and they were singing with fervor that good old hymn "Amazing

Caricature of black politician canvassing for votes (*Boston Public Library*)

Grace." The visitors stood till the verse was ended when Agery, self-controlled, called on Brother Primus to lead in prayer. Brother P. was soon hammering the bench and calling on the Lord.

"Oh," said the chief of the night riders, "this is only a nigger prayer meeting. Come, let us go."

Scouts were sent out to see that "distance lent enchantment" and the political feature of the meeting was resumed.

Mifflin Gibbs, *Shadow and Light* (Washington, 1902)

George Roper, an Alabama plantation orator who had served in the Forty-fourth Colored Infantry during the war told of an incident in the 1868 campaign:

Just about as Mr. Grant was going to be elected, we were advising the colored people who to vote for—to vote for justice and right, as we thought. And all the time I was making a speech down in the courthouse yard to them these white men were standing off, cursing me and saying, "Every time that we get the colored people right, some damn nigger gets up here and spoils them all."

We were telling them how to vote. I said, "You all come here today to hear the truth, to find out who is the best man to vote for. I don't want any sinking Peter or doubting Thomas, but look to the future that is coming. Remember you are your own men, and each of you say 'I am my own man now.' Every day that you lose is lost. There is nobody now to give you anything. Every day that you take sick and lie in your bed is a day lost. Your house-rent, six or seven dollars a month, is going on and nobody to pay it for you.

"Now look around for yourselves and don't allow a man to look for you. Here you go into a store to buy you a pound of sugar and they will book against you maybe twice the amount that you have. Listen to that and then go and learn your children so they can read and write for you and see if these men book wrong against you."

Well, when I said this, these men all looked at me and cursed. I says, "My friends, I can't speak to you as I want to speak, because men is abusing me now but when the election comes, let us go for General Grant."

Saturday night before the election when I got to the courthouse gate I said, "Hurrah for Grant and Colfax." It looked to me as if there was twenty or thirty men, and they hollered, "Halt there." I stopped. One may says, "What is that you said?" Says I, "Hurrah for Grant and Colfax." He says, "What is that in your hand?" Says I, "It is a gun." Says he, "Give that up, damn you." "No, sir," says I. He says, "God damn you," and the first shot he fired turned me clean around, and the blood run out of my eyes. I turned around quite genteel and humble and says, "What are you shooting me for?" He says, "You didn't give up that gun." I says, "It's my gun. I have it to hunt squirrels with." Then he shot me in the arm.

That is the truth, before God. They took a great many arms from the colored people; pistols and guns and I don't know what. They told me, "You were a colored soldier?" I said, "I was a soldier and don't deny my name." This man says to me, "You were a colored soldier. You was a man that fought against your master." I said, "Yes, sir, I was in the Union Army, and fought for my liberty."

Hiram R. Revels

2. Group Portrait

The first issue of *The New Era* (later *The New National Era* and *The New National Era and Citizen*), a weekly published in Washington by Frederick Douglass and his sons, carried a correspondent's report:

Hiram R. Revels taking oath of office as U.S. senator from Mississippi

There was a grand procession of the military, fire companies &c. Because a black regiment was allowed in line all the fire companies left. We really do not see what is to be done with this "pestilential colored individual." He sets legislators by the ear. He will ride in the wrong car, go to the wrong school and get in the wrong box at the theatre. Now he's been worrying the firemen, completely spoiling their day's sport. Well, we suppose he will continue to crop up this way and people may as well try and get used to seeing him everywhere. What is to be done? He will be in Congress next.

The New Era, January 20, 1870

He was. Only a week later *The New Era* reported the election of Hiram R. Revels as U.S. senator from Mississippi. Over the next years, until the newspaper went out of business in 1874, it chronicled the progress of the black men who came to Congress:

[February 3, 1870]

Senator Revels called at the editorial rooms of *The New Era* on Monday last, immediately after his arrival. We were with him at the Capitol and were pleased to know that Democrats were as cordial in receiving him as a prospective member of the Senate as Republicans.

[December 22, 1870]

Hon. Joseph H. Rainey, Representative of the First Congressional District of South Carolina was sworn in and took his seat Monday last, being the first colored man who has held such a position in this country. He was born in Georgetown, D.C., in 1832 from humble parentage, his father and mother both having been slaves. Mr. Rainey's early education was limited, never having attended school in his life, but he took every opportunity to acquire a knowledge of books and improved rapidly. His parents having purchased their freedom, he removed with them to Charleston, S.C.

[January 19, 1871]

Georgia is represented today in the House of Representatives by one of her long-despised sons. Hon. Jefferson Long of the Fourth Congressional District is an American citizen of African descent and has in the old era been inventoried as property in the very district he now represents as a man. And he is a man—a gentleman. Mr. Long is about thirty-five years of age, of a light brown complexion and gives the impression of a man actuated by a high sense of duty and of the position he occupies.

[February 2, 1871]

Five Negroes in Congress! Five kinky-haired, long-heeled, thick-lipped semi-barbarians to sit in the halls of Congress and enact laws to govern thirty millions of intelligent Caucasians.

[Reprinted from the] Joliette *Signal* (Copperhead)

Will the indignant *Signal* man tell us how many of the "thirty millions" are as "intelligent" as are those five "kinky-haired" representatives of the four million Negroes in the United States? We undertake to say that those "five Negroes" are intellectually and morally as much superior to the mass of the Democratic party as black diamonds are more valuable than snow images.

[Reprinted from the] Chicago *Journal*

[March 13, 1873]

We have in the 43rd Congress, [eight] colored members, Pinchback, Lynch, Elliott, Rainey, Rapier, Walls, Cain, Ransier. This is an increase of three members and a decided advance as to ability. Pinchback, Rapier and Cain are all men of mind, of nerve and fidelity, who will be seconded in their labors by the experience of parliamentary life gained in the last two years by Elliott, Walls and Rainey. In the presence of such men our cause ought not to suffer.

[February 19, 1874]

All hail Mississippi! The brightest star of the galaxy of Reconstructed states! Hon. B. K. Bruce was elected yesterday for the long term in the U. S. Senate with scarcely an effort. The first ballot in each house wrought the victory. No flinching, no dodging, no wincing by white Republicans because their Bruce is a Negro.

[May 7, 1874]

For the first time in the nation's history, a colored man, Hon. Joseph H. Rainey of South Carolina, presided over the deliberations of the House of Representatives. The earth continues to revolve on its axis.

A Currier and Ives engraving which once hung in black people's parlors across the land shows seven of the black men who served in Congress in the 1870s. Their frock coats and gold watch chains, their postures and facial expressions resemble those of their white colleagues, but their role in history set them apart. All were tough-minded realists whose ability as practical politicians fed the hatred of those who called them "kinky-haired barbarians."

The black congressmen left few letters and fewer autobiographical writings but contemporary newspapers, the records of Congress and of their home states offer some insight to their personalities.

Hiram R. Revels, the first to appear on the national scene, was the least typical. Northern-born, college-educated, older than the other black congressmen, he went to Mississippi in 1865 as a presiding elder of the A.M.E. Church. John R. Lynch, who became a congressman from Mississippi in 1873, described the almost accidental nature of Revels' election. (Until 1913 U.S. senators were chosen by the state legislatures rather than by popular vote):

THE FIRST COLORED SENATOR AND REPRESENTATIVES.
In the 41ˢᵗ and 42ⁿᵈ Congress of the United States.

(Library of Congress)

When the legislature convened at Jackson in January 1870, it was suggested to Lieutenant Governor Powers that he invite the Reverend Dr. Revels to open the senate with a prayer. That prayer made Revels a United States Senator. It was one of the most impressive and eloquent prayers that had ever been delivered in the senate chamber. It impressed those who heard it that Revels was not only a man of great natural ability, but also a man of superior attainments.

The duty devolved upon that legislature to fill three vacancies in the United States Senate. One was a fractional term of about one year, the remainder of the six-year term of which Jefferson Davis had been elected before the breaking out of the war. The colored members insisted that of the three United States senators to be elected one should be a colored man. The white Republicans were willing that the colored man be given the fractional term. The next step was to find the man. The name of the Reverend James Lynch was first suggested. But he had just been elected secretary of state for a term of four years. The next name suggested was that of Reverend H. R. Revels. Those who heard his able, eloquent and impressive prayer delivered on the opening day of the Senate were outspoken in their advocacy of his selection.

The Autobiography of John Roy Lynch, John Hope Franklin, ed.
(Chicago, 1970)

On the Senate floor, Revels acquitted himself with dignity if not distinction. He argued against the admission of Georgia's senators until blacks were guaranteed protection in the state, spoke in favor of integrated schools in the District of Columbia and urged amnesty for Confederate leaders who had been disfranchised. After a year in office, Revels retired from politics to become president of Alcorn University in Mississippi. *The New National Era* summed up his Senatorial career:

Considering his brief stay and his training he did well. We could have wished for more activity in a virgin field for Negro talent where every vein was full of precious ore and every blow of manhood would have been echoed by Negro progress; but on the whole we are content. The precedent itself was something. A Negro was occupying a seat in the United States Senate—he was occupying the seat of a man who had last used it to plot against the nation's life —he was occupying it as a representative figure of Negro

Robert Brown Elliott, congressman from South Carolina
(*Boston Public Library*)

interest, hope and possibility; and by the blacks he was
hailed with joy as the harbinger of a brighter period for
the black man and the nation.

The New National Era, January 2, 1873

By the time Revels returned to Mississippi there were six black
congressmen on Capitol Hill. Nine more arrived in the next four
years. They were all young men—only two were over forty—and ten
of the fifteen had been slaves. Although outwardly self-possessed,
each man knew that everything he did and said affected the lives of
five million black Americans. Robert B. Elliott (who proved to be an
eloquent speaker) described his feelings when he first spoke in
Congress:

I shall never forget that day, when rising in my place to address the House, I found myself the center of attraction. Everything was still. Those who believed in the natural inferiority of the colored race appeared to feel that the hour had arrived in which they should exult in triumph over the failure of the man of "the despised race" whose voice was about to be lifted in that chamber. The countenances of those who sympathized with our cause seemed to indicate their anxiety for my success, and their heartfelt desire that I might prove equal to the emergency. I cannot picture to you the emotions that then filled my mind.

The New National Era, March 19, 1874

Washington was still a southern city and blacks, regardless of their standing in public life, often met discrimination. Joseph H. Rainey talked with a reporter:

"Do you think it right that when I go forth from this capital an honored member of Congress that I shall be subjected to insults of the lowest fellow upon the streets?"

"But you are treated pretty well here in Washington?"

"Pretty well, but we have to live about as we can and are charged more for living than any of the white members. I was never openly insulted but once in Washington and that was at Falf's, opposite the post office. I went in there and asked for a glass of beer. The waiter handed it out and said the charge was 50 cents. I said, 'Is this because I am a colored man?' 'Yes,' said he. I went away very much mortified.

"We don't want any law making us socially equal but we do want that when we are orderly and decently dressed that we shall be allowed to purchase for our needs the same as anyone else. Why, look at us, members of Congress and voting upon important legislation, and yet when we go out

Joseph H. Rainey, congressman from South Carolina

it is with fear and trembling that we may be openly insulted."

Rainey says that upon the boat between here and Norfolk
he, a member of Congress, would have to wait for the
second table with the waiters and pay full price. The way
he obviates this is to carry a lunch, as he says he would
starve before he would take kitchen fare with servants.

Pittsburgh *Evening Leader*, reprinted in
The New National Era, June 18, 1874

Congressman James T. Rapier of Alabama

James T. Rapier, a native of Alabama, had been United States commissioner to a World's Fair in Paris and his state's representative at a Vienna Exposition. Speaking in the House, he contrasted the treatment he received at home and abroad:

I affirm, without the fear of contradiction, that any white ex-convict may start with me today to Montgomery. All the way down he will be treated as a gentleman, while I will be treated as the convict. He will be allowed a berth in a sleeping-car while I will be forced into a dirty rough box with the drunkards, apple-sellers, railroad hands. Sentinels are placed at the doors of the better coaches with instructions to keep persons of color out. If we are compelled to lay over, the best bed in the hotel is his if he can pay for it, while I am turned away, hungry and cold, to stand around the railroad station until the departure of the next train. There is not an inn between Washington and Montgomery, a distance of more than a thousand miles, that will accommodate me to a bed or meal.

Some time since a well-dressed colored man was traveling from Augusta to Montgomery. The train stopped at a dinner-house. The crowd around the depot, seeing him well-dressed, fine-looking, concluded he must be a gentleman and straightway commenced to abuse him. And, sir, he had to go into the baggage-car, open his trunks, show his cards, faro-bank, dice &c, before they would give him any peace. He was forced to give evidence that he was not working to elevate the Negro before they would respect him.

Sir, in order that I might know something of the feelings of a freeman, a privilege denied me in the land of my birth, I left home last year and traveled six months in foreign lands. The moment I put my foot upon the deck of a ship that unfurled a foreign flag, distinctions on account of color ceased. I am not aware that my presence on board the steamer put her off her course. We made the trip in the usual time. In other countries than my own I was not a stranger. I could approach a hotel without the fear that the door would be slammed in my face. Sir, I feel this humiliation very keenly; it dwarfs my manhood and impairs my usefulness as a citizen.

Congressional Record, 43rd Congress, 1st session

The New National Era reported a rare application of black power.

The visit of Hon. R. B. Elliott to a restaurant in this city so disturbed a young man sitting at the next table that with much indignant comment he left the restaurant. Subsequently Mr. Elliott ascertained that the young man was employed in the Treasury Department, from which, upon a representation of the case, he was promptly dismissed. And it served him right.

The New National Era, December 7, 18᾿ı

On the floor of the House, treatment of black members by their white colleagues ranged from appropriate courtesy to rank racism. An interchange between Samuel Cox, Democrat, of New York and Joseph H. Rainey:

Cox: If there ever was a corporate body thoroughly and disgracefully corrupt with detestable putrescence, it is the state government of South Carolina, both black and white, and especially the black.

Rainey: I have not time to vindicate fully the colored people in South Carolina. We are certainly in the majority there. We are two to one. I ask this House, I ask the country, I ask white men whether the Negroes have presumed to take improper advantage of the majority they hold by disregarding the interests of the minority? They have not. Our convention, which met in 1868 and in which the Negroes were in a large majority adopted a liberal constitution, securing equal rights to all citizens, white and black, male and female. Mark you, we did not discriminate, although we had a majority. We have never attempted to deprive any man of the rights to which he is entitled. You cannot point to me a single act passed by our legislature which had a tendency to oppress any white citizen of South Carolina.

Cox: I shall not attempt to answer the member from South Carolina who has received a little applause from the Republican side of the House. This applause proceeds on the principle on which the artist received credit for making a wonderful painting. The painter, although his work was a wretched daub, was applauded because he painted it with his toes.

The New National Era, March 14, 1872

And a flurry between John T. Harris, Democrat, of Virginia and Alonzo J. Ransier:

Harris: There is not a gentleman on this floor who can honestly say he really believes that the colored man is created his equal.

Ransier: I can.

Harris: Of course you can, but I am speaking to the white men of the House and I do not wish to be interrupted again. . . . Admit it is prejudice, yet the fact exists and you, as members of Congress, are bound to respect that prejudice—that the colored man was inferior to the white.

Ransier: I deny that.

Harris: Sit down. I am talking to white men. I am talking to gentlemen.

Congressional Record, 43rd Congress, 1st Session

On another occasion, Ransier, who excelled in the give-and-take of debate, replied to Congressman James Beck of Kentucky:

Congressman Alonzo J. Ransier of South Carolina (*Library of Congress*)

It is feared by the gentleman from Kentucky that if colored people are put upon a plane of civil equality in law —going into the same schools, hotels, places of amusement, and in the jury-box and cemetery—we, by virtue of our intellectual superiority and our moral and physical force will absorb the race to which he belongs. Let me thank him, in the name of the colored people, for the compliment he has, perhaps unconsciously, paid them, but I must deny that there is a serious intention on our part to thus destroy those for whom he speaks.

The bugbear of "social equality" is used by the enemies of political and civil equality in place of argument. I would most certainly oppose the [civil rights] bill if I believed that its operation would be to force upon me the company of the member from Kentucky, for instance.

The New National Era and Citizen, January 8, 1874

The most concentrated dose of racism was administered to a man who did not appear in the Currier and Ives group portrait. Pinckney Benton Stewart Pinchback was twice elected to the U. S. Senate by the legislature of Louisiana and once to the House. He was never seated in either chamber. The story of the senator-who-wasn't-there is a significant one.

Pinchback's father, Major William Pinchback, was a wealthy planter, his mother, a slave. The major freed his black family and sent his sons to school in Ohio. At the major's death when Pinckney was eleven, white relatives deprived the black Pinchbacks of their inheritance and threatened to sell them into slavery. For a dozen years, young Pinchback worked on Mississippi and Missouri riverboats as cabin boy and steward and, it was rumored, assistant to a gambler. Convicted of wounding his brother-in-law in a fight, he served three months of a two-year sentence in the workhouse. Subsequently, he became a captain in the Louisiana Native Guards. After the war he started a cotton factorage business in New Orleans and entered politics.

As a state senator, Pinchback sided with Governor Henry C. Warmoth rather than with Lieutenant Governor Dunn and Warmoth helped him become lieutenant governor after Dunn's death. However, the two men were on opposing sides during the 1872 campaign when Warmoth backed Horace Greeley who was running for

Pinckney Benton Stewart Pinchback

President with Liberal Republican and Democratic support while Pinchback campaigned for Grant. The month before the election found him in New York:

I entered the rooms of the Republican Committee at the Fifth Avenue Hotel and found Henry Wilson [candidate for vice-president] and William E. Chandler, secretary of the Republican National Committee in earnest consultation.

Turning to me Mr. Chandler asked, "What are the prospects for our carrying Louisiana?" I answered, "None in the world," and explained to him the character of our election laws. These laws could be turned into terrible engines of fraud if administered by dishonest men. This fact had become so apparent that the legislature at the close of the session of 1871–2 passed new laws. Governor Warmoth espoused the cause of Mr. Greeley. It was not likely that he would sign these bills and deprive himself of the great power they conferred upon him.

At the conclusion of my explanation, Mr. Chandler said, "Governor Warmoth is here in New York, at this very hotel. It would be a grand thing if you would go home and sign those bills." I was lieutenant governor and, in the absence of the governor from the state I could legally exercise all the power of the governor. If I could reach the state, sign those laws while the governor was outside its borders, they would be valid and the chances of the Republicans carrying the state doubly multiplied. The control of the government of Louisiana and possibly that of the Federal government was involved.

It was Saturday. If I left that night I would have twenty-four hours, as there were no trains leaving for the South Sunday morning. Mr. Chandler assured me he would keep me posted on Governor Warmoth's movements and should [the governor] start home would notify me by telegram.

At nine o'clock I left New York. Next morning I arrived at Pittsburgh and was much annoyed to find that a delay of six hours was before me on account of no trains running on Sunday. At Cincinnati the train missed connection and I lost six hours more, but as I heard nothing from Mr. Chandler I thought I was all right.

About eleven o'clock at night when the train arrived at Canton, Mississippi, I was aroused from sleep by a rude shake. I saw a man with a lantern in his arm standing in front of me. He asked, "Are you Governor Pinchback? There is a telegram in the telegraph office for you." Remembering Mr. Chandler's promise to wire me should Warmoth become apprised of my movements, I rushed out of the car, into the telegraph office. I knew by the manner of the man in the office that something was wrong. He seemed to be in no hurry to hand me the dispatch. On reaching the door to return to the train I found it locked on the outside. It was too late. I saw only the rear end of the train disappearing around the curve in the road.

Governor Warmoth had learned of my departure from New York. He instantly put the telegraph wires to work and started after me. At Humbolt, twelve hours behind me, he took a "special" and came rattling along at the rate of forty, fifty, and even sixty miles an hour where the road would stand it. The money and intelligence, the telegraph and railroads of the entire section of the country through which I had to pass after leaving the Ohio river were on his side.

I shall never forget the triumphant expression upon his face as I saw him standing upon the front platform of his special car in Canton that morning and the taunting manner in which he exclaimed, "Hello, old fellow, what are you doing here?" I replied with the best grace I could command, "I am on my way home. What are you doing here?" He said, "I am after you." "Well, you have caught me," was my reply, "and if you have no objection I will go on with you the balance of the journey."

My railroad race was a desperate and hazardous adventure. I have been told by one of the men who helped entrap me at Canton that every railroad entering New Orleans from the North was picketed for miles from the state line and the orders were to prevent my entrance into the state in advance of the governor if it required the sacrifice of my life.

P. B. S. Pinchback in William J. Simmons' *Men of Mark* (Cleveland, 1887)

Grant was re-elected but in Louisiana both William P. Kellogg, Republican candidate for governor, and his Democratic opponent claimed victory. As presiding officer of the state senate, Pinchback held the key to the election. He could decide to swear in either the senators certified by Kellogg or those backed by the Democrats. The night before the legislature met, Warmoth and C. A. Weed, publisher of the New Orleans *Times,* called on him with a proposition. He gave his answer in the state senate the next day:

Pinchback stated in the Senate that Governor Warmoth and Weed of the *Times* went to Pinchback's house at 12 o'clock last night and offered him $50,000 and the appointment of a large number of officers if he would pursue the course which they would point out.

Mr. Ingraham then offered a resolution that the senate resolve itself into a high court of impeachment. He stated that by the resolution impeaching Governor Warmoth, Lieutenant Governor Pinchback became Governor of Louisiana, which was agreed to. Lieutenant Governor Pinchback qualified as Governor, took possession of the office and received the congratulations of friends.

The New National Era, December 12, 1872

With characteristic boldness Pinchback immediately telegraphed to Washington:

New Orleans, December 9, 1872

President Grant:

Having taken the oath of office and being in the possession of the gubernatorial office, it devolves upon me to urge a favorable consideration of the request of the General Assembly requesting the protection of the United States Government. Be pleased to send the necessary orders to General Emery. This seems to me a necessary measure of precaution although all is quiet here.

P. B. S. Pinchback, Acting Governor of Louisiana

New Orleans, December 11, 1872

Hon. Geo. H. Williams, Attorney-General

I have the honor to acknowledge the receipt of your dispatch. May I suggest that the commanding General be authorized to furnish troops upon my requisition upon him for the protection of the legislature and the gubernatorial office. The moral effect would be great, and in my judgment would tend greatly to allay any trouble likely to grow out of the recent inflammatory proclamation of Warmoth. I beg you to believe that I will act in all things with discretion.

P. B. S. Pinchback, Acting Governor

Henry Clay Warmoth, *War, Politics and Reconstruction* (New York, 1930)

"You are recognized by the President as the lawful executive of Louisiana," the attorney general replied. "All necessary assistance will be given to you to protect the state from disorder and violence." For five tumultuous weeks, until Kellogg's inauguration, Pinchback was governor of Louisiana. The Democrats had organized a legislature of their own and threatened to install their man as governor, but Pinchback stood firm. In a formal address to the state, he said:

We recognize the right of free discussion and of free assemblage. But when any class of men propose to organize as lawmakers, in conflict with the existing authorities, such parties are revolutionists and guilty of treason against the state and must be dealt with as such. The Governor-elect will be inaugurated and the legislature recognized by the

Blacks crowded House and Senate galleries during debates
(*Boston Public Library*)

President will meet. The whole force of the state shall be
used for this purpose.

The New National Era, January 2, 1873

The day after he turned over the government to Kellogg, Pinchback, who had been elected to the House in the November elections, was also elected to the U. S. Senate. He hastened to Washington to take his seat. President Grant and the Republicans in Congress
recognized the Kellogg administration as the lawful government in
Louisiana. White congressmen with credentials signed by Pinchback when he was acting governor were seated promptly. But two
years after his election, the House voted not to admit Pinchback;
the Senate kept him waiting for three years before even giving him
a hearing.

Pinckney Benton Stewart Pinchback was something new on the national scene—a black man who said, "I quit playing second fiddle and hereafter intend to use the first violin." A black man who said to the House, "I demand simple justice." A black man who said to the Senate, "I don't base my claim to a seat as a favor, but as a right." A Washington correspondent's description of his personal style and appearance would apply in considerable detail a century later to another black Congressman—Adam Clayton Powell:

Pinchback glides around the Senate Chamber like a bronze Mephistopheles. His features are regular, just perceptibly African, his eyes intensely black and brilliant. His most repellent point is a sardonic smile which gives him an evil look, undeniably handsome as the man is. It seems as though the scorn which must rage within him at the sight of the ignorant men from the South who look down upon him on account of his color, finds play imperceptibly about his lips. His manner is reserved but polite—a model of good breeding. Mr. Pinchback is the best dressed Southern man we have had in Congress since the days when gentlemen were Democrats.

William J. Simmons, *Men of Mark* (Cleveland, 1887)

As he cooled his heels in Washington, the gossip mills ground away. Pinchback answered some of the rumors:

I see that the Sunday *Capital* and *Herald* pay me some attention, stating that I am a gambler and a penitentiary convict. During the time when slavery cast its appalling gloom over the aspirations of our race I was forced to make a living for my family in such occupations as colored men were rigidly confined to. On steamboats and elsewhere, following the example of our Southern statesmen who swarmed around card tables, I sometimes took a hand at poker. But during that time I earned my living a good deal more by my industry than by playing cards. As to the statement about my being an ex-penitentiary inmate, I brand it as an unqualified falsehood.

The New National Era, February 20, 1873

Then Pinchback's wife became an issue. Senator Revels' wife had stayed at home with her children but Mrs. Pinchback would undoubtedly come to Washington to take her place with the wives of other senators, the *Capital* pointed out. *The New National Era* replied:

It was bad enough that his brains, his courage and even his personal appearance and ample means had produced an effect in reverse of that usually produced by such qualities because the Negro Senator would not furnish sufficient foil to the superiority of his white colleagues. But to find his family made a barrier to the high position to which he has been elected is worse still. Is it not rather late for these blue-blooded people to take the blues over the entrance of a colored lady into white society? Is it not shameful that the rights of a whole race and the just dues of their representatives are withheld from them under the flimsy pretext that society will not tolerate, upon terms of equality, the wife of a colored Senator?

The New National Era, April 9, 1874

It remained for Henry M. Turner, another proud black man, to pronounce the last word on Pinchback's rejection:

Why did the Senate adjourn without seating Mr. Pinchback? Was it because he is not able to fill the position? Certainly no such flimsy objection could have been urged. In natural genius and sweeping eloquence he is the superior of half of the Senators and a far better statesman. Take that miserable old mummy, Joshua Hill of Georgia, whose speeches read like a schoolboy trying to read Latin backwards. He would not make an intelligent wagon-driver. And yet the Senate seated that mummy, without half the claim to his seat that Mr. Pinchback has.

Mr. Pinchback has proved himself a statesman of the first order. The snap and strategy displayed in his contest with Warmoth and the vim with which he executed his plans and saved Louisiana from the voraciousness of Democrats and Negro-haters entitles him to the gratitude of the Republican party.

If Mr. Pinchback had been white he would have been seated with applause. The trouble is Mr. Pinchback is colored and he is smart.

The New National Era, April 24, 1873

Pinchback was finally rejected by the Senate in 1876. Perhaps as a sop to troubled consciences, he was awarded $17,000 in back salary and expenses, a sum which became the basis for a sizable personal fortune. He continued to hold state and federal posts and was a delegate to Republican national conventions for many years.

Pinchback's cool, self-assertive style was unique. The other black congressmen, though not lacking in dignity, were less abrasive to white sensibilities. In a time when politicians were obliged to face their audiences in person instead of through a television screen, oratory was an important political art in which a number of them excelled. Schooled in the Negro ministry and in the power of its traditional preaching techniques, Richard H. Cain could evoke laughter or tears from visitors in the House gallery. Speaking in reply to Congressman Robbins of North Carolina, he said:

Congressman Richard Cain of South Carolina

The gentleman wishes that we go to Africa or to the West Indies or somewhere else. I want to enunciate this doctrine upon this floor. We are not going away. We are going to stay here. We propose to stay here and work out the problem. We believe that God Almighty has made of one blood all the nations upon the face of the earth. We believe we are made just like white men are.

Look. I stretch out my arms. See; I have two of them, as you have. Look at our ears; I have two of them. I have two eyes, two nostrils, one mouth, two feet. I stand erect like you. I am clothed with humanity like you. I think, I reason, I talk, I express my views as you do. Is there any difference between us? Not so far as our manhood is concerned, unless it be in this: that our opinions differ and mine are a little higher up than yours. (Laughter)

The gentleman talks about the colored people deteriorating. Sir, who tills your lands now? Who plants your corn? Who raises your cotton? I have traveled over the Southern States and have seen who did this work. Going along, I saw the white men do the smoking, chewing tobacco, riding horses, playing cards, spending money; while the colored men are tilling the soil and bringing the cotton, rice and other products to market.

Sir, we are part and parcel of this nation, which has done more than any other on earth to illustrate the great idea that all races of men may dwell together in harmony. We will take that time-honored flag which has been borne through the heat of a thousand battles. Under its folds Anglo-Saxon and Africo-American can together work out a common destiny, until universal liberty, as announced by this nation, shall be known throughout the world.

The New National Era and Citizen, February 5, 1874

Robert Smalls, who served five terms in Congress and remained the most influential politician in his district until the twentieth century, was a public speaker of a different order. Forthright but pedestrian in the House, he had a slashing style when he campaigned back home. There he put aside his Prince Albert suit and manner and spoke the language of his constituents, the sharecroppers and small farmers of the Sea Islands. On the stump he was blunt and earthy. "Put a corn-cob in that Democrat's mouth," he shouted on one occasion when a heckler interrupted him. During the stormy campaign of 1876 when Wade Hampton was the Democratic

Congressman Robert Smalls of South Carolina

candidate for governor, Smalls called on black women to keep their husbands loyal to the Republicans. Two black men quoted from his speeches.

John Bird:

Robert Smalls said to the women that if their husbands vote the Democratic ticket to throw them out of the house. "When John went to Massa Hampton and pledged to vote for him his wife told him, 'She would not give him any of that thing if you vote for Hampton.' John gone back to Massa Hampton and said, 'Massa Hampton, I can't vote for you, for woman is too sweet, and my wife says if I vote for you she won't give me any.' And ladies, I think if you all do that we won't have a Democratic ticket polled on Parris Island." (These are the words of Robert Smalls.)

John Mustifer:

The last meeting we held in the camp-ground, Mr. Robert Smalls give us to understand, if a gentleman vote the Democratic ticket, to don't marry him. Those what is married "don't service them in bed." He got a little wife and if he was to talk of voting the Democratic ticket, his wife would throw hot lead in his throat when sleeping; and in going to the polls he wants every womens to follow her husband with her club in hand and dare him to vote any Democratic ticket.

House of Representatives Miscellaneous Document No. 11, 45th Congress, 1st Session

Robert B. Elliott demonstrated not only oratorical power but a sound knowledge of constitutional law when he debated Alexander Stephens, former vice-president of the Confederacy. The contrast between Stephens, white-haired and ailing, who came to Congress in a wheel chair, and his young, vigorous opponent seemed to many observers a symbol of the old order and the new. In his speech which was widely praised, Elliott said in part:

Sir, it is scarcely twelve years since [Stephens] shocked the civilized world by announcing the birth of a government which rested on slavery as its cornerstone. The progress of

Robert B. Elliott delivering civil rights speech (*Peggy Lamson*)

events has swept away that pseudo-government which rested on greed, pride and tyranny; and the race whom he then ruthlessly spurned are here to meet him in debate and to demand that the rights enjoyed by their former oppressors shall be accorded to those who kept their allegiance to the Union. Sir, the gentleman from Georgia has learned much since 1861, but he is still a laggard. Let him put away entirely the false theories which have so greatly marred an otherwise, enviable record. Let him accept, in its fullness and beneficence, the great doctrine that American citizenship carries with it every civil and political right which manhood can offer. Let him lend his influence to complete the proud structure of legislation which makes this nation worthy of the great declaration which heralded its birth and he will have done that which will most nearly redeem his reputation in the eyes of the world.

Congressional Record, 43rd Congress, 1st Session

Although they were accepted as members of the Republican caucus, the black congressmen lacked the seniority required for important committee assignments. Too few in number to put through significant legislation of their own, they introduced local bills for the relief of their constituents and argued for federal aid to education and federal intervention in the Klan-wracked South. As a group, their major achievement was the passage of the Civil Rights Act of 1875. A comprehensive bill forbidding segregation in public places, it was introduced by Charles Sumner in 1870 and was passed a year after his death, largely through the efforts of the black congressmen.

Much of their work was done outside of Congress. Hiram Revels had been in office less than a month when *The New Era* reported:

Senator Revels says the number of letters addressed to him from all parts of the country is innumerable and that the labor of dictating replies to his amanuenses has been enough to wear him down. Add to this the amount of walking required in running about the Departments, pressing claims for appointments—favoring others with his influence which just now is supposed to be all-powerful—in receiving visitors, in being civil, polite, courteous and amiable, in spite of headache, rheumatism and general exhaustion, and the Senator says one can have some idea of what it is to be a Negro Senator.

The New Era, March 31, 1870

The system of political patronage, often called the spoils system, had a double significance for black officials. In addition to rewarding loyal supporters, they were able to place blacks in federal agencies that had heretofore been lily-white. Black congressmen in Washington meant black postmen in Mississippi, black customs inspectors in South Carolina, black internal revenue agents in Alabama, and black cadets at West Point. Revels looked back with pride on his role in breaking down barriers in the U. S. Navy Yard:

I got colored mechanics in the United States Navy Yard for the first time. A delegation of intelligent influential colored mechanics from Baltimore called upon me at Washington. The object of their visit was to get employment in the United States Navy Yard. I conducted them to the office of the Secretary of War and he assured me that as soon as possible they would be appointed. In a comparatively short time they received their appointments.

"Hiram Revels' Autobiography," manuscript, Carter Woodson Papers, Library of Congress

The men who followed Revels had several years of political experience in their states before coming to Washington. Cain, who brought thousands of new members to the A.M.E. Church in South Carolina, was equally skilled at getting out the vote. A letter to Robert K. Scott, South Carolina's governor from 1868–72:

Columbia, December 12, 1870

Gov. R. K. Scott

Sir:

I send you a list and the names of men whom I employed, according to your request, to canvass in behalf of your Election. The prices you will see which I promised them. Those men have served faithfully, made a sacrifice of everything in this campaign. Some of them are now *without a home, and shelter for their wives and children,* having been *driven* from the *lands* of [Democrats] because they took sides against them. I regret that my own circumstances do not permit me to pay them without applying to you for aid. I did hope that I might be in a position to do so myself and forego the humiliation of asking you, but their constant *appeals* to me for immediate *help* compels me to trouble you again in their behalf.

R. H. Cain

South Carolina Archives

In the 1872 campaign, Cain and Martin R. Delany, friends from prewar days, supported Franklin J. Moses for governor, an action they would later regret. After Moses' election, Cain wrote:

Columbia, May 8, 1873

To his Excellency Gov. F. J. Moses, Jr.

Dear Sir:

You will remember the mutual pledges made prior to your nomination for Governor, relative to Charleston appointments. I do not ask you to do anything that would embarrass your administration or make the appointment of a man who would do harm. I have felt much concern about my friend Delany and my pledges to him made before he consented to abandon his opposition to your nomination for Governor. It was principally on my personal representations to him that you had been grossly maligned that I brought him over from the opposition. He became your advocate and our mutual friend. I had assured him on the honor of a gentleman that you would not break faith.

Permit me to say that it is impolitic to break faith with friends however insignificant they may be. It would be better to have one unwise officer than to have a thousand of his friends against you in the future. Gov. Scott broke faith with those who served him faithfully, and when the time came none would trust him. I hope, Sir, you will not make his mistake.

Delany's condition is a needy one. He has staked all on *your word*. For heavens sake, do not cast him away. He has many strong friends who sympathize with him and desire to see him placed where he may render the state some services while he makes a living for his wife and children. You know, doubtless, what it is to be without money, without friends, without a position, with pressing necessities.

Dear Sir, you will pardon this seeming importunity on my part. Nothing but the unbounded regard and confidence in your noble and generous consideration would have prompted me to venture this freedom.

R. H. Cain

South Carolina Archives

When Moses failed to keep his promise to Cain, another Republican leader found a post for Delany in the U. S. Customs House in Charleston.

John R. Lynch, youngest of the black congressmen, was speaker of the Mississippi house and a power in state politics before going to Washington. He described a call he paid on President Grant:

After paying my respects to the President I informed him that I very much desired to have Postmaster Pursell removed and a good Republican appointed in his stead.

"What is the matter with him?" the President asked. "Is he not a good postmaster?"

John R. Lynch, congressman from Mississippi

"Yes," I replied. "He may be—and no doubt is—a good and efficient postmaster, but politically he is worthless. In my opinion, there ought to be a man in that office who will not only discharge his duties in a creditable manner but who will also be of some service to the party and to the administration under which he served. We lost [his] county by a small majority. If an active and aggressive man had been postmaster the result might have been different. I therefore earnestly recommend that Pursell be removed and Mr. Garland be appointed to succeed him."

The President replied: "You have given good and sufficient reasons for a change. Leave with me the name of the man you desire to have appointed and his name will be sent to the Senate as soon as Congress meets."

John R. Lynch, *The Facts of Reconstruction* (Boston, 1913)

Robert B. Elliott was also an astute politician. He might have become a statesman if he had had more time. Daniel A. Straker, his law partner in the 1870s, later wrote:

Elliott was chairman of the State Executive Committee. It was his duty to maintain, preserve and uphold the Republican party in the state. He knew the political condition of every nook and corner throughout the state and at a moment's notice was ready with the needed action. His county and precinct chairmen were ever ready to follow and obey him.

Another characteristic of this man as a politician was his bravery. On one occasion when he was about to deliver a political speech his audience comprised four-fifths of the most bloodthirsty white men of the precinct, who attended the meeting for the purpose of breaking it up. Mr. Elliott ascended the platform erected for the speakers, placing a book containing the Constitution of the state and of the United States on his left and two large Colt revolvers on his right, stating as he commenced that he was going to speak of the rights of citizens under the Constitution and had brought with him the necessary means of enforcing the same. Mr. Elliott delivered his speech without interruption.

He was particularly methodical in his politics. He knew every important person in every county, town or village and the history of the entire state as it related to politics.

Daniel A. Straker, "Brief Sketch of the Political Life of Robert Brown Elliott," *A.M.E. Church Review*, April 1893

Senator Blanche K. Bruce of Mississippi (*Moorland-Spingarn Research Center, Howard University*)

In 1872, Elliott campaigned for election to the U. S. Senate but was defeated by a white Northerner who spent thousands of dollars to buy the votes of legislators. The second black man to go to the Senate was Blanche K. Bruce of Mississippi. Bruce was an ex-slave who had been educated with his young master and had attended Oberlin College after the war. In quick succession he became tax assessor, superintendent of education, alderman and sheriff of Bolivar County, Mississippi. A sheriff's job was an important one because he controlled the selection of juries, appointed election registrars and collected state and county taxes. Paid by fees for his services, he could earn up to twenty thousand dollars a year, an enormous sum in the 1870s. There is no record of Sheriff Bruce's compensation but by the time he entered the Senate he owned rich cotton lands in the Delta as well as a townhouse and other real estate. An incident in his campaign for sheriff illustrates his quick wit:

At my first canvass for sheriff, my Democratic opponent, a man of considerable force as a public speaker, challenged me to debate. We agreed to divide time at a meeting in a precinct where the Democrats were in the majority. After eloquently portraying his services to the Democratic party and his participation in the war, my competitor said he had nothing against me—that I was a decent man for my color, but that I had been a slave and performed menial offices and was unfitted to fill the office of sheriff.

When my turn came to speak, I frankly admitted that I had been a slave, but it was a misfortune for which I was not responsible. True, I had been compelled to perform menial offices, but I served my master honestly and faithfully. Now, however, I had managed to rise to better position. I had outgrown the degradation of slavery and was a free man and a good citizen. But the difference between my adversary and myself was well defined. Had he been a slave probably he never would have risen superior to his original condition and would be performing menial offices even now.

This sally was so well received by my opponents, my competitor never invited me thereafter to debate with him.

Kansas City *Times*, October 17, 1886

Senate Chamber U. S.,

Dec 7 1875

Sir:

You are requested to attend a meeting of **REPUBLICAN SENATORS** *on Wednesday Dec. 8* *at 11½ o'clock, at the Reception Room of the Senate.*

Very respectfully,

Isaac Bassett

Assistant Doorkeeper.

The Honorable

Mr. Bruce

Bruce's invitation to Republican caucus meeting (*Moorland-Spingarn Research Center, Howard University*)

Bruce entered the Senate in March 1875, too late for the debate on the Civil Rights Act and almost too late for Radical Reconstruction which came to an end in Mississippi eight months afterward. As a Republican senator from a state that had gone Democratic, he argued for an investigation of the Mississippi elections, urged the seating of Senator-elect Pinchback and supported such nonpolitical issues as flood control on the Mississippi and the refund of a cotton tax paid by farmers. Off the Senate floor, Bruce quickly became the nation's leading black politician. Until the rise of Booker T. Washington, he was the man to see about a job. He was one of the

Frederick Douglass, Jr. (*Moorland-Spingarn Research Center, Howard University*)

few black men of his time whose correspondence has been preserved. A selection from the letters he received during his first years in office gives, in Revels' words, "some idea of what it is to be a Negro Senator."

When *The New National Era* was discontinued after four financially disastrous years, Frederick Douglass, Jr., turned to Bruce rather than to his illustrious father for help:

Washington, D.C., November 4, 1875

Hon. B. K. Bruce

Dear Sir:

I am in a bad way pecuniarily and am desirous of an appointment on the Capitol Police force. I have been informed that if a demand on the part of a U. S. Senator was made I could be so employed. Will you be kind enough to make the demand? I ask this because I have lost everything in maintaining the *New National Era* in the interests of the Republican Party and I am sure that a number of Republican Senators will, if necessary, second such a demand.

Hoping you will give this matter your earliest attention as I think there is a vacancy.

Frederick Douglass Jr.

Blanche K. Bruce Papers, Moorland-Spingarn Research Center,
Howard University

A soldier seeking a promotion wrote:

Fort Brown, Texas, February 18, 1876

Honorable B. K. Bruce

Dear Sir:

I have been very strongly recommended by all my officers for appointment as Commissary Sergeant and had I not been a colored man, I would have been appointed long since. Ordinarily such matters are not brought to the notice of Senators but, as in my case, they will never be acted on favorably by the military authorities unless forced upon them, I am compelled to appeal to you as a representative of my race at the Capitol.

Will you have the kindness therefore, to call on the President and urge my appointment, also on the Secretary of War and Commissary General (all such appointments are made on the recommendation of the latter officer). In these, like all other matters they are inclined to give the colored man the cold shoulder.

Will you allow me to suggest to you, to ask one or two or more representative colored men to go with you to these gentlemen, and urge my appointment as a matter of justice, as not a single colored man has ever been appointed to any position outside his regiment, all such appointments being given to white men, on the plea that they are longer in the service than we are, while there are instances in which they have *not* been in service as long as many colored applicants.

James W. Sullivant, Sergeant Major, 24th Infantry

Blanche K. Bruce Papers, Moorland-Spingarn Research Center,
Howard University

As chairman of the Select Committee on the Mississippi River Levees and a planter in the flooded area, Bruce received many appeals from flood victims:

Greenville, Mississippi, April 18, 1876

Hon. B. K. Bruce
Dear Sir:

I write to inform you of the Condition of our County. We are worst overflowed than we were in 1874 and the People are suffering for the wants of Something to Eat. Many of them have not Bread nor no way to get it. Senator, I don't know what you can do for the Poor Sufferers but I hope you will consider our district and do all you can to get Congress Pass a Relief Bill. The water is from 2 to 4 Feet over my Place. I hope you will do all you can for our People.

G. W. Gayles

National Archives

When John R. Lynch wrote the following letter he had been defeated for a third term in the House by James Chalmers, a Democrat. He was contesting the election, charging Chalmers with fraud and intimidation. The Democratic-dominated Committee on Elections subsequently rejected Lynch's claims.

As handsome young bachelors, Lynch and Bruce were much sought after in the black social world of Washington in which Christian A. Fleetwood, winner of a Congressional Medal of Honor, was also prominent. A Democratic newspaper had advised Bruce not to marry, in order to avoid embarrassing other senators' wives. He married "Miss Wilson of Cleveland" in 1878.

Natchez, December 15, 1877

Friend Bruce:

Your interesting letter was received some time since. I would have been in Washington before now but I knew it was not necessary. I was satisfied that no contested election cases would be disposed of prior to the Christmas holidays. I have been kept fully informed, however, through my attorney, as to what has been done. I will leave here about the 9th of January, will remain a few days in Jackson, and reach Washington on or about the 18th. I am satisfied that I can beat Mr. Chalmers if I can get the case reported to the House on its merits. I must confess that I don't much like the composition of the Committee. But I will keep up the contest until the case is decided.

I regret very much that I cannot spend Christmas in Washington. I suppose you will have a good time. I received a letter from Fleetwood the other day and he told me that quite a number of ladies from abroad would spend Christmas week there. You will have a favorable opportunity of seeing more of Miss Wilson of Cleveland—the one about

whom we were talking. If I were there I would phrenolo-
gize and physiognomise her head and face for you. I remain your friend,

J. R. Lynch

Blanche K. Bruce Papers, Moorland-Spingarn Research Center,
Howard University

IV · THE PEOPLE

"What is the condition of your people?
How are they getting along?"

"They are getting along, I might say,
tolerable. They work hard and make
very little."

A Florida freedman, 1871

1. A Way to Live

As the new citizens slowly put their lives in order, families that had been torn apart by slavery sought reunions. For more than a decade after emancipation, black newspapers printed "Information Wanted" advertisements from freedmen who were hunting for their relatives, as well as letters like the following:

Orphan asylum in Memphis, Tennessee. In the aftermath
of war thousands of children were separated from their
parents (*Boston Public Library*)

Richmond, July 20, 1874

To the Editor:

Richmond feels highly flattered by the visits of so many excursion parties. On the 3rd of July a large company arrived from Georgia to search out relatives and friends from whom they had been separated by the cruel necessities of slavery. Aged women and grayhaired men journeyed to Virginia from far-off Georgia hoping to hear some word or, perchance, to meet sons and daughters whom they bade farewell at the auction block. Many had the good fortune to find those they sought, and their greetings were pathetic beyond description.

A curious circumstance deserves mention. It was a custom for us to be known by the name of our masters and whenever a change of ownership took place, our names were also changed. So when our Georgia friends came here it required considerable ingenuity to trace the various pedigrees, as many had assumed different names since their departure from this State.

B.

The New National Era, July 23, 1874

To the Editor:

I have a mother somewhere in the world. I know not where. She used to belong to Philip Mathias in Elbert county, Georgia, and she left four of her children there about twenty-three years ago, and I have never heard of her since. I ask all who read this to inquire for her. Her name was Martha and I heard that she was carried off to Mississippi by speculators. If any of you can give me information about her it will be gladly received. I am a member of the M.E. Church.

Rev. E. W. Johnson, St. Louis, Missouri

Colored Citizen, November 8, 1879

The colonies in Canada where thousands of runaway slaves had once found refuge emptied out as former slaves headed south again. James Davis, who wrote the following, found work in Boston, but was still hungry for news of home. The Reverend Leonard Grimes, mentioned in his letter, was a leader of Boston's black community and also a native of Virginia.

East Boston, May 22, 1865

Dear Brother:

I arrived safe here on Tuesday evening. I have gone to work at McKays. They all was very glad to see [me]. Mrs. McKay hugged me & said she was a great mind to kiss me but she thought that I would not like for white women to kiss me. I told her I was not particular about kisses.

Mr. McKay return from Washington today with President Lincoln's horses which he bought at the sum of $1500, so he has the span of horses which the late president had for his carriage. I send you here some of their mane to make a ring for your finger out of Uncle Abe's horse hair.

I learned that Mr. Grimes had been to Richmond so I called and asked him if he was in Petersburg. He said he was. Then I asked him if he got acquainted with a person named John Hill. He said, "Oh yes, I stopped with him a day and a night." He says that this John Hill keeps a restaurant near the depot & is a carpenter by trade, [and] that Mr. Hill was a very dark man with a very short neck. Then I felt confident that he had seen my uncle. Mr. Hill told him that he had brother in Canada.

Write me word how Johnny is getting on. Tell me if you hears from Petersburg or Richmond. I am in East Boston but I feel very lonesome. I don't see any colored ladies & gentlemens unless I go over to the city.

James R. Davis

Carter Woodson Papers, Library of Congress

Henderson, Texas, March 29, 1867

Dear Sister:

After looking impatiently for some time I last night received your kind & interesting letter which was to me a great pleasure. My daughter Martha is living in the same town. Roy is living here, [trying] to make a support for his little family. John is here working at his trade, doing very well. Sissie is gone to Louisiana.

Since you heard from me last I have married again and, what you will think stranger, a young and pretty girl about sixteen. She was from Alabama. She formerly belong to a Dr. Deloach. I found her a girl of good character, well-behaved and sensible, so she and I talked the matter over and she told me she liked me well enough to try to take care of me, and I promised to do the same for her. So far I am very much pleased with her. She does as I direct. What is my pleasure seems to be hers. She listens to my counsels and I think strives to do right.

My children were, like all children, opposed to the marriage but she is so respectful to me and to them that I think it will wear off. Her name is Mariah. We had the first license that were issued to colored people. She is industrious as far as she knows and I think will learn very readily.

You and many others no doubt will say I could, the few days I have to remain on earth, remained unmarried. It may be, but I was lonely, wanted some kind hand to smooth my pillow, and a soft sweet voice to cheer my gloom. My health is as good as I could expect. I am able to do good work yet, stock plows, make wheels, reels and such things.

A South Carolina freedwoman

Our country is in a deplorable condition. I reckon it is the same everywhere. Money is scarce, except traders who have hoarded it away. I have a very good home, a shop &c. I generally make a good garden. My house is convenient to churches which I like very much. I always attend preaching.

I wish we all lived near each other. It would be so pleasant to converse, sing, pray with each other, but Fate has otherwise decreed. Mariah sends her love to you and so do the children. Write soon.

Jesse McElroy

Mrs. Johnson also heard from Celia Johnson, probably her sister-in-law, who was doing housework in Charleston. Jesse McElroy wrote his own letters, but neither woman could read or write.

Charleston, South Carolina, July 2, 1868

Mrs. Epsey Johnson
My dear friend:

I received your kind letter and was very glad to hear from you all. I have been quite poorly but am better now. I will try to get home as soon as I can. It is hard to get away from Mrs. Campbell and hard to get money. Cousin Mary is working with me and sends howdy to all.

Tell Mrs. Boykin that I went to the jail and gave the letter to her brother David but he could not get it read. Nobody was able to read it. He said he was going to see if any of the Yankees could read it for him. He will be out of jail in August.

Your last letter was very plain to read. You must get whoever wrote it to write all of your letters for the first one was too bad.

I spent last Sunday night with sister Mary Stewart and went to meeting to the African Church. We heard a blind man preach and had good times.

Give my love to all enquiring friends. I want to get home to see you all. Times are here very hard, and hard to get money. I remain your true friend and sister,

Celia Johnson

P.S. Excuse this short letter as I am very busy ironing. All the way I will get to go home is to promise to come back in October. If I don't I will make hard feelings. I spent a very pleasant day with Mrs. Fisher. She says you must get the smoothing irons, the looking glass and sifter from Harmon Jones and keep them for her. I have been sleeping upstairs so long that you will have [to] get me an upstairs room when I get there. I won't know how to sleep downstairs.

Celia Johnson

South Caroliniana Library, University of South Carolina

In Washington and the big cities of the South, a small but growing middle class was emerging. Government workers, teachers, lawyers, doctors lived comfortably, sometimes luxuriously. The wedding described below, which took place in Washington, had its counterparts in New Orleans and Charleston. The father of the bride, George T. Downing, was a well-known caterer who ran the restaurant of the House of Representatives. A friend of Charles Sumner's and other statesmen, he had been a leader in the northern freedom movement for many years.

The long-anticipated matrimonial affair in high colored circles came off this evening. About one hundred ladies and gentlemen, the *elite* of colored fashion and high life, were assembled. Among the more prominent present were Senator Revels of Mississippi, Frederick Douglass, Professor Wilson, cashier of the Freedmen's Savings Bank, Dr. Purvis. The bridal party arranged themselves at one end of the parlor, Bishop Brown facing them. The ceremony was then performed.

Wedding in Vicksburg, Mississippi (*Boston Public Library*)

The bride, Miss Cordelia Downing, is a young lady of twenty-one years, petite in figure and of more than ordinary beauty. Her wedding toilet consisted of a heavy moire antique, round point lace and train three yards in length, headdress of orange blossoms, diamonds and pearls. The bridesmaids wore white tarlatan puffed, white satin panniers and pearl ornaments. The groom, Mark R. De Mortie, is at present engaged in business in Richmond, Virginia, where he is one of the owners of a manufactury of oil of sassafras.

The array of presents was very large and some were costly and elegant. A very fine ring, with twelve diamonds encircling a large ruby was the gift of the groom. George T. Downing and lady gave a full set of china containing the bride's initial. A very fine assortment of laces was also presented.

The guests retired to an elaborate supper, prepared in an apartment fitted up for the occasion, the ceiling being made up of American flags. After supper, dancing followed and was kept up well into the morning. The happy couple were accompanied to the depot by about forty friends, the ladies being all attired in white in honor of the bride.

The New Era, May 26, 1870

With black men in charge of the catering business in most parts of the country, the suppers served on important social occasions were elaborate indeed. Frederick Douglass was away on a lecture tour when the dinner described below was held at his Washington home.

A number of gentlemen united in a subscription dinner to Gov. Pinchback on Wednesday night last at the residence of Frederick Douglass. Mr. Samuel Proctor was the caterer and the following bill of fare was served:

Potages:
Soup à la Paysanne.

Poisson:
Salmon à la Maintenou.

Entrées:
Fillet de Boeuf à la Provençale,
Poulet à la Florentine,
Punch à la Romaine.

Removes:
Pheasants à la Dauphinaise,
Turkey à la Perigneux.

Rôts:
Canvasbacks,
Aspic de foie gras en Belle vece.

Entremets:
Pudding Diplomade, sauce Sambayon,

Charlottes Russe,
Glaces, Fruitage.
Ice cream.
Nougats en Pyramids.
Jellies &c.
Coffee.

The New National Era, February 20, 1873

All over the country, young men were beginning to play baseball, a game that had become popular during the war. Charles Douglass, son of Frederick Douglass, was secretary of the Mutual Base Ball Club of Washington. In the letter which follows he arranged for a game with the Pythians of Philadelphia. Douglass was then a clerk in the Treasury Department; his correspondent, Jacob C. White, was a school principal.

September 10, 1869

J. C. White, Esq.
Secretary, Pythian Base Ball Club
Dear Sir:

I am directed by the Mutual Base Ball Club of this City to negotiate with you for a game or series of games between your organization and our own. I was instructed to propose that if you would come here we will secure the National Grounds, share with you the proceeds of the gates and assume no other responsibility except to direct you to a suitable boarding house, the same as you did on our last trip to play your club. I understand that such is the rule with all Clubs.

I have no doubt that a large crowd would be out, as you have gained considerable notoriety of late and as yet but one game between colored clubs has been played on the National's new grounds. I have been promised the use of the grounds whenever I shall apply for them.

Boys playing marbles (*Boston Public Library*)

Trusting that your organization may consider our suggestions favorably,

        Charles R. Douglass, Cor. Sec. Mutual B.B.C.

P.S. We would like the game to take place this month, as the Nationals will be out of town.

Baseball was a segregated sport. Even in the North, the Pythians were not permitted to join the Pennsylvania Convention of Base Ball Players. But long before the federal Civil Rights Act of 1875 was passed, blacks were demanding desegregation of public facilities. The New Orleans *Tribune* led the way with a campaign against "star cars"—the streetcars marked with stars which were reserved for black passengers:

Pythian Base Ball Club scorecard (*The Historical Society of Pennsylvania*)

On Monday evening, Mr. William Nichols, one of our citizens, entered a city car and was informed by the driver that he would have to leave because it was not a star car. Mr. Nichols said that he intended to remain where he was unless ejected by force. Whereupon the driver and starter both took hold of the passenger and ejected him from the public conveyance. Policeman Briant then arrested Mr. Nichols and the starter made a complaint at the station charging him with having "forcibly taken possession" of a city car. Mr. Nichols was released on bail.

The New Orleans Tribune, *April 30, 1867*

The star cars are still in existence. In April and December 1865, in May and June 1866, we brought this question before the authorities. From General Hurlbut's administration down to General Sheridan's we have applied to the military to abolish that absurd distinction. The conclusion we had to come to was that the distinction will disappear only when the colored man will be in power or when a civil action will be brought before a court of competent jurisdiction.

The New Orleans Tribune, *May 4, 1867*

The car question is now settled. We called yesterday upon the president of one of the car companies and were informed that all the companies had come to the understanding of admitting our citizens into all the cars, without any distinction as to color. The Chief of Police has issued the following order: "Have no interference with Negroes riding in cars of any kind. No passenger has a right to eject any other passenger no matter what color. If he does so he is liable to arrest for assault or breach of the peace. —Thomas E. Adams, Chief of Police."

The New Orleans Tribune, *May 8, 1867*

After their victory on the streetcars, black citizens organized Equal Rights Clubs and tackled other barriers:

Several men of color had on Sunday called at the confectionery store of Max Nihoul, at the corner of Rampart and Bayou Road, to obtain a drink of soda water and were refused on account of their complexion. Mr. Nihoul preferred to close his establishment than sell refreshments to persons of color. Yesterday some other parties called and asked for soda water and were refused, whereupon a discussion ensued which attracted a considerable number of persons. The fire alarm bells were rung and firemen with an engine and hose carriage and a large number of citizens soon arrived on the spot. They were armed and seemed well prepared to do work of blood and death. A general beating and knocking down with chairs began and even children were not exempt.

The New Orleans *Tribune*, May 14, 1867

Mr. V. E. Macarty, a respectable gentleman of polished manner was [put] out of the Opera House on Tuesday evening because he is a colored man. There was perhaps not a man in the whole audience who was more fit than Mr. Macarty to frequent a refined society. Prejudice and nothing else was the cause of the outrage. Let the members of the Legislature set down this outrage upon their notebook and when the moment comes to vote for the Civil Rights Bill to do their duty by passing that instrument.

The New Orleans *Tribune*, January 21, 1869

A month later the Louisiana legislature passed a civil rights bill which forbade discrimination on railroads and steamboats and in all places of public resort. Over the next years, similar bills were

A Pullman sleeping car

passed in South Carolina, Mississippi, Florida, Arkansas. South
Carolina's law provided for a one-thousand-dollar fine and up to
three years imprisonment for violators. The new laws, however, did
not end discrimination. The burden of enforcing them was left to
black people. This was particularly true on the railroads which re-
served first-class cars and the new Pullman sleeping cars for white
travelers and shunted blacks into dirty and crowded smoking cars.

Cartoon poking fun at civil rights laws (*Boston Public Library*)

Francis Cardozo, a consistent battler against segregation, ran into difficulties in Georgia which had no civil rights law. He told about his experience in a letter to the Columbia *Daily Union:*

Columbia, South Carolina, April 20, 1872
Editor of the *Daily Union:*
When we arrived at Augusta we went into the sleeping car to engage berths for the night. The conductor refused to accommodate us. I then showed him a letter from Mr. Pull-

man, President of the Palace Car Company. Last January I
was ejected from one of Mr. Pullman's sleeping cars and
brought suit against him for $5,000. He proposed the follow-
ing as a compromise: 1st. He should issue a general order to
all his conductors to make no objection to any man on account of his color. 2nd. He should give me a letter permit-
ting me to ride at any time on the same terms as others,
should conductors object. 3rd. He should pay all legal expenses incurred by me.

After reading my letter [the conductor] told me *I* could
stay but my friends must leave. I told him I would keep
with my friends. The conductor ordered the porter not to
make up our beds and the intended sleeping car was to us a
waking car.

During the night the conductor said he wished to show
the letter to Mr. Pullman's agent. I handed him the letter,
requesting him to send it to me at New Orleans the next day.
He never sent it. On our return from New Orleans I arrived
in Atlanta and immediately went to the sleeping car to obtain a berth, which was promptly denied me. I then asked
the conductor (a different person from the one that took us
down) if he had my letter. He said he did not. I then asked
if he had heard of it. "I have indeed," he said. "Do I understand that you refuse me accommodations?" I asked. "I
do," he replied. I then said, "Mr. Conductor, you have the
power to keep me out, but I give notice that I will renew my
suit against Mr. Pullman and will not accept any compromise this time."

I then attempted to go into the regular first-class day car.
The doors were locked and the conductor informed me that
I must go into the smoking car. At this point ten or twelve
white men gathered on the platform. A young man asked
me if I was Cardozo, the secretary of state of South Carolina. I told him I was. He then took me by the arm and attempted to drag me off the platform among the crowd. I

stepped backward into the smoking car. He pursued me there and drew off to strike me. The conductor then interfered and ejected this person from the car. I am satisfied that this was a deliberate conspiracy to assault me and murder me if I resisted.

F. L. Cardozo, Secretary of State, South Carolina

The New National Era, May 16, 1872

Adelina Cuney, wife of a Texas politician, used more direct methods to gain a seat in a first-class railroad car. Her daughter wrote:

My uncle Joseph had gone to the depot with mother to see her off to Houston, where she was to join father. The conductor of the first-class coach saw them coming and quickly locked the door of the coach as he knew from experience that no argument could compel mother to enter a second-class car. After locking the door he disappeared. It was then nearly train time and the coach was filled with passengers. Mother looked around and then said: "Well, Joe, I see but one means of entrance and that is the window, so give me your hand as a mount." And then, as if mounting a horse, she got in the window and took her seat demurely. It was now time for the train to leave so the conductor hastened forward, saw only Uncle Joseph, unlocked the door and cried with great satisfaction, "All aboard." Entering his coach to collect tickets he was bewildered to see mother sitting there with perfect ease and indifference.

Maude Cuney-Hare, *Norris Wright Cuney* (New York, 1913)

Three months after Mississippi's civil rights bill was passed, Thomas W. Cardozo reported efforts to evade it. When, in the following, he spoke of "looking in the glass" he was, of course, referring to his light skin, inherited from a white father. Pinchback and Lynch were also the sons of white men; Rainey and Ransier had some white forebears.

Vicksburg, Mississippi, May 19, 1873

To the Editors:

All of the proprietors of hotels have resorted to a contemptible dodge by hanging out signs that they no longer keep public hotels but that their homes are "for the accommodation of selected guests and personal friends"! And the proprietors of places of amusement generally give notice "that no one will be admitted but those who have special invitation."

Now when we ask for our last remaining right there goes up a terrible howl about social equality. Why, Mr. Editor, there is no class of persons in this country who have demonstrated their love of social equality as those white citizens of the South have. I see a practical demonstration of it whenever I look in the glass. And next winter, when the bill is sprung in Congress and the old howl of social equality is made let Pinchback, Rainey, Lynch, Ransier and others stand up as living monuments of social equality.

Thomas W. Cardozo

The New National Era, May 29, 1873

Although blacks as well as whites expressed a distaste for intermarriage there were a number of interracial romances during the Reconstruction years. In Mississippi, Albert T. Morgan, a white state senator, married Carrie Highgate, a black New Yorker who had gone south to teach. And in Washington where foreign diplomats were often ignorant of American folkways, Paul Gerard, a Frenchman, married Marie Wormley, member of a wealthy and cultured black family. Gerard wrote to *The New Era:*

Washington, February 3, 1870

Dear Sir:

A short time ago I joined myself in alliance with your people by marrying Miss Marie B. Wormley. I am extremely interested in every step of the struggle in which you are engaged, especially for securing social privileges.

A well known gentleman in Washington says about my marriage that "it belongs to the twentieth century." Although in his mind it was a condemnation of my course, yet I accept this as a compliment. Knowing by experience that in your people are found the same capacity and virtues as those of which the white race shows itself so proud, and less vices sometimes, perhaps the twentieth century will effect the reconciliation. This desired fusion between all the races I long for and expect.

Paul Gerard

The New Era, February 10, 1870

At Wormley's Hotel in Washington, owned by Marie Gerard's uncle, at the St. Charles in New Orleans, and in other capital cities of the South, black men of power were beginning to socialize with whites. When Hiram Revels took his Senate seat, George T. Downing invited prominent white Republicans to meet him:

Last night Mr. George T. Downing gave a very pleasant entertainment in honor of Senator Revels. Among those present were Senator Wilson, Hon. William D. Kelley, the entire Mississippi delegation, Major Bowen and others, in all about forty persons. A very agreeable evening was passed in social converse. Late in the evening the host served a magnificent supper. The guests were entertained with vocal and instrumental music.

The New Era, February 3, 1870

Home of Congressman Robert B. Elliott in Columbia, South Carolina (*Peggy Lamson*)

Soon afterward, John W. Forney, publisher of the *Washington Chronicle*, had black guests at a party attended by President Grant and members of his cabinet. *The New Era* commented:

Col. Forney dared to extend invitations to these colored gentlemen. The ostracism which has heretofore characterized American society renders this action of his a noticeable mat-

Congressman Robert Smalls's home in Beaufort, South Carolina

ter, but we doubt not that, in the newer and better life upon which we have now entered, the color of the skin will cease to be a bar to the recognition of gentlemanly qualities in the United States.

The New Era, February 22, 1870

A white official of the Freedmen's Bureau felt similar optimism when he visited Columbia, South Carolina. From his letter to General Howard:

I have been much interested in witnessing the social elevation of the freedmen at this place. The Governor, General R. K. Scott, in his receptions makes no distinction among the members of the legislature (125 of whom are colored). All are taken equally by the hand with the graceful urbanity for which his honor is distinguished. All alike, on such occasions, crowd around his luxurious refreshment tables where, as his accomplished lady told me, no invidious distinctions are made.

You will remember at the dinner party given on your account by the Governor, and at which I had the honor of being a guest, his secretary of state, the Hon. F. L. Cardozo and lady (both colored) received equal attention with other officials, and ladies and gentlemen of the highest standing. I could but feel as I looked around upon that agreeable circle that equality of character and culture were the true conditions of equality in social life. I learned of other occasions when the Governor had followed the same rule, and in conversation he assured me he could allow himself to adopt none other.

The New Era, June 16, 1870

In the same issue of *The New Era,* however, members of the Texas legislature protested because blacks had been excluded from a state ball held in the legislative chambers. The protest, excerpted:

We, the undersigned, members of the House of Representatives, dissenting from the action of the House in regard to the "Grand State Ball" given at the Capitol do offer this, our solemn protest, for the following reasons:

That no invitation was extended to eleven members and as the admission was by card they were excluded whereas

This portrait was titled "A Gentleman of Color" (*Boston Public Library*)

we believe in all affairs of State no such distinction should have been made [and]

Because we believe the whole affair to have been in violation of the rights of certain members as representatives of the people, and calculated to work political evil, the parties having been excluded on account of the "prejudice of color."

The New Era, June 16, 1870

Emblem of the Tenth Regiment, U. S. Cavalry (*National Archives*)

The civil rights struggle was waged, for the most part, by the black elite. The issue had little meaning for the freedmen-farmers whose life-style precluded dinner at hotels or first-class seats on trains. In the complicated world of American race relations, one group of black men actually opposed integration. After the war when the army was reorganized, four black regiments were formed: the Ninth and Tenth Cavalry and the Twenty-fourth and Twenty-fifth

Buffalo Soldier, sketch by Frederic Remington (*National Archives*)

Company B of the 25th Infantry (*National Archives*)

Infantry. These segregated regiments, officered by whites, gave black men their first opportunity to serve in the regular army. When Congress considered a bill to integrate the armed forces they resisted it:

Washington, D.C., February 23, 1873

To the Editors:

Permit me a few remarks concerning the bill now before Congress having for its object the amalgamation of white and colored soldiers and doing away with the colored organizations. If the bill is carried out, the colored soldier will be a thing of the past.

There are in the army about twenty-four thousand white and two thousand colored soldiers. Divide the two thousand colored among twenty-four thousand white and you will see that each company of fifty men will have only four colored men in it. These men, being in such a minority, would be detailed to perform all the menial offices in the company and would take the place of the African under-cooks who were in service before the war.

The Negro does not want to be put into the same regiment with white men, neither are white men anxious to be amalgamated with colored. I trust that the friends of the colored soldier will see that no changes are made. I speak on behalf of the two thousand colored men in the regular service.

W.E.H.

The New National Era, March 6, 1873

Although the bill failed to pass in 1873, it was brought before Congress again. This time the intent of its sponsors was clear, as a soldier explained to General Benjamin F. Butler. The general, a prominent Radical Republican, had enlisted black troops during the war.

Brownsville, Texas, December 7, 1876

General:

I have taken the liberty to write you, knowing that since Charles Sumner is dead, you are the only champion of the Negro who is willing to give him justice. Last session of Congress, a series of assaults was kept up by the Democrats against the colored soldiers with the intention of disbanding the Colored Regiments. A good many of the officers on recruiting service are opposed to colored troops and try all they can to keep them from enlisting, by requiring all kinds of credentials, also to read and write, which they don't require from the white recruits. They then raise the cry that the Colored Regiments can't get recruits.

General, you are too well aware of the way that the haters of the Negro put their falsehoods before the public. They claim they have a desire to enlist both white and colored men in the same Regiment. Neither the white nor the Colored Soldier desire such a thing. As soon as the Colored [Regiments] are done away with they will refuse to enlist any more colored men and the colored soldier would soon be a thing of the past. And even if they are mixed, they will be so few Colored men in a Company that by the time you take out the Cooks, Officers' Servants, and Teamsters which will be all colored you will never see a Colored man either on parade or guard.

A good many of the Officers of Colored Regiments are in favor of mixing the soldiers simply because they are ashamed of being in a Colored Regiment and fancy they are looked down upon. I think if any man is ashamed of the way in which he earns his bread he should look for some other means to get a living.

General, I trust you will use your influence against putting white and colored men in the same Regiments.

E. K. Davies

National Archives

Private Davies' letter, written in a neat, legible hand, had a wider circulation than he anticipated. Reading it hastily, Butler thought that it came from E. J. Davis who had served under him during the war and had afterward become governor of Texas. Butler sent it to the Secretary of War as an expression of opinion from an enlightened white Southerner. Reading with equal haste, the Secretary forwarded it to General W. T. Sherman. Whether Sherman realized that Davies was black is not known, but he pronounced the letter a "libel on the army" and recommended that the black regiments be abolished.

When the bill to end racial distinctions in the army came up in the Senate, Blanche K. Bruce, ignoring the opinions of men like Davies, spoke in favor of dissolving the black regiments:

We believe that, clothed with all the powers and privileges of citizens, we are able, if I may use the expression, "to paddle our own canoe" and, indeed, if we fail to do so successfully, I do not know but that it is about time for us to sink.

Let every man who wants to go into the Army present himself to the recruiting officer, and let him be accepted or refused, not because he is white or black, but because he fills the requirements of the military service. I hope we have passed the critical period in our history in which race distinctions even for protection are to be considered necessary and that we will forget the question of complexion and go forward hand in hand as American citizens.

Congressional Record, 45th Congress, 2nd Session

But white Radical Republicans believed, with Davies, that the bill would end the recruiting of black soldiers. They voted to postpone the measure indefinitely—and the United States Army remained segregated for seventy more years.

Serving on the westward-moving frontier, black cavalrymen found themselves cast, ironically, in the role of Indian fighters. They became known as the Buffalo Soldiers because their hair, the Indians thought, was as tightly curled as the buffalo's. Traditionally, black and red men had been sympathetic neighbors and sometimes allies. Indians had sheltered runaway slaves, intermarried with them—and sometimes enslaved them—and blacks had fought for the Indians in the Seminole wars in Florida. But there is nothing to indicate that the Buffalo Soldiers were half-hearted about helping to drive the Plains Indians from their lands.

Most of the recruits in the black regiments were freedmen who found the army pay of thirteen dollars a month, plus food and clothing, more than they could earn at home. Emanuel Stance of South Carolina was nineteen years old—and barely five feet tall—when he joined the army in 1867. Three years later, as a sergeant in the Ninth Cavalry, he was the first black regular to win a Congres-

sional Medal of Honor for "gallantry and good judgment" in skirmishes with the Indians. One of his reports to his commanding officer:

Fort McKavett, Texas, May 26, 1870

Lieutenant:

I have the honor to make the following report of a scout
after Indians. I left camp on the 20th of May, taking the
Kickapoo Road. When some fourteen miles out I discovered
a party of Indians making across the hills, having a herd of
horses with them. I charged them and after slight skirmish-
ing they abandoned the herd and took to the mountains. I
[took] the horses, nine in number. I resumed my march to
Kickapoo Springs and camped for the night. The following
morning, I decided to return to the Post with my captured
stock as they would embarrass further operations, as my
command was small, numbering ten all told.

About 6 A.M., when about ten miles from Kickapoo, I discovered a party of Indians, about twenty in number, making
for a couple of Government teams three miles in advance of
us. They evidently meant to capture the stock as there was
only a small guard with the teams. I immediately attacked
by charging them. They tried hard to get their horses off,
but I set the Spencers to talking and whistling about their
ears so lively that they broke in confusion and fled to the
hills, leaving us their herd of five horses. Resuming the
march towards camp, they skirmished along my left flank to
the eight-mile waterhole, evidently being determined to take
the stock. I turned my little command loose on them and after a few volleys they left me to continue my march in
peace. I reached camp at 2 P.M. of the 21st with 15 head of
horses captured from the Indians. The casualties of this scout
was one horse slightly wounded.

Emanuel Stance, Sergeant, Co. F, 9th Cavalry

National Archives

At the same time that Emanuel Stance was fighting Indians in Texas some fifteen or twenty thousand former slaves of the Choctaw, Cherokee and Chickasaw Nations were appealing to Congress for their rights. These Indian nations had fought for the Confederacy during the war. The terms of their peace treaty with the U.S. government required them to give their ex-slaves full citizenship rights and land. In 1870 the Committee on the part of the Colored People of Choctaw and Chickasaw Nations declared:

Although freed from slavery by the result of the late war, we enjoy few, if any, of the benefits of freedom. Being deprived of every political right, we are still wholly in the power of our late masters, who were almost a unit on the side of the rebellion against the government, and who, from having been compelled to relinquish their ownership in us, regard our presence among them with no favorable eye. That we, under these circumstances and in our helpless condition, have suffered, and still do suffer, many ills and outrages, even to the loss of many a life, is a notorious fact.

The New Era, March 31, 1870

During the next years, *The New National Era* reported:

The colored people that were held as slaves by the Indians until freed by the 13th Amendment are uneasy about their status. Their position is an anomalous one. They are not enumerated or claimed as members of any tribe and they are much disturbed by the rumors that they will have to leave the Territory. They have determined to pick out their land and claim equal rights with the Indians in all tribal property.

The New National Era, May 2, 1872

The Choctaw Legislative Council has just adjourned. In the Treaty of 1866, Congress agreed to give the Choctaws $300,000 for the strip of country known as the "leased district" provided the Choctaws would, within two years, adopt into the nation and make citizens of about three thousand Negroes, formerly their slaves, and give forty acres of land to each individual. The time expired without action being taken and from Council to Council the Government has extended the time. So strong is the prejudice against allotting their lands that they have again refused to pass the act of adoption.

The New National Era and Citizen, November 13, 1873

Under pressure from Congress, the Cherokees and Choctaws finally granted land and partial rights to their ex-slaves—making them the only freedmen in the country to receive the forty acres of land that all had dreamed of. The Chickasaws continued to resist, pointing out in one resolution passed by their legislature, "The Chickasaw people cannot see any reason or just cause why they should be required to do more for their freed slaves than the white people have done in the slave-holding states for theirs."

---

2. We Need This Land

In the agricultural South, the freedmen's hunger for land showed no signs of abating. Even the most ignorant among them realized that without farms of their own they would be at the mercy of their former masters. Families who had been driven from their land along the coast when the Sherman field order was rescinded pooled their resources and tried to buy land elsewhere. After Tunis G. Campbell's colony on St. Catherines Island was broken up, the settlers leased a plantation on the mainland, south of Savannah, and farmed it cooperatively. The constitution of their Farmers Association:

Belle Ville, McIntosh County, Georgia, March 4, 1867

We the undersigned citizens, Farmers & Laborers of Belle Ville, McIntosh Co., Georgia, feeling the necessity of improving our status, have this day formed ourselves into an association to be known as the Belle Ville Farmers Association and have nominated and duly elected the following named persons to serve in their several capacities for the ensuing year:

For President & General Agent	Tunis G. Campbell, Sen.
" Vice Presidents	Tunis G. Campbell, Jr., Reamus Elliot
" Treasurer	William Williams, Sen.
" Recording & Corr. Secretary	Edwin E. Howard
" Sheriff & Collector	Lunnon Spaulding
" Deputy Sheriff	James Spaulding
" Constables	William Williams, Jr., Reamus Elliot

Farmers bring produce to market on Saturdays (*Boston Public Library*)

" Fence Viewer	Toby Maxwell
" Road Master	Bristoe Hopkins
" Market Inspector	John McKeiver
" Janitor of Buildings	William Williams
" Hog & Cattle Reeve	Charles Campbell

Rules governing Belle Ville Farmers Association:

I. The President shall preside over all meetings; and in his absence either of the Vice Presidents may act as Chairman.

II. The duty of the Treasurer shall be to receive all moneys from the hands of the Secretary, paying them out by order of the President at the desire of the Association, also keeping a regular account which may be at any time audited as necessity requires.

A country store (*Boston Public Library*)

III. The duty of the Secretary shall be to keep a true account of all the deliberations of the Association, attend to all correspondence, keep a record of the working of the Association in order to demonstrate to all feasibility of this plan of working and to show to the people of the State & Country that we can be, are, and with Freedom will be a producing tax-paying element.

IV. The duties of the other officers shall be in accordance with their several appointments: the Sheriff to serve and make returns of all writs, to be also assisted by the Deputy and by the constables who shall preserve good order. The Fence viewer to take charge of all fences, keep up all gaps, see that the gates are closed. The Road Master to see all Public Roads cleared of brush and dirt, and all byroads cleared of debris, filth and unnecessary nuisances.

The Hog & Cattle Reeve to keep all hogs, cattle & horses within inclosures, impounding all not so cared for, allowing none to be released without paying damages. The Market Inspector to see that no diseased meats or vegetables are disposed for sale, confiscating all such and reporting the person so selling.

The Janitor of buildings to take charge of all public buildings, keeping them clean and lighted as required.

And we hereby pledge ourselves, our interest and our labor to the successful issue of this the first permanent [organization] for our welfare and hope thereby to merit the approbation of our friends who have assisted us and the disappointment of our enemies who seek our downfall.

Respectfully submitted,
T. G. Campbell, President & General Agent

Edw. E. Howard, Secretary

National Archives

The black farmers of Edisto Island continued their struggle for land. Conscious of their new political power, they turned to the governor they had helped to elect when they ran into difficulties:

Bulow Plantation, St. Andrews Parish, South Carolina
November 26, 1868

To His Excellency Gov. R. K. Scott
Dear Governor Scott:

We the people petition you for information. We emigrated from Edisto Jan. 29th '67 to this plantation, under the invitation of H. Knight to sell us a homestead, a lot not exceeding 30 acres at a value not exceeding two hundred and four dollars. The said Knight request of us to pay one hundred and four dollars. He agreed with us to pay the remaining one hundred dollars in two installments, fifty dollars Jan. '68, fifty dollars Jan. '69. So Jan. '68 Knight came to the plantation and excuse us from meeting that installment because of the great Deluge & the multitude destroying insects which you know, sir, destroyed two third of the whole country produces. Now Knight are pressuring us to pay for the land or pay him interest. We do not propose to pay Knight a Dollar more for we understand that the heirs of Bulow are in controversy for the property and Knight have no power [over] the plantation. We cannot tell who are the right owner of the property so we write to obtain information & to have you advocate our cause.

We want the land. We wants to finish pay for the 30 acres to make ourselves a Homestead. We do not matter who the plantation belong to. We are willing to finish pay the owner for our 30 acres (the whole tract of land estimated over three thousand acres). We have paid the ½ value already and whosoever the plantation belong to if he will request of us to commence to pay him we willing to do so.

We hold in our hand a receipt showing how much each person paid & for what. Sir, we ask your immediate Reply telling us what step best to pursue.

James Russell, President [of] Meeting

Edisto Island, December 3, 1870

To His Excellency, Governor R. K. Scott

Dear Sir:

We, the undersigned citizens of Edisto Island in a mass meeting convened on Sat. Dec. 3, 1870, petition Your Excellency to take in consideration our want of Homes and lands to cultivate and do what you can to relieve us.

We understand a plantation on Edisto is for sale containing 900 acres of land. We need this land, and wish you or anyone you can refer us to to purchase it for us and in due time will refund the money.

Dear Gov., we have stood by and supported you throughout this last campaign almost to a man. We take no credit to ourselves, for we would not have done so, had we not believed you were a gentleman of principle having the good of the poorer classes in view as well as that of the rich. We ask you to stand by us that our confidence may ever remain unshaken. Dear Gov., let us hear from you at the earliest opportunity that we may know the right policy to pursue to attain our desired object.

James Hutchinson, Chairman
On behalf of the Citizens of Edisto Island

South Carolina Archives

South Carolina was the only southern state to appropriate money to help freedmen buy farms. A Land Commissioner was empowered to buy plantations when they came on the market, subdivide and sell them, on easy credit terms, to small farmers. When Charleston's bankers refused to lend money to the members of another co-operative group, the Atlantic Land Company, because they were black Republicans, they wrote to the Land Commissioner:

Charleston, February 18, 1870

Hon. C. P. Leslie
Dear Sir:

The undersigned citizens of Charleston, representing a large, intelligent and influential portion of the Republican Party in their section of the State, respectfully bring to your attention the following facts.

One year ago they purchased, with the view of benefitting themselves, and giving employment to their colored Fellow Citizens, a valuable tract of land known as Bull's Island, near the city of Charleston. They have spent a large sum of money in improving said Plantation and are now in possession of all the materials required to insure their success in their planting operations.

It is impossible for them at the present time, in the depressed state of their business, to pay the Bond executed in part payment of the purchase money, and proceedings for foreclosure have been instituted. They require the sum of $6,000 on property valued at least at $15,000 to save them from a sale of their property and the consequent failure of an enterprise of vast importance to the colored citizens of Charleston and its vicinity. They have made every effort to obtain the money and have met with those difficulties which you, as a prominent member of the Republican Party, can well appreciate. It does seem to us that as members of that Party we are entitled to some consideration at the hands of our Representatives and that with such undoubted security we offer we are entitled to the benefit of the Laws enacted by the General Assembly. It is currently reported that the favorable Report of your Agent here means nothing—that it is a matter of form and intended for delay.

We desire to know what is to be done in our behalf. We intend to have a final answer, if necessary, through the medium of our Representatives. We have enclosed a copy of this communication to Gov. Scott, who is deeply interested in our success.

[71 signatures]

South Carolina Archives

The sharp tone of the letter was not accidental. It had become increasingly evident that C. P. Leslie, a white Northerner, was speculating in land for his own benefit, with the connivance of Governor Scott. Under pressure from black legislators, Leslie resigned his office two weeks after the above letter was written. The affairs of the

Land Commission were eventually taken over by Francis L. Cardozo and Henry E. Hayne, but meanwhile the members of the Atlantic Land Company, caught in a squeeze between enemies and "friends," lost their plantation. Another co-operative enterprise in nearby Colleton County was more successful. The following article was headed "Colored Communism":

In this country, the colored people own some of the largest plantations. A number of them, in some cases so many as fifty, form themselves into a society, elect officers and adopt by-laws. A specified amount is paid into the treasury by each member. When sufficient is accumulated a suitable plantation is selected and the purchase made. The land is equally distributed. Each is free to work as suits him and each can dispose of his crop as he deems proper. The only thing required is honesty and a prompt payment of all dues which are usually light.

All sick are cared for by the society if unable to care for themselves. All disputes arising between members are brought before the society and the officers endeavor to amiably arrange dissensions.

These societies are principally formed from people who work for hire, fifty cents a day being the sum generally. But few own any animals, their small resources being expended in the purchase money and erection of houses. Upon those that have been in operation three or four years, the land has been paid for and the members are generally prosperous.

The New National Era and Citizen, September 25, 1873

Farm co-operatives were established in other parts of the South, but the most impressive success story came from Mississippi. During the war, General Grant had settled freedmen on plantations belonging to Jefferson Davis and his brother Joseph. The colony

Jefferson Davis' plantation in 1866 (*Boston Public Library*)

was broken up at war's end so that the land could be returned to the Davis family. Soon afterward, Benjamin T. Montgomery who had been a Davis slave leased the property. In 1866 he advertised:

To the Colored People: The undersigned have secured for a term of years the Hurricane and Briarfield plantations from Joseph E. Davis, Esq., the proprietor proposes, on the first day of January, 1867 to organize a community composed exclusively of colored people to occupy and cultivate such plantations and invites the co-operation of such as are recommended by honesty, industry, sobriety and intelligence. A tax to be assessed by the council will be collected to provide for the education of the young and the comfortable maintenance of the aged and helpless.

The New Era, March 3, 1870

Frances E. W. Harper

Before long, Montgomery was able to buy the plantations out-right. To black visitors from the North, Davis Bend was a dream come true. Frances E. W. Harper, a poet who had been active in the antislavery movement, wrote to a friend in Philadelphia:

Mobile, July 5, 1871

My dear friend:

It is said that truth is stranger than fiction. If ten years since someone had said you will be a welcome guest under the roof of the President of the Confederacy, though not by special invitation from him, that you will see his brother's slave a man of business and influence, that hundreds of colored men will congregate on the old baronial possessions, that a school will spring up there like a well in the desert dust, that this former slave will be a magistrate, and that under the moulding hands of this man and his sons will be developed a business whose transactions will be numbered in hundreds of thousands of dollars, would you have smiled incredulously? I have lived to see the day when the plantation has passed into new hands, and these hands once wore the fetters of slavery.

Mr. Montgomery, the present proprietor of between five and six thousand acres of land, has one of the most interesting families that I have seen in the South. They are building up a future which if exceptional now I hope will become more general hereafter. Every hand in his family is adding its quota to the success of this experiment of a colored man both trading and farming on an extensive scale. Last year his wife took on about one hundred and thirty acres of land and with her force raised about one hundred and seven bales of cotton. She has a number of orphan children employed and not only does she supervise their labor, but she works herself. One daughter, an intelligent young lady, is postmistress and assistant book-keeper. One son attends to the planting interest and another daughter to one of the stores. The business of this firm of Montgomery & Sons has amounted, I understand, to between three and four hundred thousand dollars in a year. I stayed on the place several days and was hospitably entertained.

William Still, *The Underground Railroad* (Philadelphia, 1872)

During the first years of Radical Reconstruction there was wide-spread optimism about the progress that the freedmen-farmers were making. An editorial from the South Carolina *Missionary Record:*

From observations among the colored people in this State there is a steady growth in prosperity and accumulation of lands and other property. Purchases of large tracts of land are being made and they are building up homesteads and becoming taxpayers, producers and good citizens. Thousands of acres of land are being cultivated this year more than last and many thousands more will be taken up next year.

The New National Era and Citizen, September 4, 1873

To encourage freedmen to save money to buy land, Congress had chartered the Freedmen's Savings and Trust Company as a bank for black people. In 1870, the bank reported:

The increasing thrift of the colored people is shown by the returns of the Freedmen's Savings Bank. It has 42 branches in the Southern States. The depositors number 44,395, with an average deposit of $284 each. The total deposits amount to $12,605,782, of which $663,149 have been drawn out for the purchase of land. The freedmen, in addition, have spent $296,918 in purchasing homes and $941,736 for seeds, teams and agricultural equipment.

The New National Era, September 22, 1870

The situation was less rosy than this report indicated because 44,395 depositors represented only 1 per cent of the black population of the South. And even these exceptional or lucky freedmen were doomed to disappointment. The bank's original charter required that at least two thirds of the deposits be invested in government securities. This was later amended to permit investments in real estate. The hard-earned savings of the freedmen were loaned to speculators; after the financial panic of 1873, most of these loans were worthless. To restore confidence in the bank, its trustees offered the presidency to Frederick Douglass. Assured that the institution was basically sound, he accepted the job and even loaned the bank ten thousand dollars of his own money. But he had underestimated the dishonesty and incompetence of his predecessors. After two months in office he wrote to a friend:

Despite my efforts to uphold the Freedmen's Savings and Trust Company it has fallen. It has been the black man's cow, but the white man's milk. Bad loans and bad management have been the death of it.

Gerrit Smith Collection, George Arents
Research Library at Syracuse University

Largely as a result of Douglass' efforts, depositors were eventually paid up to fifty cents for each dollar they had deposited. Most of the small depositors, however, could not be located. Still on file in the National Archives are the names of thousands of freedmen who lost their first savings in the government-backed Freedmen's Bank.

William Wells Brown, an ex-slave who became a successful writer, described the impact of the bank's failure:

The hope of everyone seemed to center in the Freedmen's Savings Bank. "This is our bank," said they and to this institution the intelligent and the ignorant, the soldier, farmer, day laborer and poor washerwoman all alike brought their earnings. Deposits in the Bank increased from three hundred thousand dollars in 1866 to fifty-five million dollars

BLOOD MONEY.

After failure of Freedmen's Savings Bank, Thomas Nast equated northern speculators and Ku Klux Klan (*Boston Public Library*)

in 1874. These deposits were the first installments toward purchasing homes, or getting ready to begin some business. The announcement, therefore, of the closing of the Bank had a paralyzing effect upon the blacks everywhere.

Large numbers quit work; the greater portion sold their bank-books for a trifle. Many who had purchased small farms and had paid part of the purchase money, became discouraged, gave up the lands and went about as if every hope was lost. Verily, the failure of the Freedmen's Savings Bank was a National calamity, the influence of which will be felt for many years.

William Wells Brown, *My Southern Home* (Boston, 1880)

Although the failure of the Freedmen's Bank blasted the dreams of thousands of would-be black farmers, the attitude of southern planters was even more calamitous. In state after state, plantation owners refused to sell or rent to blacks. The *Commercial Bulletin* of New Orleans reported in 1869 that "planters and landowners are forming combinations and societies pledged not to rent land to Negroes." Two years later, Emanuel Fortune told congressional investigators:

They will not sell our people any land. They have no disposition to do so. They will sell a lot now and then in a town, but nothing of any importance.

Q—What could you get a pretty good farm for—how much an acre?

A—Generally from $10 to $15 an acre. Very poor people cannot afford that.

Q—You can get it if you have the money?

A—They will not sell it in small quantities. I would have bought forty acres if the man would have sold me less than a whole tract. They hold it in that way so that colored people cannot buy it. The lands we cultivate generally are swamp or lowlands.

Q—Is there not plenty of other land to buy?

A—Not that is worth anything. I do not know of any Government land that will raise cotton.

Asked if blacks were getting homes of their own, Robert Meacham answered:

Very few of them. For want of means, that is one reason. Another reason is that they do not have a chance to buy the land. Those who have it will not sell it to colored men and they ask so much for it that colored people will not buy it.

I have been told by gentlemen that there is a thorough understanding among them in the way of seeing that the colored people shall never have much. They are united one with another to see that that is done.

Condition of Affairs
(Washington, 1872)

The story was the same in Mississippi:

Q—Do the white people here favor the colored people buying lands?
A—No, sir. They say that if you suffer the colored people to own land they cannot get any laborers.
Q—So the white owners of the soil are opposed to your people becoming owners of land?
A—Yes, sir, or stock in any way. They don't believe in that. I have known a great many that have lost their stock. Sometimes the employers would go out and shoot the stock down.

Condition of Affairs
(Washington, 1872)

And in South Carolina:

Men of rebel proclivities throw obstacles in the way of freedmen purchasing lands, especially in some sections of South Carolina. They either raise the price on colored purchasers, refuse to sell to them or refuse to give them time on a purchase. Whenever a colored man, by the industry of

himself, wife and two or three children accumulates sufficient means to purchase a few acres, the planters offer him
land on rent rather than he should buy land. One of the features of rebel policy toward the Negro is to keep him out of
land and thereby control his labor and his vote.

The New National Era, March 16, 1871

**When a freedman did manage to buy land, his white neighbors
often conspired to take it from him. A Louisiana farmer reported:**

I am a colored man. I settled a place on overflood land
about three and a half miles west of Shreveport, near the
lake. I have about nine or ten acres improved and four
houses built on it and I have lived on the place for the past
five years. In 1875, in December I went to Natchitoches to
the United States land office and I paid them $15 and got
my title to the land. The land agent told me to carry my papers to W. D. Willey and tell him to have them recorded for
me in the courthouse at Shreveport. Mr. Willey charged me
$9 to have them recorded yet he did not have my land re-
corded, nor did he give me my money back, neither my papers. In January, 1876 Mr. Jewell told me to leave that place.
Mr. Jewell told me he would send me to state prison if I did
not leave and leave everything there that I had built. Nor
would he let me move anything. I am about eighty years of
age, have a wife and one child. I had a good garden, but
they had turned the stock in on it and destroyed it. I also
had a very nice lot of fruit trees, such as apples, plums,
peaches &c., and he would not let me move any of them.
This is the truth, so help me God.

his
Caesar × Robinson
mark

Senate Report 693, 46th Congress, 2nd Session

In this 1869 cartoon planter wants laborer jailed because
he refuses to work without pay (*Boston Public Library*)

Unable to obtain land of their own, the vast majority of freedmen
were obliged to hire themselves out to white planters. Whether
they worked for wages or for a share of the crop, they had little to
show for their labor at the end of the year. The planters kept the
account books. By juggling the figures, they could keep freedmen in
perpetual debt. Henry M. Turner described how this system of
virtual peonage began in Georgia:

Q—You say that colored men employed in the country have not been able to get anything for their labor. Why is that?

A—During the year there is very little money paid to them and if they want to obtain provisions or clothing they are given an order on some store. At the end of the year these little bills are collected and however small a quantity of things have been taken, almost always the colored man is brought into debt. That is alleged as a reason why they should be bound to stay with their employers and work out what they say they owe them.

Q—A sort of practical peonage?

A—Yes, sir. Whenever there is fear that the laborer will go to work with someone else the following year, he is apt to come out $25 to $30 in debt and his employer calls upon him to work it out.

There was a bill introduced the other day to make it a penal offense for a laborer to break his contract. For instance, a white man writes out a contract. He reads the contract to the black man and, of course, reads just what he pleases. When the black man takes it to somebody else and gets him to read it, it reads quite differently. Among other things there is a provision in the contract that he must not go to any political gathering or meeting. If he does, he will lose $5 for every day that he is absent, and yet he is to receive only $50 or $75 a year. Every day that he is sick, a dollar or a dollar and a half is to be deducted. The man may want to quit and work for some person else who will pay him better wages.

Q—The effect of the legislation would be to render the laborer practically a slave during the period of his contract?

A—Or else he would be liable to punishment by imprisonment. There is no doubt that they will pass some kind of law to that effect.

Q—With a view to harmonize the relations of labor and capital?

A—Yes, sir, that is the phrase.

Condition of Affairs
(Washington, 1872)

Other Georgians told of their experiences. Cane Cook of Americus:

I worked for Robert Hodges last year. I had my own stock and rented land from him, agreeing to give him one-third of the corn and one-fourth of the cotton for rent. We divided the corn by the wagonload and had no trouble about that. I made three bales of cotton, weighing five hundred and six, five hundred and eleven and four hundred and seventy pounds. He told me he would buy my cotton and pay the market price which was twenty-one cents [a pound]. I got some meat and corn and other things from him during the year and he paid me $50 in cash, Christmas.

I went to him last Friday for a settlement. When he read over his account he had a gallon of syrup charged to me. I told him I had not had any syrup. He asked me if I disputed his word. I told him I did not want to dispute his word but I have not had any syrup. He got very angry and took a large hickory stick and came toward me. He is a strong man and I did not want any trouble with him. I went backwards to the door and he followed me. As I turned to go down the steps he struck me a powerful blow on the back of my head and I fell to the ground.

I could not move hand or foot. Two colored men carried me [home]. My hands, arms, back and legs are almost useless. I have to be fed like a baby. I have not gone before any of the courts. I have no money to pay a lawyer and I know it would do no good. Mr. Hodges has not paid me for my cotton. While I lay before his door he told me that if I died he would pay my wife $50. I hope there will be some law sometime for us poor oppressed people. If we could only get land and have homes we could get along, but they won't sell us any land.

Henry Warner of Schley County:

I am a blacksmith. I engaged to work a year for Aaron Hooks for $350 and do the blacksmithing for six gangs of hands. During the year I went to Mr. Hooks as he was about to start on a journey and asked him how much he had charged against me for what I had drawn on my wages. He said $72.40. While he was away I asked Mrs. Hooks for $5. When Mr. Hooks returned he told me he found $168 charged against me. I told him I had had only $5 and it could only be $77.40. Mr. Hooks said it was on the books and must be right. I afterward agreed to take two old mules at $75 each. It was a great more than they were worth. I took two hogs at $5 each and bought $5 worth of stuff—in all $242.40. When we had our settlement at the end of the year he said he owed me $12 and that was all I could get.

The New Era, March 3, 1870

Louisiana freedmen had similar stories to tell:

My name is Simon Dickson. I worked for Miss Lizzie Dickson on her place, in 1873. I made six bales of cotton and each bale weighed about six hundred pounds. I was to give her one hundred pounds to the acre but she took all

Blacks gin cotton under watchful eye of overseer (*Boston Public Library*)

I made that year for the money I owed her, $20. In 1874 I made eight and a half bales of cotton, weighing on an average five hundred and twenty-five pounds to the bale. I was to give her one-half of what I made. But she again took all. I then owed her about $40. She said I owed her $115 so she taken all of my crop every year for what she claimed I owed her, yet she would never tell me what anything cost.

My name is Hiram Smith. I live on Joe Williams' place. I asked Mr. Williams to pay me what he owed me on my cotton; also $75 he had taken from me. He jumped on me and beat me so badly I fear I cannot live. He made me crawl on my knees and call [him] my God, my master, the God of all power, all because I had asked for a settlement. That was done on the 16th of March, 1876.

Senate Report 693, 46th Congress, 2nd Session

In Florida where Radical Republicans controlled the legislature a new law offered some protection to farm workers. Robert Meacham explained:

Q—How has it been with their contracts? Have they had trouble in settling up fairly and getting their pay?

A—A great deal. In the first place, the farmers draw up the contracts in writing and read it to them. The colored people are generally uneducated and when a contract says this or that they hardly know what it means. Another reason why they do not get much is that in August and September when the crops are laid by, the slightest insult, as they call it, or the slightest neglect is sufficient to turn them off and according to the terms of the contract they get nothing. Now that is remedied a little. There is a law in this state that allows a man to get what he works for, unless it is proven that he has willfully neglected or violated any of the articles of agreement. It provides that whenever the tenant has worked anywhere for a length of time he shall be paid for that portion of his work. You cannot turn a man off without a good and lawful excuse and without paying him for the time.

Condition of Affairs
(Washington, 1872)

However, as Radical control weakened, more and more black families found themselves working as they had in slavery times, with little hope of ever becoming independent farmers. The best firsthand description of these farmers-without-land came from Henry Adams, a Louisiana freedman. After a three-year stint in the army, Adams and other veterans undertook their own investigation of life in the rural South. He explained the purpose of the investigation to a group of senators:

Well, in 1870, after I had left the Army, a parcel of we men that was in the Army thought that the way our people had been treated during the time we was in the service— we heard so much talk of how they had been opposed. So a parcel of us got together and said we would organize our-selves into a committee and look into affairs and see the true condition of our race.

Some of the members was ordered by the committee to go into every State in the South where we had been slaves, and post one another from time to time about the true condition of our race. We worked our way from place to place and from State to State, and worked amongst our people in the fields to see what sort of living our people lived. We wanted to see whether there was any State in the South where we could get a living and enjoy our rights. At one time there was five hundred of us. About one hundred and fifty went from one place or another. The information they brought to us was very bad.

Q—The committee, as I understand you, was composed en-tirely of laboring people?

A—Yes, sir. No politicianers didn't belong to it because we was afraid that if we allowed the colored politicianer to belong he would tell it to the Republican politicianer and, from that, the men that was doing all this to us would get after us.

Adams worked in Louisiana and traveled to neighboring states making notes of what he saw. From his memoranda which he turned over to the Senate committee:

I have seen colored children barefooted, half naked and even starved on their way to school, and in [some] parishes there was no public schools. The colored people works for shares of the crop, one-third they makes and their em-ployers find them something to eat and farming utensils, giving them rations for man and wife per month the follow-ing: two bushels of meal and twenty pounds of pork, nothing else.

Most black families lived in the old slave cabins

Meals were cooked in the fireplace

Weighing the cotton was always a white man's job (*Boston Public Library*)

The white people rob the colored people out of two-thirds of what they make. For instance, the contract [is] for one-third or one-quarter of the crop. They take every bale and will not divide it at the gins but ship it to the city. Then when the cotton is sold they figure and figure until there is but little left to the colored man.

White men would sell cotton for colored persons in Shreveport, and the bale of cotton bringing $65, they would pay them $49 and tell them that was money enough for a nigger to have. They would buy cotton from colored people when cotton was selling at twelve and a half cents and pay them six to seven cents. I was present and saw with mine own eyes.

I picked cotton of Forster plantation and I seen the white men that weighed the cotton. When the draught would weigh seventy-five pounds they would check fifty pounds. Yet they were charging colored people fifteen and twenty-one cents per pound for meat; ten pounds of flour for $1; tobacco sixty cents per plug; sugar fifteen to twenty cents per pound and coffee in proportion.

I worked on James Hollingsworth's plantation and the same thing was practiced on that place. On Dr. Vance's plantation where I often worked, I have seen the same. From the mouth of Red River to Jefferson, Texas, no difference can be seen. Even in Arkansas and Texas where I traveled I see the same, as it was my business to look around and ascertain as far as possible into the treatment of colored people by whites.

In going from Shreveport to New Orleans I seen along the banks of Red River colored people who were afraid to talk to me at landings. I asked several of them, "Do you not live well?" They told me, "No, the whites take all we make and if we say anything about our rights they beat us." I told them, "If the men you all live with this year do not give you all what belongs to you just like he has promised, you all must leave that place and go to another, and if he does not fulfill his contract leave that place also." They told me, "If we do that we will have to be all the time going from plantation to plantation for all the white men are alike on this Red River. What one of them says to us, they all say, and what one of them do to us, they all do. We have been working hard since the surrender, and have not got anything."

Senate Report 693, 46th Congress, 2nd Session

John M. Langston

3. All That We Want Is the Greenback

When John M. Langston traveled through the South as general inspector of schools for the Freedmen's Bureau he was impressed with the number of skilled black workers he saw. In one of his reports to the Bureau he wrote:

More than one-third of the colored population of North Carolina are mechanics. They are nearly six to one as compared with white mechanics. All the mechanical occupations are represented by them: blacksmiths, gunsmiths, wheelwrights, millwrights, machinists, carpenters, cabinetmakers, plasterers, painters, shipbuilders, stonemasons and bricklayers are found among them in large numbers. There are also many pilots and engineers. The two most trustworthy pilots in North Carolina are freedmen. The engineer on the boat run by this pilot is also a freedman. One of the most interesting sights which it was my good fortune to witness was the building of a steamboat by a colored shipbuilder, with his gang of colored workmen.

The New Era, January 13, 1870

These workmen were in a better position to bargain with their employers than the field hands were. During the first summer of peace, black spokesmen in Virginia wrote:

Everywhere your late owners are forming Labor Associations for the purpose of fixing and maintaining, without the least reference to your wishes or wants, the prices to be paid for your labor. We say to you, "Go and do likewise." Let Labor Associations be at once formed among the colored people throughout the length and breadth of the United States, having for their object the protection of the colored laborer, by regulating fairly the price of labor, by affording facilities for obtaining employment by a system of registration and, last but by no means least, by undertaking on behalf of the colored laborer to enforce legally the fulfillment of all contracts made with him.

The Liberator, September 8, 1865

Workers on Mississippi river boat

The next years saw a spurt of union organizing all over the country. In 1867 black waterfront workers struck for higher wages in Mobile, Savannah and Charleston. A riot on the docks in New Orleans was averted when the head of the Freedmen's Bureau, General Joseph Mower, ordered contractors to pay freedmen the wages due them:

Yesterday morning a crowd of colored stevedores, numbering about five hundred, assembled on the levee. For some time the contractors who undertake to load and unload boats have been practicing a swindle upon the workmen and the latter were determined to prevent any further such abuses. The workmen were generally paid only one-half of what was due them by these contractors.

Stevedores on the docks in New Orleans (*Boston Public Library*)

Under this state of excitement the working men seized a contractor named Moses and attempted to lynch him, but the man was rescued by the river police. The contractor employed in discharging the steamer *Irene* was also attacked but the swiftness of his legs put an end to the assault.

Mayor Heath, with the Chief of Police, went to the scene and made an effort to appease their riotous dispositions. But as the Mayor has lost much of the affection of the colored people, very little attention was paid to his remarks. The disturbers proceeded toward the New Basin for the purpose of catching some other contractor, but passing the headquarters of General Mower the rioters were advised to desist in their conduct which they did.

The New Orleans *Tribune*, May 17, 1867

Black workmen had to battle on two fronts—against employers and against white workers who would not work alongside of them. When Lewis Douglass, who had learned to set type on his father's first newspaper, got a job in the Government Printing Office, white printers threatened to strike. Frederick Douglass said:

Lewis Douglass (*Moorland-Spingarn Research Center, Howard University*)

It is alleged that he has worked at a lower rate of wages than that fixed upon as the proper one by the Printers' Union; that he has worked in a city where such Unions existed and did not become a member; that he has served no regular apprenticeship. Analyze these excuses and they but aggravate the very crime they are intended to defend. Douglass is made a transgressor for working at a low rate of wages by the very men who prevented his getting a high rate. He is denounced for not being a member of a Printers' Union by the very men who would not permit him to join.

He is not condemned because he is not a good printer, but because he did not become such in a regular way, that regular way being closed against him by the men now opposing him. There is no disguising the fact—his crime was his color.

The New York Times, August 8, 1869

Two years after Lewis Douglass first applied, the Columbia Typographical Union of Washington agreed to accept black members. In nearby Baltimore, however, white shipyard workers went on strike to force employers to fire a thousand black men. Under the leadership of Isaac Myers, a caulker, the men who had lost their jobs formed a co-operative:

He conceived the idea of the colored people buying a shipyard and marine railway. He called meetings in all the colored churches, organized a company, and within four months raised $10,000 in shares of $5 each, exclusively from colored people; purchased [a] yard and railway for $40,000 and three hundred colored caulkers and carpenters found immediate employment. He secured a government contract against the combined competition of ship builders of Wilmington, Philadelphia, Baltimore and Alexandria. The entire debt of the shipyard company was paid off in five years from the profits of the business.

"The Late Isaac Myers, of Baltimore, Md."
A.M.E. Church Review, April 1891

Myers went on to organize a Colored Caulkers Trade Union Society in Baltimore and a Maryland State Labor Union. In the face of similar organizing efforts in Philadelphia and New York, white union leaders began to discuss an alliance. In 1869, the National Labor Union, a federation of white trade unions, invited Myers and other black men to attend their annual convention. Myers was lis-

Isaac Myers

tened to respectfully when he appealed for unity between black and white workers, but the convention, not yet ready for integration, recommended that blacks form separate unions which could affiliate with the NLU. Later that year, leading black men met in Washington to organize a Colored National Labor Union. From their "Address to the Colored People of the United States":

We call your attention to the necessity of immediate organization in every State. We regret that our white fellow citizens have organized "Trades Unions" to the exclusion of colored members—that they will not permit colored men to work in their shops. This opposition on the part of a large number of the white mechanics must be met and overcome, not in angry dispute or open hostilities but by organization.

We therefore advise the calling of a State Labor Convention in all the states. In any city or county where there are seven or more mechanics, artisans or laborers of any particular branch, we advise their immediate organization. Having your labor organized, you can advertise it for sale in the daily papers. Although the white mechanics may refuse you work with them, contractors will be governed by self-interest and will negotiate with you as readily as with any other association of mechanics and laborers. Thousands of colored mechanics could obtain immediate employment if they would adopt the above course.

In most of the States it is a necessity at this time that you organize cooperative mechanical associations. Let each one lay by a small sum weekly for the purchase of the necessary tools, then take his labor as capital and go out and build houses, forge iron, make bricks, run factories, work plantations &c. This is being done by our white fellow citizens and can be done by you.

To acquire a Homestead should be the ambition of each man in the land. This can be done by organizing building associations. We shall aim to furnish you with the most improved plan of organization.

You will please furnish [our] Bureau [of Labor] with all information that will assist us in finding out our real condition and that will aid us in the promotion of the moral, social, intellectual and industrial welfare of our people.

Isaac Myers, President, George T. Downing, Vice-President

The New Era, February 17, 1870

The leaders of the Colored National Labor Union were more conservative than their white counterparts. Many white trade unionists supported the International Workingmen's Association founded by Karl Marx in 1864, and the NLU backed a Labor Reform Party in the United States. Myers and other black spokesmen saw no conflict between capital and labor, deprecated strikes and maintained their allegiance to the Republican Party. At a mass meeting in Richmond, Myers said:

We wish to establish the most friendly relationship between labor and capital, because we believe their interests to be inseparable, because we know in proportion as the laborer is remunerated for his labor and encouraged, in proportion is capital safe and productive. I know an establishment where the mechanics get $3.25 a day and so much percentage on all the work turned out. The result is, the shop turns out a third more work than any other establishment of the same kind in the State.

How can labor be made respectable and productive and protect its rights? We answer, by being organized. Is there a necessity for the colored mechanics and laborers of the United States organizing? My answer is, there is the greatest necessity; and unless you do organize in a few short years the trades will pass from your hands—you become the servants of servants, the sweeper of shavings, the scrapers of pitch and the carriers of mortar.

And why do I make such a broad and positive assertion? It is because I find the white mechanics of the North and South organized for the extermination of colored labor and because I do not find the colored men organized for their protection, and because I know if you do organize you will preserve your labor, command employment, and educate your children in the trades.

The New Era, April 21, 1870

Despite their middle-of-the-road position, black trade unionists were sometimes criticized for being too radical. The following letter to Frederick Douglass, who became president of the Colored National Labor Union in 1870, was written by Richard T. Greener, Harvard University's first black graduate and a teacher at the Institute for Colored Youth in Philadelphia. At the time he wrote, trade unionists were asking that the prevailing ten-hour work day be cut to eight hours.

Philadelphia, October 11, 1871

To the Editor:

I notice that the [Colored] National Labor Union is soon to meet in Columbia, South Carolina. Having followed the course of this society and read its somewhat incongruous speeches and indefinite resolutions and having noticed how it is gradually drawing into its net most all of our prominent men, yourself among the number, I am led to ask what is the object of this *National Bureau of Labor?* Is it merely another name for Communism? Does it propose to make labor the equal of capital—or to give ten hours pay for eight hours work? Or is it merely a colored offshoot of the notorious *Internationale* which proposes to overthrow stable government in England and to give us a mobocracy in America?

South Carolina phosphate workers (*Boston Public Library*)

As I have yet to read a clear statement of its object from its high priest, Karl Marx, down to Myers in America, I should like to know what these gentlemen propose. Are we to be emancipated who do our eight or nine hours work and then work several more hours to get ready for the next day's labor? How many editors, how many lawyers, how many capitalists—ogres that they are!—how many teachers would not hasten to join this movement if [it] would guarantee to us also eight hours pay for six hours work and a chance to spend our evenings in the beer shops.

It is because I, like you, have sprung from the ranks and have shaken off the service of Vulcan, preferring to follow Minerva, even though she bid me work fifteen hours a day that I am alarmed. Do you long for the ship-yard again?

I surely do not ask for the drudgery of a store without the prospect of promotion. Will the National Bureau of Labor inform a former "laborer"?

Richard T. Greener

The New National Era, October 19, 1871

Greener's distaste for unions was not shared by black leaders in the South where men like Henry M. Turner, Robert B. Elliott and James T. Rapier called Labor Conventions and backed demands for a minimum wage and a nine-hour day. Although the Colored National Labor Union went out of existence in 1872, southern workers continued their efforts to organize. When *The New National Era* criticized a strike of Pennsylvania ironworkers, an Alabama union man wrote:

Wetumpka, Alabama, May 16, 1874

To the Editor:

I note in your paper an article headed "The Folly, Tyranny and Wickedness of Labor Unions" to which, as State Agent of the Alabama Labor Union, I beg space to reply. I condemn as much as you the evil practices of demagogues but to class the *entire* Labor Unions of the country in the same category, I think unjust.

In this State, the laboring men are almost entirely colored, but they have organized themselves into a Labor Union for their mutual protection. The institution in this State is intended to do that for the laboring masses what they are not as individuals capable of doing for themselves—that is, they have men in whom they confide to investigate and supervise their contracts and to see that their interests are not compromised. The Labor Union of this State is supplying a want that has long been felt by our people.

William V. Turner, State Agent,
Alabama Labor Union

The New National Era, May 28, 1874

In the cities, longshoremen, bricklayers, teamsters, even waiters, joined unions and had some success in improving working conditions. But attempts to organize the bulk of southern laborers—the men and women on the big plantations—largely failed. There were times, however, when an upwelling of resentment was so strong that the farm workers organized without the help of state or national leaders and won their demands. The most successful of these "risings"—as the planters called them—took place in the rice fields along the Combahee River in South Carolina in 1876. The strike started because each planter paid his workers with "checks" which could not be turned into cash money for as long as four years from date of issue. These bits of paper could only be used to buy goods at the planter's store. A typical check:

---

50 Due   —Fifty Cents —   .50
                to Jonathan Lucas
or Bearer, for labor under special contract.
Payable on the first January 1880
                J. B. Bissell

Savannah *Tribune*, September 2, 1876

Refusing to harvest the rice crop, hundreds of men and women patrolled the fields with clubs to keep would-be scabs away. At meetings they sang "the greenback song" a parody of the wartime song sung by General Sherman's troops—"Marching Through Georgia."

We are not afraid to work
We will labor every day.
All that we want is the greenback.
When the day's work is ended,
Come and bring the pay.
All that we want is the greenback.

Women in the rice fields (*Boston Public Library*)

Greenbacks, forever, come, planters come.
Up with the greenback
And down with the check.
We will labor in your fields
From the morning until night.
All that we want is the greenback.

G. G. Martin, don't you know
That we told you at your store,
All that we want is the greenback?
Henry Fuller, don't delay.
J. B. Bissell, what you say?
All that we want is the greenback.

Beaufort *Tribune*, August 30, 1876

When panicky planters telegraphed Governor Chamberlain to tell of the "rising," Chamberlain did what governors have traditionally done when faced with a serious labor conflict—he called out the militia. However, in 1876, South Carolina's militia was largely black and the brigade commander in the Combahee region was Congressman Robert Smalls. Instead of leading troops to the rice fields, Smalls went alone to talk to the strikers. Afterward, he wrote to the governor:

Beaufort, South Carolina, August 24, 1876

To His Excellency Gov. D. H. Chamberlain

Sir:

I received a telegram from the Attorney General to call out the Militia if necessary to put down the riot on the Combahee. I found no rioters, but I did find a large body of men, about three hundred, who had refused to work for checks, a sample of which you will find enclosed. The rice planters issued these checks instead of money, and they are only redeemed in goods purchased at exorbitant prices at the stores of the planters. As these checks are payable in 1880, other storekeepers will not receive them, nor will they buy medicines or the services of a physician in case of sickness. Several of the strikers informed me that they had been unable to get money enough to pay their taxes.

The abolition of this check system will restore quiet among the laborers in the rice districts. I found no lawless disposition among the strikers. Many of them belonged to the Militia and as such had arms, but not one appeared upon the ground with any weapon except a club or stick, but I found from forty to sixty white men, mounted and armed with Spencer rifles, sixteen shooters and double-barreled shotguns. The presence of these armed white men did much to alarm and excite the strikers.

Warrants had been issued by Trial Justice Fuller for seven strikers who were charged with whipping two men of their own number who had gone to work contrary to the agreement made by them in their club. I asked those to come out of the crowd against whom warrants had been issued. The seven men gave themselves up. They had previously objected to arrest by armed white men. The prisoners then walked into Beaufort, fourteen miles distant, without a guard and were in Beaufort hours before the arrival of the Sheriff.

I would suggest that Mr. Fuller, the Trial Justice, be removed as he is a large planter, and one who issues checks to his laborers. Therefore there must be, naturally, dissatisfaction on the part of laborers when brought before him.

I find that the prices charged for goods where checks are taken are as follows: grits $2 per bushel, regular price $1; bacon 25¢ per lb., regular price from 10 to 15¢; molasses $12 per gal., regular prices $4, and other articles in proportion.

I hope you will be able to adopt a remedy to cure the evils of the check system and thus add to the peace of the rice district and the prosperity of the laborer.

Robert Smalls

South Carolina Archives

The strike continued for another month, spreading to the Georgia border. With the rice rotting in the fields, the planters were forced to give in. When they agreed to pay the harvesters $1.50 an acre, in cash, peace was restored to the Combahee.

V · THERE IS A BRIGHT FUTURE

I wants my children to be educated because I can believe what they tells me. If I go to another person with a letter in my hand, he can tell me what he pleases in that letter and I don't know any better. But if I have got children who read and write, they will tell me the contents of that letter and I will know it's all right.

A Louisiana freedman

1. Send Us Teachers

One by one, the benefits of emancipation were being wrenched from the freedmen's grasp. But despite the diminishing hopes of the present, they held fast to their belief in the future. For the future belonged to their children and education was the magic key that would open the doors of opportunity.

The older generation had faith in the future of their children

During the first years of Reconstruction, the schools supported by northern philanthropic groups continued to expand. Robert Harris, a black Ohioan who was teaching in North Carolina, reported to the American Missionary Association:

Fayetteville, North Carolina, April 3, 1869

Rev. E. P. Smith, Gen. Field Agt., A.M.A.

Dear Sir:

We are now occupying our new schoolhouse and have graded our school into two classes, Primary and Grammar. We are yet without curtains or shades. We borrowed chairs &c and were obliged to provide other necessaries at our own expense. Grading, setting out trees, digging well &c we have defrayed by a subscription among the citizens.

The colored people came from far and near to attend the "Dedication" of the first schoolhouse built for colored children in this county. The whites are a little jealous, as it

The Penn School in South Carolina was supported by the
Pennsylvania Freedmen's Association

surpasses all of theirs. We now have two excellent schools
which, we trust, will not languish for lack of means.

As yet our State has done nothing for Education and the
prospect is not encouraging. The Legislature will probably
pass a school bill, but the State has no money.

Three of my scholars leave me this month to take charge
of country schools. I am continually importuned for
Teachers. We are very desirous of having a library for the
advanced department and beg of you to put us in the way
of getting one. We have now one hundred and seventy
scholars and constantly increasing. We are surely "Marching On."

Robert Harris

American Missionary Association Archives,
Amistad Research Center

The missionary teachers offered the freedmen's children the same kind of training that they had received in New England and New York. The orphan boy who wrote the following had been given a home and name by Frances Wells, principal of Trinity School in Alabama. His letter was addressed to a class of white Sunday-school children in the North:

Athens, Alabama, February 15, 1868

Dear Children:

I am a little black boy. I don't suppose I'll ever be white. I'm free, though. My mother is dead, my father went off with the Yankees. I lived in the camps one year with the Yankee soldiers. I used to dance around the camp for sugar and bread. Now I has a nice home with Miss Wells. She teaches me to be good and I am trying to be the best boy in the world.

I have read through the First and Second Reader and now I am in the Third Reader. I have very nice clothes with pockets in them; I eat with a fork. I used to sit on the floor and eat with my fingers, and get grease and molasses all over myself. I didn't have any manners nor anything to eat hardly. Now I have everything nice and I try very hard. I am a temperance boy. I don't drink any rum and I never will.

I learn Latin, too, when Miss Wells' class recites their lesson: *Ille, illa, illud. Sum, esse, fui.* I shall study Latin and history too. History tells about George Washington who never told a lie and Abraham Lincoln who made us free.

Perhaps I shall get on the cars some time and come to see you. Would you speak to a black boy? I shall be 8 years old next May.

George Wells

Linda W. Slaughter, *The Freedmen of the South*
(Cincinnati, 1869)

In the District of Columbia, which had its own popularly elected government during Reconstruction, the schools for black children were considered the best in the nation. A black Bostonian who had been teaching for twenty years reported:

To the Editor:

I have been so fortunate as to attend several of the [Washington] schools during their examinations. I cannot forbear to record my gratification with the closing exercises of the preparatory high school. The reading was especially fine. The original essays showed thought and research. It was, however, in Latin grammar and algebra that the most perfect triumphs were achieved. The recitations, consisting of parsing and translations, were nearly perfect, there being scarcely a hesitation, and no failures. In algebra, too, a like satisfactory result was attained. Problems involving one, two and three unknown quantities were stated with an ease which prophesied a successful elucidation.

Susan Paul Vashon

The New National Era, June 20, 1872

Statesmen and foreign dignitaries visited the schools to observe the rapid strides that the students were making. Richard T. Greener who became principal of Sumner High School in Washington in 1873 recalled:

When the great Senator [Sumner] brought the Marquis de Chambrun to visit my school I took occasion to call out one of my pet pupils, a handsome little black boy, since distinguished as the first colored class-day orator at Harvard. He recited Lincoln's Gettysburg Address. Mr. Sumner sat with rapt attention and at the close sprang to his feet and said, "My dear Professor Greener, I was at Gettysburg and heard Mr. Lincoln deliver that wonderful address, and let me assure you he did not do it better!"

Life and Writings of the Grimké Family.
Anna J. Cooper, ed. (n.p., 1951)

These schools, however, were a far cry from those that most freedmen's children attended. In the rural South teachers often knew little more than their pupils. Columbus and Aury Jeter, who taught in Georgia until Klansmen broke up their school, described their qualifications to congressional investigators:

Columbus Jeter: I and my wife generally taught night-school at home until 9 o'clock at night. The neighbors would come into the school and I would give them lessons as far as I knew how. I did not charge them for it.

Aury Jeter: I was teaching a day-school and he had a night-school for those who could not come in the day-time, for the old settled men in the country.

Q—How much education have you and he?

A—I have studied geography, arithmetic, and grammar, and reading and spelling. In slave times we had a colored man who knew how to spell a little, and unbeknown to the others I learned my letters. I went to school in Knoxville, and awhile in Memphis and two months here since I was free.

Q—How much education had your husband?

A—He can just read and can spell pretty well. I taught him what little he knows. I can write some, not much. The hardest thing I have tried to learn has been writing. I can make the letters, but I cannot write a letter very well, for it takes me so long.

Condition of Affairs
(Washington, 1872)

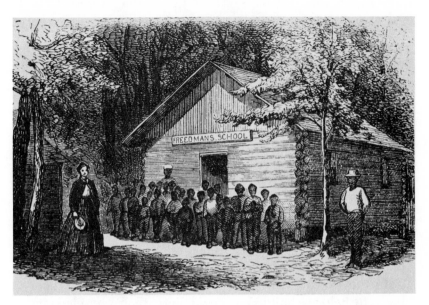

A plantation school in North Carolina (*Boston Public Library*)

People in the country districts pooled their resources to establish schools, but their efforts were often frustrated by the whites who lived nearby. The following letter was addressed to the Freedmen's Bureau:

Forsyth, Georgia, July 22, 1867

Dear Sir:

I write to inform you of a most Cowardly outrage that took place last Saturday night. Our teacher whom we have employed here was shot down by a crowd of Rebel Ruffians for no other cause than teaching School.

General, this is the second teacher that has been assaulted. The Rebels make their brags to kill every Yankee teacher that they find. We do not know what we may do if

the Military does not assist us. The Freedmen are much excited at such an outrage.

George H. Clower, William Wilkes &c, Freedmen

National Archives

Richard Reese, another Georgian, said:

Last spring we built a schoolhouse and hired a white lady
to teach. Friday night, February 5, our schoolhouse was
burned up. We have a deed of one and a half acres but there
is no timber on it and the owners of the land around have
put up a paper forbidding us to cut a stick on theirs. See how
tight they have got us. We want the Government or somebody to help us build. We could burn their churches and
schoolhouses but we don't want to break the law or harm
anybody. All we want is to live under the law.

The New Era, February 17, 1870

The new state constitutions provided for public schools, but, in the
first years of Reconstruction, most states failed to appropriate the
necessary money. *The New National Era* summarized the educational
scene at the end of 1870:

We copy from a report made to the National Teachers
Association which will show how little attention has been
paid in the South to Common schools:

1. Delaware without school supervisors and no provision
for the blacks.

2. Maryland only educating colored children in Baltimore.

3. Virginia just putting a free school law on her statute
book.

"SUFFER LITTLE *WHITE* CHILDREN TO COME UNTO ME."

A Thomas Nast cartoon comments on southern attitudes toward schools for black children

4. Kentucky just enacting a new school law, but giving no opportunity to colored youth.

5. Tennessee, by Conservative Democratic triumph, delaying the whole Republican school system.

6. North Carolina at the close of the last year, not a school in the country districts under the State law.

7. South Carolina slightly in advance of North Carolina.

8. Georgia where she was before the war, utterly against schools.

9. Alabama, with a free school system of her own, yet so connected with the old order of things as to rob it of its usefulness.

10. Florida with her system partly organized.

11. Mississippi just making its school laws.

12. Arkansas with an efficient system only partially organized.

13. Louisiana efficient in theory, but by no means perfect in practice.

14. Texas without legislation, the Senate refusing to confirm the Superintendent nominated by the Governor to carry out the idea of popular education.

The New National Era, December 8, 1870

When public schools were established during the next years, their administrators faced an acute teacher shortage. The majority of southern whites not only refused to teach in "the nigger schools," but persecuted the white teachers who came from the North. Black newspapers printed many letters like the following:

Creswell, Texas, November 29, 1871

To the Editor:

We need immediately five hundred teachers for colored schools in Texas. The colored people in this State cannot supply the demand. There are but few white Republicans who can engage in the profession of teaching and rebels will not teach them. Therefore our only prospect is to get teachers among the educated colored people of the North or Christian white people who are willing to endure privations among the heartless whites of the "sunny South." The late elections have opened the South, I trust, for the introduction of civilization. Send us teachers.

W. V. Tunstall, President, Board of
School Directors, Houston County

The National Era, December 14, 1871

Uniontown, Alabama, January 10, 1872

To the Editor:

I have been solicited by the leading colored men of this section to ask you to procure two first-class colored teachers —one for the male school and the other for the female school in this town. We have a free school fund of about

$1,000 which would run two first-class schools about five or six months. I am paying $60 a month which I consider a fair compensation.

The services of these teachers are needed right away. I prefer colored teachers from the fact that the prejudices of the Southern whites against Northern whites are so great it would be difficult for them to obtain board. This difficulty the colored teachers would not labor under.

James H. Houstin, Superintendent of Education,
Perry County

The New National Era, January 25, 1872

Even in states with Radical Republican governments the school funds were not always fairly distributed:

Grenada, Mississippi, March 29, 1873
To the Editors:

There was an indignation meeting held at the M.E. Church by the colored citizens of Grenada on the 26th of March. The colored children have been left out in the cold ever since the free-school system has been established. The school board has given the white children eight months free school and the colored children only four months. These men who do this are pretended Republicans.

After deliberation the following preamble and resolutions were passed:

Whereas Miss Fanny Isom has been teaching a school in an open house without any fireplaces or any stove. She has had for the last two months over forty scholars, with only three puncheon seats with no backs to them and the Board of School Directors refuse to do anything for said school because it is for colored children;

And whereas the directors of sub-district No. 1 in the town of Grenada have made contracts with the teachers of the white schools for eight months and with the teachers of the colored schools for but four months;

Therefore, be it *resolved by the colored people of Grenada county,* That we condemn the course pursued by the Board of School Directors in that they are defrauding the colored children out of their just rights.

Resolved, That we know our strength in this county and will use it when we come to the polls and try to put trusty men in office.

Alex Phillips, Chairman

The New National Era, April 10, 1873

In Georgia, scarcely any money went to schools for black children. When the following letter was written the state had 1,379 schools for whites and 356 for blacks:

Savannah, December 4, 1873

To the Editors:

The common schools of Savannah since 1866 have been managed by a Board of Education appointed for life and with power to elect their successors. This Board is composed of Democratic politicians. The Board received last year the sum of about $64,000 and expended less than $3,000 for the support of colored schools, notwithstanding the colored children are in excess of the whites. The colored people have held several indignation meetings and have demanded equal schools.

Flint

The New National Era and Citizen, December 11, 1873

Because of the inequities in the distribution of school funds, black congressmen and their supporters on Capitol Hill fought for a national education bill. From a speech by Congressman Josiah T. Walls of Florida:

I am in favor of a national system of education because I believe the national Government is the guardian of the liberties of all its subjects. The question for solution: can [Negroes] be educated under the present condition of society in the States where they were freed? Can this be done without the aid of the Government? No, sir, it cannot.

While the Democratic party adhere to the principles that they have now it would be against their interests to educate the Negro. Can we suppose that these firm adherents to slavery and States rights are willing to educate the Negro and loyal whites and thereby enable them to wield the controlling power of the South? No, sir, I should think not.

Congressman J. H. Rainey of South Carolina, whose state school system was the best in the South, told the House:

I find in the report of the superintendent of education of the state which I have the honor to represent, the following statement: there are 206,610 school children between the ages of 6 and 16, with total attendance of only 66,056, the greater portion of the remainder being unable to attend for the want of educational facilities.

Think of it, only 66,056 children attending school out of a school population of 206,610 in one State of this union. But the people are eager for knowledge. I have seen gray-headed old men, formerly slaves, learning the alphabet after

A New Orleans classroom before the city's schools were integrated

the hard toils of the day. The delight with which they behold their little children striving to read is pleasurable to behold. What we want is schools and more of them.

Mr. Speaker, ignorance is widespread; it is not confined to any one state. This mental midnight is a national calamity, not sectional. The great remedy is free schools, established and aided by the Government throughout the land.

The New National Era, February 15, 1872

Their bill failed to pass, in part because its opponents feared that nationally supported education would mean integrated schools. The new constitutions of South Carolina and Louisiana called for schools open to both races but New Orleans was the only southern city to put this into practice. Opening the campaign for integration, The New Orleans *Tribune* used arguments that sound familiar a century later:

We do not see why the city should go to the expense of organizing twenty or thirty new schools when she already has a sufficient number. Discrimination among children on account of religion and language would certainly be better justified than a distinction based on their complexions. The idea of having schools over the doors of which will be inscribed the words "for children of fair complexion only" or "for children with blue eyes only" and of other schools set apart "for children of dark complexion" is of itself ridiculous, and brings a smile on the lips of every reader, outside the Southern States.

Even a distinction based on the occupation of parents would be better justified than a distinction on color. Yet nobody thinks of setting apart in schools children of merchants and of mechanics, of tradesmen and of laborers. It is not proposed to separate bad children from good ones. Why? Because such distinctions are against the democratic principle of American society.

The next step, therefore is to do away with the distinction of race in the public schools.

The New Orleans *Tribune*, May 9, 1867

New Orleans' schools were integrated in January 1871. Thomas W. Conway, the white Northerner who was Louisiana's superintendent of education from 1868 to 1873 reported on their success:

In New Orleans when I proclaimed the free schools open as well to the black as to the white children, the pupils of the latter class were advised to take their books and leave the schools. I must confess that for a day or two I was pained at the scene being enacted before my eyes. There, on the one hand, came the colored pupils to enjoy their rights, and on the other the white scholars, seeing the former enter the building, seized their books and rushed for the street, as excited as if they were flying from an approaching army. And there stood the teachers, as pale as ghosts, wondering whether their school was ruined and their vocation gone. And the neighbors, black and white, stood half bewildered and half frightened.

All the newspapers in the city, except the *Republican*, advised the white people not to send their children to the public schools. The white pupils all left and the school-house was virtually in the hands of the colored pupils. This was the picture one day. In a few days I went back to see how the school was progressing and, to my surprise, found nearly all the former pupils returned to their places; and that school, like all the schools in the city, reported at the close of the year a larger attendance than at any time since the close of the war. A year ago I visited the same school and saw therein about as many colored children as whites, with not a single indication of ill-feeling.

The New National Era, June 4, 1874

The issue of "mixed schools" was debated in other states. The following editorial appeared in the Austin (Texas) *Reformer:*

To us it is self-evident that all public institutions of learn-ing must very soon be opened to all persons. In the grand old Commonwealth of Massachusetts people were first ex-cited upon the question in 1849. In 1854 the legislature set this matter at rest by abolishing the separate schools. The mixed school system thus inaugurated has given universal satisfaction.

In Michigan the question was settled by the Supreme Court. In that State, the schools have been mixed but little more than a year. In Kansas where the colored population is rapidly increasing the schools are being mixed every-where without opposition.

Throughout the greater part of the North mixed schools have been established by choice of the white people as

Blacks and their white supporters dreamed of public schools open to children of all races (*Boston Public Library*)

the colored element is there politically insignificant. In the South which contains so large a proportion of colored votes we are not to expect any political party will long persist in insisting on separate schools for the races. And inasmuch as thousands of colored youth in every Southern State must forever be debarred from the benefits of the public school fund from any system of caste schools, the issue forces itself upon us.

We think we do not mistake the aims of the Republican party of Texas when we assume that it is the unalterable purpose of its leading spirits to make all the public schools free to every color.

The New National Era, October 19, 1871

When Thomas W. Cardozo wrote the letter which follows he was superintendent of public instruction in Mississippi:

Jackson, Mississippi, June 26, 1874

To the Editor:

The great hobby seems to be the school clause! Well, what of that? Are not the public schools of nearly every Northern city already opened to colored children? And ought not the public schools of the South be opened to them? Those in New Orleans are already mixed. In some of them there are as many colored as whites, not separated in classes, but recite and sit by the side of each other. Louisiana, Arkansas, Florida and Mississippi have colored men as Superintendents of Public Instruction, yet the system is not marred and everything goes on smoothly. I presume they visit the white schools (I know our Superintendent does) and are treated courteously.

Thomas W. Cardozo

The New National Era, July 2, 1874

To many educators the issue of integrated schools was less important than the kind of education the children were receiving. School Superintendent Jonathan C. Gibbs introduced black history to the schools of Florida:

Tallahassee, Florida, October 9, 1871

To the Editor:

I have been writing a number of sketches of distinguished colored men for the newspapers of Florida and they have been widely copied. My object was to incite the colored youth of this state to acquire knowledge and fit themselves for the higher walks of usefulness. Among the sketches was one of Benjamin Banneker. A gentleman in this State sent the sketch into Kentucky and it is fiercely denied that any such man as Banneker existed and I am charged with inventing the sketch for sensational purposes.

To enlighten the "hunters of Kentucky," I propose that some of your correspondents in Baltimore seek out the publishing house of Goddard & Angell who published Banneker's "Almanac" and send me a letter for publication of the transactions between the firm and Banneker.

The fact is that the flood of light that has ruled the minds of men since the late war concerning the mental, moral and physical possibilities of the Negro as the coming man of a higher and better civilization, strikes terror to the hearts of men who have so long trampled him underfoot. What Banneker, Aldridge, Alexander Dumas—how few when reading ["The Count of] Monte Cristo" or "The Three Guardsmen" think of attributing it to the genius of a Negro—have done to exalt our common humanity, you, young men of Florida may do under far more favorable circumstances. The future is, to the young man of color who is in earnest, glorious. Everything is before us; everything to win!

Jonathan C. Gibbs

The New National Era, October 19, 1871

However, in states where black voters had little power, whites ran the black schools. After a trip to the South, William Wells Brown reported:

All the white teachers in our colored public schools feel themselves above their work and few have any communication whatever with their pupils outside the schoolroom. Some have been known to announce to their pupils that under no circumstances were they to recognize or speak to them on the streets. These people have no heart in the work they are doing and simply go through the mechanical form of teaching our children for the pittance they receive as a salary. While teachers who have no interest in the children they instruct are employed in the public schools, hundreds of colored men and women are idle, or occupying places far beneath what they deserve.

William Wells Brown, *My Southern Home* (Boston, 1880)

As they gained control over the schools, whites began to write textbooks that gave their version of recent history. Lee's school, mentioned in the following letter, was Washington and Lee University. Time has softened the image of Robert E. Lee, but in the 1870s black people and many white Northerners still thought of him as a racist and traitor.

Creswell, Texas, June 10, 1873

To the Editors:

The news comes pouring in that the Southern people, as fast as they can get into power, are going to foist upon our children a series of school books got up by Southern traitors. Think of it! Lee's school, got up to educate boys to hate the Union and to get the next generation ready to accomplish what they undertook and failed, writing textbooks for a land they have drenched in blood. Forbid, Almighty God!

We have had to rely upon the General Government to save us in every crisis and we must again appeal to her to establish some sort of educational supervision in all the States and adopt a uniform series of textbooks from Maine to Texas. I do not ask for books abusive of the South or laudatory of the North, but books patriotic and national in tone.

This "university series" as they are called, are got up at Lee's school and has for its primary object the rearing up of the young chivalry to revere the "Lost Cause" and its worthies, and secondarily to infuse the same spirit into the minds and hearts of our children. I would suggest Jeff Davis, in the character of Mother Goose, write the nursery tales of the series.

William V. Tunstall, Superintendent of Public Instruction,
Houston County

The New National Era and Citizen, June 26, 1873

In this Nast cartoon, the boy is saying, "What! won't those stupid White Geese even let me go to School without hissing and biting at me?" (*Boston Public Library*)

Actually, almost all textbooks—from the North as well as the South—treated black people as inferior. Faith Lichen, a regular contributor to *The New National Era*, wrote a perceptive essay on the tribulations of a black schoolboy. His geography book, which was published in Philadelphia, described Europeans as "scientific and learned" and Africans as a barbarous people who "show little signs of intelligence." Excerpts from Ms. Lichen's essay:

Reader, were you ever a colored boy? Have you ever gone to school and been obliged to walk around a crowd of white boys because they put themselves right in your path, and had "cuff that nigger!" yelled into your ears, and after doing all that one pair of fists could do against half a dozen

Advertisement for book on "The Uncivilized Races"

pairs, were you unmercifully beaten (two or three police-men passing meanwhile) until some old woman came along and rescued you?

Released at length, have you made your appearance just in time to "hold out your hand, sir" for the reception of six or eight stinging blows from a heavy rattan in the hands of a white teacher whose one article of faith was "spare the rod and spoil the child"?

Have you ever studied Smith's *Geography* with that very worst type of Negro presented in painful contrast to the most perfect of the Caucasian on the opposite page? Have the words "superior to all others," referring to the latter, ever stuck in your throat and defiant pride made you "go down" while some other boy, no more ambitious but less sensitive, "went up"?

Have you ever tasted the sweet revenge of sticking pins into the eyes of the soul-driver in the picture of a cotton field at the head of the lesson on Georgia? No! Then you don't know what a jolly experience belongs to nine-tenths of the colored men in this land of liberty.

The New National Era, January 25, 1872

2. We Were Devoured with Ambition to Do Our Best

By the end of Reconstruction less than one third of the black children of the South were receiving any kind of formal education. There were, however, a fortunate few—perhaps one in a thousand —who were able to go beyond the three Rs to normal school or college. The road from illiterate slave to bachelor of arts took ability, luck and dogged determination. In the following autobiographical account, Samuel McElwee, a member of the Tennessee legislature, described his educational odyssey:

I was born a slave in Tennessee, June 30th, 1858. I learned my alphabet by looking over my sister's shoulder while the white girls to whose parents we belonged taught her. At the close of the war I could read and spell in the First Reader. My father started me to a district school in 1867. As I had to work on the farm I attended school during the winter months only. But by studying until twelve and one o'clock at night, in spite of a hard day's work on the farm, I could return to school on examination day and receive my promotion. This continued until 1874, at which time I accepted the position of school teacher in Lee County, Mississippi. After a session of five months I went to Oberlin College. I waited on the table, washed windows and picked currants for my board. Returning to Mississippi, I again taught five months and then went to Alabama in search of a school. Not succeeding, after days of privation and nights out of doors, I returned to Tennessee. Reaching home without money, I accepted an agency for Lyman's Historical Chart and the Family Bible and at the same time sold medicine.

FISK UNIVERSITY, NASHVILLE, TENNESSEE.

Fisk University opened in 1866 as an "Academy and Normal School" (*Boston Public Library*)

Disappointed yet not discouraged, in 1877 I began the study of Latin, German and algebra under a private tutor. I walked ten miles two nights a week and recited to a young white man who was attending Vanderbilt University at Nashville. He told my story to the professors of Fisk University who wrote to me to come there. In the fall of 1878 I entered Fisk and was found qualified to enter the senior preparatory class. I found it extremely hard to keep up, but I did so, and entered college with the class. I supported myself while at school by selling maps and charts and teaching when I could get a school. I graduated in the regular college course on May 26th [1883], thus having conferred upon me the degree of B.A. I came home in June and began reading law.

The New York *Globe*, February 2, 1884

Before the war, blacks had been barred from almost all U.S. colleges and universities. Afterward, largely in response to the need for teachers, more than thirty institutions for higher education were established in the South. Most of these, including Fisk, Hampton, Talladega, Atlanta University, were founded by the American Mission-

Avery Institute in Charleston, South Carolina, which was founded by American Missionary Association, trained teachers for black schools across the South (*American Missionary Association Archives, Amistad Research Center*)

ary Association and other church groups. Some, like Alcorn and Alabama A & M, were part of state university systems while Howard University was established by the Freedmen's Bureau. At Howard a student could enter the Preparatory Department for the equivalent of a high school education, continue on through college and then take a graduate degree in law, medicine or theology. Its first classes were held in 1867; by 1870 a cluster of new buildings occupied a 150-acre site on the outskirts of Washington. Although most of the teachers at the new colleges were white, Howard had some black faculty members. John M. Langston, who headed its law department, became acting president of the institution in 1874, and Dr. Charles B. Purvis, author of the following letter, was a member of the medical faculty.

Howard University in 1869 (*Boston Public Library*)

Philadelphia, May 29, 1871

Hon. Gerrit Smith
My Dear Sir:

To show my appreciation of Howard University with which I am connected, I have volunteered to undertake to collect $2500 towards the institution, which, by reasons of its broad and Catholic principles is one of the best in the country, admitting as it does persons of every race to all of its departments. Even women are entitled to every privilege that is accorded to men. In the Law and Medical departments they attend without being subjected to the least annoyance. Furthermore the professors are not confined to any particular class, *men & women, white & black share the professional honors.* An institution so democratic deserves the earnest support of all true lovers of human equality. Being free from debt it remains but to be endowed to make it popular & successful.

I am aware you have already contributed towards the support of the institution, but feeling you would be willing

Dr. Charles B. Purvis, member of Howard's medical faculty and chief surgeon at Freedmen's Hospital

to assist us still more if the great work we are doing was thoroughly explained to you, is why I wrote. I trust the appeal will be favorably received.

Charles B. Purvis

Gerrit Smith Collection, George Arents Research Library at Syracuse University

Howard offered a liberal arts program with heavy emphasis on the classics. Simon P. Smith was only two years out of slavery when he entered its Preparatory Department in 1867. He was a college freshman when he wrote the letter which follows. The Reverend Edward F. Williams helped Smith enter Howard and contributed liberally to his support.

Howard University, Washington, March 19, 1872

Rev. E. F. Williams

Dear Friend:

The studies that I have recently taken up are Horace, Xenophon's Memorabilia of Socrates, Grecian and Roman Antiquity and Loomis' Geometry. I have in all five studies; the fifth is rhetoric. I also have Latin and Greek prose compositions. Every Monday I have a lesson in the Greek Testament but we only study the Acts. Every Friday at two we have a lecture on Physical Geography. I like Xenophon's Memorabilia and geometry more than the other two. I do not know how well I will do with these studies, but if I do not know them it will not be because I do not study.

I do not like to write any news that would cause you to be overanxious about me, but I am going in debt and it keeps me worried. I would not have been in debt if I could have got work but it has been impossible this year. So I have been compelled to rely upon the money that I got through your influence, which I feel a shame to do for I prefer to help myself as much as I can. If you can give me any encouragement about paying this debt I shall be very thankful.

Simon P. Smith

American Missionary Association Archives,
Amistad Research Center

Yankee teachers in the South helped their more promising pupils continue their education. When Archibald and Francis Grimké entered a public school in Charleston, their name caught the principal's eye. She knew Angelina and Sarah Grimké who, thirty years

Archibald and Francis Grimké during their student days (*Moorland-Spingarn Research Center, Howard University*)

earlier, had broken with their aristocratic South Carolina family to join the antislavery struggle. Interested in the boys, the principal arranged to send them North to school. Archibald Grimké, who was sixteen when he left home, dictated the following many years later:

The Grimké boys were enrolled in the Morris St. School under the principal, Mrs. Frances Pillsbury. When Mrs. Pillsbury heard that she had boys by the name of Grimké in her school she became very much interested in us, on account of what she knew of the sisters Grimké. She began a correspondence in our behalf and by fall she was able to inform us she had secured transportation for my brother Frank and myself to go to Massachusetts.

My mother got us ready and we left Charleston, the two first colored boys to leave the city in search of an education. We went first to Hilton Head [where] the government transport stopped on its voyage to New York. There we had letters to the Freedmen's Bureau which was to take charge of us and help us on our way to Boston.

We left N.Y. for Boston by way of Springfield, Mass., where we stopped overnight at Dr. Church's, an old abolitionist. He and his wife received us with open arms and generous hospitality. Mr. Church and his wife thought it would be well for us to go to the theater that night and see Edwin Forrest who was at that time the leading tragedian on the American stage. It was a tremendous experience for us boys. He played "King Lear." We thrilled with the overwhelming power of the great actor for half a century afterwards. The next day we were put on the cars and went to Boston.

The boys worked in Massachusetts for six months until arrangements were made for them to go to Lincoln University in Pennsylvania.

We reached Lincoln some time in April and had our first interview with the President, Rev. Isaac N. Rendall. He was somewhat disappointed [in] our size and age. We seemed quite small and we had no education of any consequence. But after questioning us he made up his mind to receive us and the next day our student life at Lincoln [began].

We had to sleep in a large room with perhaps 20 other boys, each one with his iron bedstead and in what the students called the "sky parlor." We were all enthusiasm and devoured with ambition to do our best. Almost at once the teachers took notice of us, found that they could make something of us that would be useful to ourselves and to the race with which we were identified.

Archibald H. Grimké Papers, Moorland-Spingarn
Research Center, Howard University

After two years at Lincoln, Archibald Grimké received a letter from Angelina Grimké, then the wife of Theodore Weld. She had seen his name in a newspaper article about the school. "As the name is a very uncommon one," she wrote, "it has occurred to me that you have probably been a slave of one of my brothers and I feel a great desire to know all about you." He sent her a forthright reply:

Lincoln University, February 20, 1868

Mrs. A. G. Weld:
Dear Madam:

I was somewhat surprised by receiving yours of the 15th inst. I never expected to hear through the medium of a letter from "Miss Angelina Grimké" of Antislavery celebrity. I thank you, madam, for your concern for me. I shall give you a simple sketch of my history.

I am the son of Henry Grimké, your brother. Of course you know more about my father than I do. Suffice it to say he was a lawyer & was married to a Miss Simons & she died, leaving three children. After her death he took my mother, who was his slave & his children's nurse. Her name is Nancy

Weston. By my mother he had three children, Archibald & Francis & John. He died about fifteen years ago, leaving my mother in the care of his son, Mr. E. M. Grimké. In his own words, "I leave Nancy & her children to be treated as members of the family." He told my mother that he could not give her her "free papers" because he favored a certain law forbidding masters to leave their servants free, "but," said he, "I leave you better than free, because I leave you to be taken care of."

My poor mother, with no one to care for her, for Mr. G. did not do as his father commanded, & three small children to provide for, was thrown upon the uncharitable world to struggle alone. By dint of hard labor, working her finger nails to their very quick, she kept us from perishing by hunger and from cold and sat by & nursed us when we were sick. Thus she continued until 1860 when Mr. E. M. Grimké wanted a boy to wait on him. He informed my mother that she should send me to his house. His mandate was irresistible. It was a severe shock to my mother. She could bear all the privations of this life & suffer, yea die, for her children but to be deprived of them when she could just discern the fruits of her labor was heart rending.

But this was only the beginning of her sorrows. He kept on until she was rendered childless. Her sons were groaning from the severity of their hard taskmasters & when she remonstrated at their unjust treatment she was thrown into a loathsome cell & kept there for six days.

I afterwards fled from my oppressor. Frank attempted to escape but was retaken & sold. My little bro. was next taken away. At last *Freedom* was proclaimed to *all men* & again the members of our little family were united. The public schools were flung open for all. I went to one of them where I got acquainted with Mrs. Pillsbury, the principal, a native of Mass. and the sister-in-law of Parker Pillsbury, editor of the *Anti-Slavery Standard*. Through her intercessions we (myself & Frank) were admitted here. I am supported by six men in Dr. Spring's Church, N.Y. Squire F. W. Hotchkiss supports Frank. My younger bro. is home with my mother. He cannot get a support.

I hope, dear Madam, you will excuse this badly written epistle. Perceiving your great desire to know about me, I sat down to write you as quick as possible. Perhaps you would like to see our pictures. They are enclosed. I shall hope to hear from you soon.

Archibald Henry Grimké

Archibald H. Grimké Papers, Moorland-Spingarn
Research Center, Howard University

A dramatic meeting followed—and the white Grimké sisters acknowledged to the world that the black Grimké brothers, ex-slaves, born out of wedlock, were their nephews. "I am glad you have taken the name of Grimké," Angelina G. Weld wrote them. "It was once one of the noblest names of Carolina. I charge you most solemnly by your upright conduct and your devotion to the principles of justice and humanity to lift this name out of the dust where it now lies and set it once more among the princes of our land."

The Grimké brothers did exactly that. With assistance from their aunts who helped to finance their graduate education, Archibald became a noted attorney and Francis a distinguished minister. Both were uncompromising spokesmen for their race until well into the twentieth century.

At Hampton Institute in Virginia, founded by General Samuel Armstrong as a normal school, students worked part of each day to pay for their education. Julia Rutledge, also the bearer of a distinguished South Carolina name, supported herself at school by dressmaking. Her letter was written to Sarah Chase, a northern teacher who had taught in Charleston.

The waterfront at Hampton in 1868. Girls lived in Griggs Hall, building on left. Barracks in center housed classrooms and dining hall. Teachers lived in building on right (*Hampton Institute*)

Normal School, Virginia, October 4, 1868

Dear Miss Chase:

I am here in Virginia at school, paying my own way by working. The girls work indoors and the boys on the farm. The girls have all the domestic affairs, wash for the boys, sew, all the scrubbing to do. There are about 14 girls and 22 boys.

We are very comfortably fix. Our chambers are neatly furnish and every convenience. We have water pipes in the house, a bathing room.

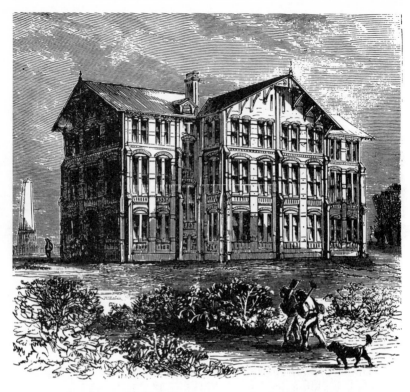

Academic Hall at Hampton was built in the 1870s
(*Boston Public Library*)

The bell ring at half-past five, allowing us half hour to dress, then it ring at six for breakfast. We dine at twelve, clear up our dining room and get in school by one. We have school from one to five and then we recreate about a half hour and the bell ring for evening prayers. After prayers we go in to supper. We study until half-past eight. The bell ring for us to get ready for bed. At nine it ring for us to out the lights.

The best of it we have such a very kind Matron. She tries in every way to make us happy. Every scholar love her.

Goodbye with a double portion of love,

Julia A. Rutledge

Dear Ones at Home, Henry L. Swint, ed. (Nashville, 1966)

Booker T. Washington as a Hampton student (*Hampton Institute*)

When Della Irving went to Hampton four years later living conditions were still rugged. After her graduation, she taught in Virginia public schools, then established the Franklin Normal and Industrial Institute, a boarding school which was patterned on Hampton. Her schoolmate, Booker T. Washington, was Hampton's most illustrious graduate.

The first night I got there when we went in to supper they had a big yellow bowl with sassafras tea, what we called "greasy bread," and a little molasses. There were three or four new students and one old student. He said, "Why don't you eat?" We said we were waiting for them to put supper on the table. He told us this was all we would get. We had sassafras tea and corn bread and syrup for supper all those years. In my Senior year things were fixed up real nice. We had tablecloths then, while we had oilcloth before.

That first night I slept on the floor with seven other girls. We were all new and there was such a rush of girls they had no other place to put us. We didn't know anything about bells and the next morning when we woke up, everybody had had breakfast and gone over to Academic. We didn't have a bit of breakfast. I had a little piece of cheese and some crackers in my trunk and I ate them.

Then they gave me a room with three other girls. They gave us ticks and we carried them to the barn and filled them with straw. We took two pillows and filled them too. We had regular wooden bedsteads. There must have been about thirty or forty girls. All the fire we had was two stoves in the corridor. When it rained it always leaked. I had an old waterproof of my mother's and I have gotten up many a time and put that waterproof on my bed, with a tin basin on the bed, too, to catch the water. I could not turn over for fear of upsetting the water. Miss Mackie [the lady principal] made me bathe every morning in cold water and I have often broken the ice in my pitcher before bathing.

They used to allow us to go bathing in the creek in front of Griggs Hall. The girls had a wharf there and could go bathing every Saturday, but they had to wear an old dress and an old pair of shoes. I wanted to swim, so one night I said, "I'm not going to put on my shoes." They all wanted me to teach them to swim. I told them to take off their shoes. They were afraid Miss Mackie would see them and punish them, but I said, "She can't see your feet in the water." I got about twelve or fifteen girls to take off their shoes. I didn't dare take them out in deep water, so we stayed in shallow water and we were kicking right on the oyster shells. We cut our feet dreadfully. The next morning our feet were so swollen we couldn't put on our shoes. We were scared to death, sure they would send us all home when they found out. We stayed in our rooms all day and didn't go to breakfast or church. They always call the roll at church, so we knew we would be missed.

Monday morning [we were] sent to General Armstrong. I thought swimming was vulgar and didn't want to say anything about it. When he asked me why I was absent from church I began to cry and said, "I went in swimming, and we had to take off our shoes so we could swim and we cut our feet with the oyster shells." The General laughed till he was red in the face and said, "You can swim? Fine, fine. You must teach my teachers." After that he always called me his little swimmer.

Booker Washington graduated one year ahead of me. The girls used to call him a country-looking fellow, and because his trousers were so short they called him "High Waters."

I got a twenty-dollar prize when I graduated. I had a speech at Commencement on "Our Work as Women." I graduated in a little pink calico dress. The President['s]

Della Irving's graduating class at Hampton, 1877 (*Hampton Institute*)

wife and some of his Cabinet were the judges and Congressman Gould was there. When I got through Mr. Gould announced the prize winners. He said, "The first prize was won by—Miss Della E. Irving of Southampton." That was the happiest day of my life.

Della Irving Hayden, "A Graduate's Reminiscences,"
Southern Workman, January 1917

Unlike most of the black colleges, Hampton emphasized industrial training rather than liberal arts. General Armstrong was often criticized for refusing to teach the classics.

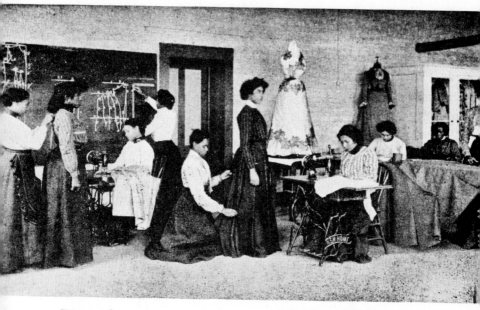

Dressmaking class at Tuskegee Institute where Booker T. Washington carried on the Hampton tradition of industrial training

Hampton, Virginia, January 26, 1874

To the Editor:

I was present at a musical entertainment given by the Hampton students on Friday evening in the assembly room of the Institute. This Institution is indeed doing a noble work. It graduates not less than twenty students a year who go forth into the waste places of the South to instruct the ignorant and helpless. I cannot agree with the principal, however, that the introduction of the classics in the school will destroy its worth and put the colored people above their race. The representative men of our race prove this to be without foundation. The men who do us the most good are those who have been blessed with a collegiate education.

C. D. Johnson

The New National Era and Citizen, January 29, 1874

Wilberforce University in Ohio, founded in 1856 by the A.M.E.
Church, offered a classical education with special emphasis on
training for the ministry. The Reverend Reverdy Ransom described
his student days there:

The most important thing that the new student has to do is to get his room fixed up. The university supplies each room with chairs, wash-stand, stove, bedstead, mattress and, we would like to say, two pillows. But that name suggests comfort and repose, both of which commendable qualities the average pillow in our day most sadly lacked. Ours were filled with a dark substance which looked like coarse hair. And to this day I cannot rid myself of the thought that my pillow was a living thing.

Sometimes that pillow would have an undulatory motion; again it would swell up large and full; at other times it would shrink almost to nothing, and again at times the *thing* would twist itself into a long hard roll, then stretch itself diagonally across the pillow case. At such times no amount of coaxing, shaking or pounding would induce it to change its shape.

The other home comforts each student must provide for himself. A coal bucket, a lamp, an oil can and a broom must be bought and used. Each student is required to sweep and cleanse his room and make his bed. This last is one of the most forcible reminders to the male student that he is away from home. Many have been able to excel in mathematics and the classics, but never as artful bed makers.

The regulations of the college are very strict regarding the observance of study hours. During these hours the students are not allowed to visit each other's room, nor to talk loud or make unnecessary noise. No matter how brightly the sun shines, students are not allowed to leave their rooms during study hours unless it be to recite. There are those who disregard authority and break the laws. Sometimes in mid-winter students run out of coal. One of these unfortunates would come shivering into a fellow student's room to "borrow a little heat" or "to study by your fire." Students who were out of oil would go to another's room to study by his light. When the professors caught a student out of his room during the study hours the favorite excuses were— "Well, Professor, I was out of oil," or "I just ran in to see where the lesson was."

Reverdy C. Ransom, School Days at Wilberforce (Springfield, Ohio, n.d.)

When the Wilberforce faculty decided that students must spend study hours in classrooms instead of their own rooms, a student revolt followed. Two letters to *The New National Era and Citizen* are tantalizingly sketchy:

Cincinnati, January 26, 1874

To the Editor:

There are some wickedly-mean and malicious stories going the rounds concerning the morals of the pupils of Wilberforce University. All sorts of looseness is charged to them, and the accounts of the actions of the young ladies are perfectly shocking.

After a quiet investigation, I am convinced that they are all based upon the unfortunate efforts necessary to induce the students to study. It seems that the faculty resolved to require all students spending their study as well as recitation hour in the school-room, instead of studying as usual in their own rooms. The senior class first, and finally, the whole institution was involved in a general revolt against what they, perhaps justly, considered a reflection upon their integrity, and since then, all sorts of falsehoods have been circulated as the occasion of their difficulties.

Depugh

The New National Era and Citizen, January 29, 1874

Wilberforce University, Xenia, Ohio

To the Editor:

I feel it my duty, as a student of the University, to deny the assertion about the conduct of the young ladies of Wilberforce. It grieves me to think that anyone identified with the black race could circulate such a slanderous report. Admitting that one or two young ladies have behaved indiscreetly and done what is perfectly fashionable in some of the gay cities of the East, does that justify the writer in using such sweeping language? Mr. Editor, there are young ladies here of high moral standing, and before they would dare to do that which is contrary to the laws of propriety, they would rather die—yes, die first.

We young ladies of Wilberforce are here to improve our minds, to become intelligent women, to prepare ourselves to go forth into the world to instruct those who have not kind friends and parents to send them to a place of learning. We are not like the beautiful butterfly, flying from flower to flower, sipping the sweet honey therein. We are like the busy bee, always seeking, always endeavoring to elevate our race.

Perhaps there is not a college in this land, but what has had rebellious spirits to encounter. If it is true, as the gentleman has asserted, that the rebellion of our college was caused on account of the inability of the Faculty to govern the students, the worthy gentleman has left the impression that there is no race capable of governing itself; for among all nations, be they black or white, there has been rebellion.

Zelia R. Ball

The New National Era and Citizen, February 26, 1874

There were rumblings of rebellion elsewhere too. At Howard, T. Thomas Fortune recalled, the chief complaint was about food:

Old Man Page who had the dining room privileges at Howard had been a poor-house keeper in Vermont. He had a red head, a red face, and the students he underfed often made him feel red. He would have some bread, cheap meats and diluted coffee for breakfast, molasses and baker's bread and water for lunch and meat pie for dinner. The menu did not vary. Those of the students who paid their own way without assistance from the college, some twenty-five in number, rebelled against the food and protested loud and long, but Old Man Page refused to budge and was sustained by the college authorities. The aggrieved students decided to strike. They went across 7th Street to Mrs. Mason's boarding house and got decent eating with some variety for $14 a month, which was big money in those days.

Norfolk *Journal and Guide*, December 3, 1927

At Hampton, perhaps in answer to student restlessness, General Armstrong established a court for the seniors and permitted them to discipline themselves. When he bypassed the court on one occasion they drew up a formal protest. Among the signers of the following petition was nineteen-year-old Booker T. Washington:

Gen. Armstrong
Sir:
We as members of Senior Cottage and its court, feeling that the case of D. F. Douglass was not carried to you in its proper form and that it was not by the consent of the court, but rather by a great abridgment of our rights, we therefore petition for said case for a legal trial. We feel that our rights should be recognized as a court, but we cannot think that

our court has any authority where cases are wrested from us as [at] present.

E. A. White, R. B. Jackson, Warren Logan,
B. T. Washington [and eighteen others]

Hampton Institute

The nature of Douglass' misconduct was not disclosed but from a letter written a year later it seems likely that he had been caught smoking—a punishable offense at many schools:

Hampton, Virginia, May 29, 1876

To the Faculty
Respected Sirs:

It pains me to give so much trouble to those whom I am under so many obligations to. My future record is the only way I can show to you whether or not you have been casting pearls before swine. As a transgressor, I am willing to suffer the consequences of my evil doings. I have considered abstaining from the use of tobacco. If I make a promise, I want to keep it. I might say I will not use it anymore, but I must confess that it has such a hold on me that I am not sure whether I can withstand the temptation. I will pledge you my word [I] *will* strive to discontinue the use of it as hard as ever I strove to do anything in my life.

Dennis F. Douglass

Hampton Institute

Oberlin College, founded by antislavery activists, admitted its first black students in 1835, far in advance of other "white" schools. However, during Reconstruction, as students grew more assertive about their rights, many complained of discrimination. Selections from letters to *The New National Era:*

Oberlin, Ohio, November 13, 1871

To the Editor:

Some four or five hundred college students are enabled to pay their expenses in college by teaching in the preparatory department, but no colored student has this privilege. The faculty says that it is *inexpedient* for colored students to teach at present as the college can't bear the pressure. They argue that if they permitted a few colored students to have equal rights it would drive hundreds of white students from the reach of their influence. During the past few years some score or more of colored students have graduated from this college, yet none could obtain a class to teach.

Yours for equal rights, Don Carlos

The New National Era, November 23, 1871

Oberlin, December 4, 1871

To the Editor:

At the beginning of each term the boarders are permitted to select the table at which they wish to sit. But, sir, could you go into that beautiful hall at meal time you would see in some obscure corner a dark object at the ends of the tables. They are placed at the ends so that their pale-faced brethren and sisters may not have to sit close to them.

At the opening of the fall term, one of our students went to the hall and was pointed to the most obscure seat in the room. He refused to take it, claiming the right, with the whites, of choosing his own seat. We quote a few words uttered by the manager:

"You colored people will have to understand that if you board in this hall you must sit where I tell you and nowhere else. You will not be mixed in with the white boarders. You ought to esteem it a great privilege to be admitted into the hall even."

He offered to pay this student what it would cost extra

in a private family. The matter was laid before the president who, like an honorable man, decided in accordance with justice.

J.W.

The New National Era, December 14, 1871

The schools with the grimmest record of discrimination were the United States academies at Annapolis and West Point. Two black cadets received appointments to West Point in 1870. After a month there, one wrote:

West Point, June 29, 1870

Dear Friend:

Your kind letter should have been answered long ere this, but really I have been so harassed that I could not do anything. I passed the examination all right but my companion Howard was rejected. Since he went away I have been lonely indeed. These fellows appear to be trying their utmost to run me off, and I fear they will succeed. We went into camp yesterday, and all night they were around my tent cursing and swearing at me so that I did not sleep two hours. It is just the same at the table, and what I get to eat I must snatch for like a dog.

The one who drills the squad is the meanest specimen of humanity I ever saw. This morning he said to me, "Stand off from the line, you d—d black ——. I want you to remember you are not on an equal footing with the white men and what you learn you will have to pick up, for I won't teach you a d—d thing."

I have borne insult upon insult until I am completely worn out. I wish I had some good news for you, but alas!

it seems to be getting worse and worse. I hope my brightest hopes will be realized, but I doubt if they will ever be here.

James W. Smith

The New Era, July 14, 1870

His father, a former slave, encouraged him to stay:

Columbia, South Carolina, July 3, 1870

My Dear Son:

I pray God my letter may find you in a better state than when you wrote me. I told you that you would have trials to endure. Do not mind them, for they will go like the chaff before the wind and your enemies will soon be glad to gain your friendship. They do the same to newcomers in every college. Do not let them run you away, for then they will say the "nigger" won't do. Show your spunk and let them see that you will fight. That is what you are sent to West Point for.

You must not resign on any account for that is what the Democrats want. They are betting here that they will devil you so much that you can't stay. Stand your ground, don't resign and write me soon.

From your affectionate father, Israel Smith

The New Era, July 21, 1870

Cadet Smith stood his ground for four painful years. Just before his graduation, a biased professor found him "deficient" in Philosophy and he was dismissed. After his return home he wrote an extensive account of his experiences at West Point. Selections from his story:

Cadet James W. Smith reading his defense at West Point court martial (*Boston Public Library*)

I reported on the 31st of May, 1870 and had not been there an hour before I had been reminded by several thoughtful cadets that I was "nothing but a d—d nigger." Another colored boy, Howard of Mississippi, reported on the same day and we were put in the same room. One night about 12 o'clock, someone came into our room and threw the contents of his slop pail over us while we were asleep. This affair reported itself the next morning at inspection and the Inspector ordered us to search among the tobacco quids and other rubbish for something which might identify the perpetrator. The search resulted in the finding of an envelope addressed to one McCord, of Kentucky. That young "gentleman" succeeded in convincing the authorities that he had nothing to do with the affair. A few days after that Howard was struck in the face by that "gentleman" "because the d—d nigger didn't get out of the way."

Those of us who succeeded in passing the preliminary examination were taken in "plebe camp" and there I got my taste of "military discipline" as the petty persecutions of two hundred cadets were called. Whenever the "plebes" were turned out to police camp, certain cadets would come into the company street and spit out quids of tobacco which they would call for me to pick up. I would get a broom and shovel, but they would immediately begin swearing at me for not using my fingers. Then the Corporal of Police would order me to put down that broom "and not try to play the gentleman" for my fingers were "made for that purpose."

On the 13th of December I was in the ranks of the guard and was stepped on two or three times by Cadet Anderson who was marching beside me. I spoke to him, saying, "I wish you would not tread on my toes." He answered, "Keep your d—d toes out of the way." Cadet Birney then made some invidious remarks to which I did not reply. Cadet Corporal Bailey reported me for "inattention in ranks." I was courtmartialed [and] found guilty as I had no witnesses. The sentence was one year's suspension but since the year was almost gone, I was put back one year. I had no counsel at this trial, as I knew it would be useless considering the one-sided condition of affairs.

One Sunday at dinner, I helped myself to some soup and Cadet Clark of Kentucky who sat opposite me asked what I meant by taking soup before he had done so. I told him that there was a plenty left. He asked, "Do you think I would eat after a d—d nigger?" I replied, "I have not thought at all on the subject, and moreover, I don't quite understand you, as I can't find that last word in the dictionary." He then took up a glass and said he would knock my head off. I told him to throw as soon as he pleased and I would throw mine. The commandant of the table here ordered us to stop creating a disturbance and gave me to understand that thereafter *I should not touch anything on that table until the white cadets were served.*

When we came back from dinner, Cadet Clark struck me from behind, but did not knock me down. He came into my room and attempted to take me by the throat. I succeeded in getting near my bayonet which I snatched from the scabbard and tried to put through him. Being much larger and stronger than I, he kept me off.

There were a great many cadets outside, looking through the window and cheering their champion with cries of "that's right, Clark, kill the d—d nigger," "choke him" &c, but when they saw him giving way before the bayonet they cried, "open the door, boys," and Mr. Clark went forth. The cadet officer of the day "happened around" just *after* Clark had *left* and wanted to know what did I mean by making all that noise.

During the cadet encampment there are dances given three times each week, known as "Cadet Hops." These "hops" are attended by the first and third classes and their lady friends and no "plebe" dream[s] of attending until he shall have risen to the dignity of a "yearling"—third classman. As soon as I became a "yearling" there was a great cry raised that the sanctity of the "hops" was to be violated by the colored cadet. Meetings were held and resolutions passed to the effect that as soon as the colored cadet entered the "hop" room, the managers were to declare the "hop" ended and dismiss the musicians.

The "hops" went on undisturbed for two or three weeks when, one day, my brother and sister, with a couple of lady friends came to camp to see me. Everyone was on the *qui vive* to get a glimpse of "nigger Jim and the nigger wenches who are going to the hops."

I was on guard that day, but not being on post was sitting in the guard tents with my friends when a cadet corporal, Tyler, ordered me to go and fasten down the corner of the first guard tent. I fastened down the corner and went back to my friends. In a few minutes, he came back and wanted to know why I hadn't fastened down that tent wall. I went back and found that either Cadet Tyler or some other cadet had unfastened the tent wall so I fastened it again.

Soon after that the drum sounded for parade and I was compelled to leave my friends for the purpose of falling in ranks, but promising to return as soon as the parade was over. Just as the companies were marching off the parade ground, the officer in charge ordered me to step out of ranks, take off my accoutrements and place them with my musket on the gun rack. That being done, he ordered me to take my place in the center of the guard as a prisoner. Of course my friends felt very bad as they thought they were the cause of it, while I could not speak a word to them as they went away. The next morning I was put "in arrest" for "disobedience of orders in not fastening down tent wall when ordered" &c.

After the usual "investigation" by the Commandant of Cadets, I was sentenced to be confined to the company street until the 15th of August, about five weeks, so that I could not see my brother and sister again. I tried to get permission to see them in the Visitor's Tent the day before they left the Point, but my permit was not granted and they left without saying "good bye."

The cadets, of course, rejoiced at my arrest and had quite a jubilee over it and boasted of "the skill which Cadet Tyler had shown in putting the nigger out of the temptation of taking those black wenches to the hops." I never thought of going to the "hops" for I should most assuredly not have asked a lady to subject herself to the insults consequent upon going. Besides, I did not go to West Point for the purpose of advocating social equality, for there are many cadets with whom I think it no honor for anyone to associate, although they will soon be numbered among the "officers and gentlemen" of the United States Army.

The New National Era, August 6, 13, 20, 27, 1874

Cadet Smith's dismissal from the Point on the eve of his graduation was a bitter blow for black people everywhere. After a movement to send him to Europe to complete his education failed, he taught at a private military academy in Charleston and at the South Carolina Agricultural Institute at Orangeburg. West Point continued its racist policies. One black man, Henry O. Flipper, was graduated from the U. S. Military Academy in 1877, two others in 1887 and 1889; then almost half a century passed before a fourth, Benjamin O. Davis, received his diploma from the Point. Several black cadets entered Annapolis during Reconstruction, but it was not until 1949 that a black was graduated from the U. S. Naval Academy.

Although the national schools were virtually closed to black aspirants, something new was happening in South Carolina. Under pressure from the legislature, South Carolina College—which changed its name to the University of South Carolina—admitted black students in 1873:

Howard University, December 26, 1873

Rev. E. F. Williams

Dear Friend:

Six weeks ago one of my classmates left. He was one of the scholars that Mr. Cardozo sent here from Charleston. Two days ago, T. McCants Stewart, another scholar Mr. Cardozo sent here left the junior class and went back to Charleston. Since which time Mr. Cardozo (the treasurer of the State of South Carolina) has written to his other boys here to come home and enter South Carolina College. They are going in January, one from the freshman class and three from my class, the Sophomore.

I would very much like to go to South Carolina College. There I understand that I shall not have to pay any tuition or room rent. I would like to go there to finish my schooling because I am a South Carolinian and was brought up in Columbia. When quite a small boy I used to wait on Southern students in that College and I remember once standing in the door of one of the buildings and [I] cried because I could not go to school. Now, thank God, there has been a great change. The mountains have been brought low and the vallies are exalted.

Simon P. Smith

American Missionary Association Archives,
Amistad Research Center

Simon Smith stayed at Howard, graduating from its theology department in 1876, while his schoolmate, T. McCants Stewart, wrote exultant letters from Columbia. Stewart who was born of free parents in Charleston in 1852 received a B.A. and law degree from the University of South Carolina and then became Robert B. Elliott's law partner. As he explained in the following, there was an exodus of white students and professors when blacks first entered the university, but many returned soon afterward.

Columbia, South Carolina, April 17, 1874

To the Editor:

The doors of the State University are now open to the people. In October 1873, a colored student applied for admission to the Medical Department. He was admitted after quite a struggle by a majority of only one vote. Every medical professor voted against the applicant, but after learning the result, expressed a willingness to abide by the issue. Not so with the outside world. Southern society flourished the whip in the face of the professors and some, fearing proscription, kissed the rod lifted to strike them. Dr. Laborde,

T. McCants Stewart

who had been connected with the institution for more than a quarter of a century, forced from her walls by two unfeeling daughters, wept like a child as he left.

Both races are represented in the University classes. In the Professional and College Departments more than one-half of the students are *white*. Within the past week twelve new students applied for admission into the College Department. More than one-third of them were *white*.

The institution is calculated to do much good for South Carolina and the Negro race. If the time ever comes when the descendants of the Rutledges and the Marions shall believe in the unlimited brotherhood of man, the University of South Carolina will have a dwelling place in the breast of every Africo-American.

T. McCants Stewart

The New National Era, April 16, 1874

Columbia, South Carolina, June 20, 1874

To the Editor:

The University now numbers one hundred and ten students. A pretty large proportion of these are of the Caucasian race. I want it distinctly understood that the University of South Carolina is not in possession of any one race. Its advantages are being enjoyed by young men who want to make their State better by themselves having lived in it. The two races study together, visit each other's rooms, play ball together, walk into the city together, without the blacks feeling honored or the whites disgraced.

A word as to our advantages. Being an old institution, we have almost every convenience for studying higher mathematics and the sciences. Our library contains thirty thousand volumes and an excellent collection of paintings and sculpture. The college literary society alone has a library of from twelve to fifteen thousand volumes. A student coming here has to look out mainly for books and board. There are no ordinary University fees.

Every Negro ought to be very much interested in this State. There is a bright future before it—bright for the friends of humanity and progress. With unshaken confidence, then, in a wise Providence, with faith in the possibilities of a Negro under a government that is democratic in deed and in truth, our efforts must be crowned with abundant success.

T. McCants Stewart

The New National Era, July 9, 1874

Richard T. Greener

When the university integrated its faculty as well as its student body, Richard T. Greener left his teaching post in Washington to become professor of metaphysics and logic and university librarian. However, South Carolina was the only one of the old state universities of the South to be integrated during Reconstruction. To keep blacks from the hallowed halls of Louisiana State and the University of Mississippi (then called Oxford University), legislators founded Straight University in New Orleans and Alcorn University in Mississippi. After the bill establishing Alcorn passed the legislature,

Governor Alcorn said, "Now let Oxford be for white Southerners and Alcorn for the children of white carpetbaggers and Negroes." Hiram Revels was president of Alcorn from 1872 until 1875 when an economy-minded state government removed him and cut the school appropriation by more than two thirds. Although some blacks were critical of Revels and Alcorn, others were grateful for the opportunities that the new school offered:

Rodney, Mississippi, February 18, 1872

To the Editor:

At last we have a University in which the colored youth of Mississippi are to be trained in wisdom's ways. The Legislature appropriated the princely sum of $50,000 per annum for ten years to Alcorn, and the same amount to Oxford University. In addition, they both get the benefit of $100,000 in Agricultural College Scrip, which was donated by Congress on condition that an agricultural chair [be] established. The interest only on this amount is available. While the faculty are teaching the students the science of agriculture, they expect to raise enough on the farm to meet expenses of provisions. By this they hope to be able to receive all students (except those with free scholarships) for the small sum of $100 per annum.

Alcorn University is located in Claiborne county, near Rodney. This University was formerly known by the name of Oakland College. The buildings were erected just prior to the war. The college was sold to the State for $40,000. A valuable farm of two hundred and forty acres was included in the purchase.

Colored people, look at your college! Here the haughty "chivalry" were taught to make the enslavement of their fellow-men a part of their creed. But lo, the change! Freedom has come, not bodily freedom alone but freedom to *think*.

Alcorn University is open to *all* students. There are two universities in the state—one for colored and the other for white—but we hope when existing prejudices have been modified to see them merged into one university greater and grander still than either of these.

Don Carlos

The New National Era, March 7, 1872

Federal funds for agricultural education also helped to finance such state colleges as Alabama A & M and Arkansas Agricultural, Mechanical and Normal College. In Georgia, however, the federal money was spent only for white students:

January 5, 1874

Editor, *Morning News*, Savannah, Ga.:

I charge our Governor with injustice to my race for the manner in which he disposed of the agricultural school fund appropriated by Congress for the use of the whole people. [The] act of Congress says in the most emphatic words, "There shall be no discrimination in its benefits." But the Governor gave every dollar to Franklin College at Athens, to establish an agricultural department where he knew no colored student could enter, without a great hubbub.

There is no excuse for not placing our share of the money where we could have access to its benefits. For there was Atlanta University with three hundred students which would have been glad to have received it. When near forty of us colored members were in the Legislature, it was agreed between us and the white Democrat members that we would never bother Franklin if the State would make an equal appropriation to our University. But the Governor fails to pay over the appropriation, and then takes away our share of the United States land scrip.

All we ask for is square right! We are not seeking to foist ourselves into white society. On the contrary, we are trying to avoid it. But treating us as the story says the Yankee treated the Indian will not do. They hunted together all day and the time came to divide spoils, but they had only killed a turkey and a buzzard. The Yankee said, "Now, Indian, you take the buzzard and I will take the turkey, or I will take the turkey and you the buzzard." The Indian replied, "But Indian take buzzard every time."

We only want our share of the turkey—nothing more, nothing less.

Henry M. Turner

The New National Era and Citizen, January 22, 1874

The best-known black collegians of the 1870s were the Jubilee Singers of Fisk University. A Colored High School when it started with help from General Clinton B. Fisk of the Freedmen's Bureau, Fisk began its first college classes in 1871. To raise money for dormitories and classrooms, students gave concerts in the North and in Europe. They sang the songs that slaves had created on the plantations of the South—and the world heard Negro spirituals for the first time. While making musical history, the Jubilee Singers raised more than $150,000 for Fisk. Their fundraising became so crucial to the university that its president, the Reverend E. M. Cravath, traveled with them much of the time.

The Jubilee Singers toured Europe twice, spending a year in the British Isles on the first trip, and three years in Great Britain and on the continent on the second. For the Singers, almost all of them former slaves, their years abroad where they sang for Queen Victoria and the Kaiser and took tea in the mansions of the wealthy, were a Cinderella-like break with the past. "But their heads were not turned by it," a Fisk official wrote. "They may feel more at home on the concert platform than they did at first, but their manners have remained as natural and unaffected—as free from 'airs' as if they had never sung outside their own schoolroom."

The Jubilee Singers (*Fisk University Library's Special Collections*)

The accuracy of this statement is attested to by a moving collection of letters from a Jubilee Singer to her fiancé back home. America Robinson and James Burrus met in 1871 when they were two of the four members of Fisk's first college class. Just before their graduation in 1875 she joined the Singers and went to Europe for three years. After receiving his B.A., Burrus taught mathematics at Fisk—the first black member of the faculty—and in 1877 went to Dartmouth College for graduate study. Month after month during their long separation, America wrote to "My Dearest James." Selections from her letters:

Jubilee Hall at Fisk was built with the proceeds from the Jubilee Singers' concerts (*Fisk University Library's Special Collections*)

Torquay, England, August 16, 1875

My Dear James:

If ever I wished for you it is tonight. My bedroom window overlooks a lovely bay and the moon has just arisen and left a silvery path on the sparkling waters. The sky is clear, and the scene is enchanting, if you were only here to share the enjoyment with me. This place was surely made for lovers. It is too lovely for other mortals. I would give the world to be with you tonight. My thoughts have been almost wholly of you today.

Portrait of James Burrus in middle age. No picture of America Robinson has been found (*Fisk University Library's Special Collections*)

I received your letter this morning after waiting patiently for three long weeks. I had begun to think that you had forgotten me. If you do not hurry and send the picture I shall begin to despair. I am truly glad to know that you had such a good time at my house. Mother wrote me that you were there. I hope you will feel free to go there whenever you go to Memphis, and feel that it is your home.

We had an Eisteddfod [gathering of Welsh singers] Saturday night in which the Jubilee Singers took part. We had a gay time.

James, I shall scold you very severely if you do not write oftener. You must brace yourself and write soon.

Your own, America

London, May 22, 1876

My *Dearest* James:

Your two letters came within a few days of each other. I am so glad to know that you are pleased with me. You say it is sweet to be believed & I think it sweet to meet *your* approval. When your letter came it affected me so that I lost my appetite really. My heart was so full that I had no inclination to eat. You spoke of being so teased about me. I have the same experience. I know I look guilty whenever your name is mentioned because my face burns so & when they tell me I blush I cannot help getting still redder.

James, you have told me about some of the things that annoy you. I wish you would confide in me more. Somehow the little things you told me have drawn me so much closer to you. I used to think that you got along so smoothly. Your life seemed to be wholly unruffled. From what you have said I know that you & I are perplexed alike & that trouble is common to us both. I cannot be with you to offer help but I can pray for you.

The photo is *very very* good. The glasses give you a stern & scholarly appearance. You look already like a professor. I think you will be obliged to send me another one soon for I may wear this one out. I cannot possibly look at it without kissing it. It is the dearest face to me there is on earth.

Last week was delightful. The first of the week I visited the Biscuit manufactory; it was very ingenious and interesting. The next day I went to Oxford & attended the races. I mean the boat races. I took tea at Jesus College. The next morning I breakfasted with a gentleman at Christ Church College. I went to Banbury on Thursday and saw the Cross. The next day we went to Bedford, the home of Bunyan. Tom, Maggie & I went out to his home in an open carriage.

We will leave for Switzerland on the 28th of June. We will sail up the Rhine which I anticipate is delightful. You wrote telling me to get Stereoscopic views. I have a few. It makes my head ache to look through stereoscopes so I thought it best to get scraps and keep a scrapbook. I think you will like the idea.

You said something about my learning French enough to teach you. I will try, knowing that I have an object in this, namely to teach such as you—a B.A.—You asked what would mother & father say when you asked for me. I think they would rather give me to you than anyone else. I am sure I would rather come to you. What will your mother think of me being your wife?

Ever true and lovingly yours, America

Leeuwarden, Holland, March 24, 1877

My Dearest James:

When we arrived here today we found the weather very inhospitable, but the people glad to welcome us. There are 1600 tickets sold today & the concert does not take place till Monday. Hundreds met us at the station. Some climbed upon the buses & Carriage to get a glimpse at us. At night when we went to the concert they had assembled at the front door of the hotel but we slipped out the back entrance through the stable yard & beat their time.

This morning when I went down to breakfast I found over half a dozen gentlemen in the room, smoking & talking. They looked like heathen to me, but it is the custom of the country. In the church where we sung men were smoking at the intermission. It seemed so irreverent. At the stations there are no suitable waiting rooms for ladies. Men smoke everywhere.

Excuse my dull letter. It is hard to write when one is tired.

Yours only, America

Arundel, England, May, 1877

My Dearest James:

You may blame me all you wish for waiting so long without writing. It is so seldom that we get to London that we must fix up our things when we are there. I only see my large trunk once a year, so the storing away of winter apparel & getting out summer &c takes abundance of time.

But this is not the sole reason that I have not written. I had expected to go home in July or August but not being certain I did not like to write until I did know. Mr. Cravath said when we were in Holland that all who were unwilling to stay another year would go home in July. And if many decided to go home, the class would be broken up & all go then. Maggie Carnes & I gave Mr. Cravath our reasons for leaving. It is simply this. Mr. Cravath was unwilling to give us new singers the same as the old & we were determined not to stay for less than they. Our salary has been inferior each year. Mr. C. wanted that we should work our way up —that we have done & now that we have reached the point where we would get the same amount, he was unwilling to abide by it, fearing the old singers would demand more.

Well, Saturday night Mr. C. and Gen. Fisk came down here from London. After tea they sent for Maggie & me. Mr. C. said he was astonished that I would let such a noble work hinge for the sake of a few hundred dollars & base my decision on money &c. He did a lot of talking, showing the Christian & not the money side, but was unable to convince me that I was wrong. Gen. Fisk told Mr. C. that he thought that the salaries should be equitable. He talked very nice to me indeed. [Mr. C.] gave me no answer as to whether he wished me on my condition until Monday. He came to my room & was very cordial. He said he was not sure the class would remain another year, but if it did why he would expect me to remain. He should be able to tell in a week or so.

Do you think I did right, James? I did not consult you about remaining another year. In the first place there was not time & in the second I was not sure whether you intended going to Dartmouth or not. If you went there would be no use of my returning. Of course, I may come home, but the probabilities are that I shall stay. Please write me what you intend to do. If you go to Dartmouth, when will you go & all about your expenses there &c.

America

Frankfort, November, 1877

My Dearest James:

We are still singing with as great success as attended our labors at the beginning of our work in Germany. James, I wish you could see the German officers. They are the finest and best-looking men in the world. Every night our concerts are full & they make the house look well. They do wear such magnificent uniforms.

I went to the Aquarium on Tuesday and saw two wonderful chimpanzees act on the Trapeze. There is a great deal to be seen in Berlin. The Americans over here are very friendly. They are rather proud of us. They see that we are courted on every side.

I am glad you are doing so well & like being there. I trust you will get through all right.

Yours, America

The long separation at last took its toll. Troubled by America's frequent references to the handsome gentlemen she met, James wrote a letter full of "cruel accusations" and she broke their engagement. When she wrote the following, the Jubilee Singers had returned home while she and several others remained in Europe to complete their education.

Valentigney, France, August 4, 1878

My Dear James:

You are still dear to me and ever will be. I always have loved you. I always shall, but the decision I came to in my last is final. My dear James, I cannot be your wife.

I will, of course, burn your letter. Burnt or unburnt, I should never peruse it again. Enough of sadness comes into one's life without searching for it. In turn, I will ask one favor of you. I do not know whether you care to keep any of my letters. If so, will you please put them together & mark them *To be burned when I am dead.* I should be better satisfied to know that no eye save yours had seen them. I shall do with yours in like manner.

I shall be here this month or perhaps longer. Then I return to my school in Strasbourg where I shall study German, French and music. If you wish to write me, occasionally or often, your letters would receive as great a welcome as ever. I should like to know all about you.

I seem doomed to be a wanderer on the face of the earth. Perhaps you may soon find a peaceful home. I shall love you where'er you are, what'er you are, what'er you do.

America

Special Collections, Fisk University Library

James Burrus never married. After teaching at Fisk and Alcorn, he became a successful businessman. When he died in 1928, leaving an estate of $120,000 to Fisk, America Robinson's letters were found in his trunk.

VI· THE GOVERNMENT OF THE UNITED STATES ABANDONS YOU

The Southern white politician who predicted
the failure of Reconstruction left no stone
unturned in making his prophecy an accomplished
fact. Intrigues, bribery, murder and rapine
destroyed the Reconstruction of the Southern
states and defeated Republican rule.

Daniel A. Straker, 1893

1. Will It Be I?

Before Reconstruction had fairly begun, its opponents—calling themselves Conservatives, Democrats, Reformers—determined to deliver the South from "Negro domination." The undeclared war began with the first elections. In Mississippi when the new state constitution was submitted for ratification in 1868, planters controlled their employees' votes:

Dick Sprauls said that I would get a bullet put through me if I voted the Republican ticket; or I would be driven from home without anything to eat and be liable to be bush-whacked. I voted the Democratic ticket only to save the lives of myself and family. My having voted the Democratic ticket, against my feelings and sense of right, so worried me last night that I could not sleep.

Sam Scott

Captain Snead said, previous to the election, I should not stay on his place, or any man who voted a ratification ticket. On election day Captain Snead got me drunk and took away from me forcibly a ratification ticket and gave me a Democratic ticket and made me vote it. He also said he would give me no meat or bread if I voted the ratification ticket.

Jordan Jackson

I went to vote and was met by a lot of white folks. Samuel Elliott asked me what ticket I intended to vote. I told him I intended to vote the radical ticket and he said, "Lord God, boy, if you vote the radical ticket you will be ruined." I said the speeches we had heard told the black people to vote for the radical ticket and why shouldn't we do so? The men gathered round and forced me to vote the Democratic ticket. Nearly all the black people wanted to vote the Republican ticket if they could have done so without fear or threats. They feel that they have been forced to do wrong.

Pink Campbell

Condition of Affairs in Mississippi, House of Representatives
Miscellaneous Document No. 53, 40th Congress,
3rd Session

White Georgians used a different tactic. As soon as the state was restored to the Union and the federal military authority withdrawn, the white members of the legislature expelled the twenty-

Henry M. Turner

seven black members. The new constitution, they said, gave blacks the right to vote, but not to hold office. While Tunis G. Campbell protested the expulsion in the state senate, Henry M. Turner spoke in the house:

Mr. Speaker:

Before proceeding to argue this question upon its merits, I wish the members of this House to understand the position that I take. I hold that I am a member of this body. Therefore, I shall neither fawn nor cringe nor stoop to beg for my rights.

Whose Legislature is this? Is it a white man's Legislature or is it a black man's Legislature? Who voted for a Constitutional Convention, in obedience to the mandate of Congress? Who first rallied around the standard of Reconstruction? Who set the ball of loyalty rolling in the State of Georgia? And whose voice was heard on the hills and in the valleys of this State? It was the voice of the brawny-armed Negro, with the few humanitarian-hearted white men who came to our assistance.

It is said that Congress never gave us the right to hold office. I want to know, sir, if the Reconstruction measures did not base their action on the ground that no distinction should be made on account of race, color or previous condition! Was not that the grand fulcrum on which they rested? And did not every reconstructed State have to reconstruct on the idea that no discrimination should be made? If Congress has simply given me political rights to make me a slave for Democrats or anybody else, let them take away my ballot. I don't want to be a mere tool. I have been a slave long enough already.

We have built up your country. We have worked in your fields, and garnered your harvests, for two hundred and fifty years! Do we ask you for compensation for the tears you have caused, and the hearts you have broken, and the lives you have curtailed and the blood you have spilled? We are willing to let the dead past bury its dead; but we ask you, now, for our RIGHTS. You have all the elements of superiority upon your side. You have our money and your own. You have our education and your own; and you have our land and your own. It is extraordinary that, with all advantages on your side, you can make war upon the poor defenseless black man.

You may expel us, gentlemen, but I firmly believe that you will some day repent it. You may expel us by your votes, today, but remember that there is a God in Heaven who despite the machinations of the wicked, never fails to vindicate the cause of Justice.

Henry M. Turner, "Speech on the Eligibility of Colored
Members to Seats in the Georgia Legislature," reprinted in
George Singleton, *The Romance of African Methodism* (New York,
1952)

Turner, Campbell and James Sims, who had also been elected to the legislature, went to Washington to protest the expulsions and Congress returned Georgia to military rule until 1870. When new elections were held that year, Turner was again elected to the legislature—and again denied a seat. He told a congressional committee how his second expulsion was accomplished:

The election lasted three days. On the third day the whites voted everything there. A circus came and they voted the whole circus—the Democratic ticket of course. They got about thirty colored Democrats. They would carry them into a room, put a cloak on them, bring them out and vote them, and then carry them back and put a high hat on and bring them out and vote them again. Repetition after repetition went on. All the wagoners that came in with cotton, everybody, whether he belonged there or not was voted. I do not think there are more than sixteen hundred Democrats in the county yet they polled twenty-seven hundred votes. If we had had a fair election we would have beaten them by five or six hundred votes. But we beat them only about thirty-eight votes.

A few days after the election, a white gentleman came up and said, "Turner, I will tell you something, but don't you tell my name. They have got the ballot-box up in that room (pointing to a building) and I think it is a damned shame." I went upstairs to see. I pulled open the door and walked right in. There were two men with their faces toward the fire;

another was sitting back in the corner, and the ballot-box was on the table and the whole table was strewn with ballots. They all looked up when I came in. One of them asked, "What do you want?" I said, "I wanted to see some gentlemen, but I see they are not here." I took a good look around and then went on about my business.

Q—Who were the men who had the ballot-box?

A—The clerk of the court was one; the two men I do not know. Neither one had any right to handle the ballots, which point I made before the committee in the legislature. A committee of three were appointed to investigate the matter. We appeared before the committee and the counsel for the Democratic claimants appeared in their behalf. The committee refused to receive what I regarded as vital affidavits, refused to take any cognizance whatever of the fact that the ballots were manipulated. Without knowing our evidence, without comparing our testimony with theirs, they just read off the decision in the house and said that the Democratic claimants were entitled to their seats and that was the end of it.

Condition of Affairs (Washington, 1872)

Election frauds and the intimidation of voters were only two of the many methods used by the leaders of the old Confederacy to return themselves to power. A white minister who traveled through Alabama in 1867 reported:

I put up with some of the leading men of the state and learned from them that they would never yield. They had lost their property and worst of all, their slaves were made their equals and perhaps their superiors, to rule over them. They said there was an organization, already very extensive, that would rid them of this terrible calamity. I asked how and they replied, "Why, suppose a man drops out here"—meaning that they would kill him. "While that is being investigated another will drop out there and yonder until the cases are so numerous that they will overwhelm the courts, and nothing can withstand the omnipotence of popular sentiment." On my arrival at Huntsville, I learned of the organization of the Ku Klux Klan. It seemed to answer precisely the design expressed by these men.

Condition of Affairs (Washington, 1872)

Founded in 1867, the Klan's announced objective was the "maintenance of the supremacy of the white race in this Republic." Before its decline five years later, it had a membership of half a million men. Robert Gleeds, ex-slave and state senator in Mississippi, explained its goals as he understood them:

We believe it had two objects. One was political, and the other was to hold the black man in subjection to the white man and to have white supremacy in the South. A paper published in Alabama said in plain words "We must kill or drive away the leading Negroes and only let the humble and submissive remain." That was in 1868. I was down there canvassing and read the paper and saved the copy. I spoke of it often—the idea of a party being built up on the principle of the open slaughter of human beings. It was startling to me, the advocacy of such a principle. And it was well carried out in Tuscaloosa County and in Pickens County. You will find but three colored men at that time who would dare speak openly of Republican principles, except where a great many colored people lived. Since then it has been a great deal worse.

Q—You call the colored people that vote the Democratic ticket traitors?

A—We call them enemies to our people.

Q—They have not a right to do as they please, like the rest of you?

A—They have the right, just like Benedict Arnold had a right to trade off the army like he did. But that does not make it justice and equity because he did.

Condition of Affairs (Washington, 1872)

By 1868, political assassinations were sending shockwaves through the black communities of the South. Benjamin F. Randolph, former army chaplain and Freedmen's Bureau agent, was one of the first to be killed:

Charleston, October 20, 1868

To the Republicans of South Carolina:

It is my painful duty to inform you of the death by the hand of assassins at Hodges Depot in Abbeville County, on Friday the 16th in open daylight of the Hon. B. F. Randolph, Chairman of the State Executive Committee of the Republican Party and State Senator from Orangeburg County. Mr. Randolph was actively engaged in the faithful discharge of duty and in the exercise of a right which is the boast of Americans—the right of free speech. He was stricken down by men instigated, if not paid to do the deed, by those who under the name of the Democratic Party would destroy a race and bring anarchy and ruin upon our State and country.

I know there are times when forbearance ceases to be a virtue. I share with you the feeling of indignation which uncontrolled would lead me and you to seek vengeance by retaliation. But bear and forbear. The day of our political deliverance is at hand. Let not these outrages intimidate you nor yet lead you to measures of retaliation by which possibly the innocent may suffer along with the guilty.

A. J. Ransier, Acting Chairman,
State Executive Committee of the Republican Party,
South Carolina

Charleston *Courier*, October 22, 1868

When South Carolina's General Assembly met to mourn Randolph, Robert B. Elliott voiced the feelings of his colleagues:

At the close of the last session of this General Assembly we all remember that it had been threatened that a conflict should begin. We all felt that there were persons in this State who were waiting to do their murderous work. We asked ourselves, will it be I? will it be I? and each wondered whether he should be the first martyr to the cause of truth, justice and liberty. None could tell who would be the first to fall; or if any should meet again in this House, which of us would be absent. We have met. We see a vacant seat today and look in vain for the person who occupied it. He has been murdered.

Journal of House of Representatives, South Carolina, December 1, 1868

The killings and beatings were stepped up in the next years until victims were numbered in the thousands. Republican governors received innumerable letters like the following:

Greenville County, South Carolina, January 14, 1871

Dear Sir:

Please allow me to say that I am yet here and it is about all that I can say. Since the election it have been so that I cannot stay at home in peace. On Friday night, there came a crowd of men to my house and after calling, knocking, climbing and shoving at the door they said that I was the President of the [Union] League and at the head of the militia organization and if I did not stop then I would have to abide by the consequences. They said they intended to give me another call and they did but I was not at home. I lay in swamps and woods.

Dear sir, it is a plot to drive me out of the country because I am a school teacher. They say I shall not teach school any longer in this country. Please, your honor, send some protection up here.

Thomas S. Jones

South Carolina Archives

Each week *The New National Era* published reports under the headline KU-KLUXISM!

A correspondent from South Carolina gives the particulars of the cold-blooded murder of Mr. Anthony Johnson, a colored trial justice. Mr. Johnson was suddenly attacked by an armed band of ruffians, his door shot to pieces and broken down and his mother ordered to procure a rope with which to hang her son. Not satisfied with taking his life, they gratified their hellish instinct by placing their pistols against his head and shooting it to pieces.

The New National Era, January 12, 1871

Ku Klux Klansman

The facts as narrated by Mr. Simeon Young (colored), who is chairman of the Board of City Commissioners:

I live in the town of Newberry and on Sunday morning last between 1 and 2 o'clock my wife woke me up, saying there was Ku-Klux outside. I jumped out of my bed and took my rifle. They broke in the window of the bedroom and threw a turpentine ball into the room which I smothered with a blanket. They then went to the front door, burst that in and threw several turpentine balls into the room and then burst open the bedroom door and fired some ten or twelve shots, wounding my wife and child as they lay in bed. I fired upon the nearest man, wounding him. I then jumped through the window and as I was running through the crowd I received two shots in the thigh.

The New National Era, May 25, 1871

When the friends of Lieutenant-Governor Oscar J. Dunn of Louisiana and Florida's Jonathan Gibbs believed that the two men had been poisoned, they were not being paranoid. Every black leader echoed Elliott's question, "Will it be I?" Urging Congress to pass a bill to curb the Klan, Joseph Rainey said:

As to our fate, we are not wood, we are not stone, but men, with feelings and sensibilities like other men whose skin is of a lighter hue. When myself and colleagues shall leave these Halls and turn our footsteps toward our southern home we know not but that the assassin may await our coming. Be it as it may we have resolved to be loyal and firm, and if we perish, we perish! I earnestly hope the bill will pass.

Congressional Globe, 42nd Congress, 1st Session

A month later, Rainey received a warning from the Klan. It was written in red ink, to simulate blood.

K.K.K.
Beware! Beware! Beware!
(Skull and Cross Bones)
Your doom is sealed in blood
Special Order: Headquarters 17th Division, Cyclopian
Cyclop Commandery

At a regular meeting of this post on Saturday it was unanimously resolved that notice be give to J. H. Rainey and H. F. Heriot to prepare to meet their God.

Take heed, stay not. Here the climate is too hot for you. We warn you to flee. You are watched each hour. We warn you to go.

The New National Era, May 25, 1871

Elliott also spoke in Congress in support of the Klan bill. The day he left Washington for South Carolina, he wrote:

October 13, 1871

Dear Wife:

I write to inform you that I shall leave for home at 7 o'clock tonight by the Richmond and Danville R.R. and expect to reach home on Sunday morning. If anything should happen to me, I have a draft on the Bank for $1,800. If it should be stolen, write immediately to Hon. N. G. Ordway, Sergeant-at-Arms of the House of Representatives and have

"Dam Your Soul. The Horrible *Sepulchre* and Bloody Moon has at last arrived. Some live to-day to-morrow "*Die.*" We the undersigned understand through our Grand "*Cyclops*" that you have recommended a big Black Nigger for Male agent on our nu rode; wel, sir, Jest you understand in time if he gets on the rode you can make up your mind to pull roape. If you have any thing to say in regard to the Matter, meet the Grand Cyclops and Conclave at Den No. 4 at 12 o'clock midnight, Oct. 1st, 1871.

"When you are in Calera we warn you to hold your tounge and not speak so much with your mouth or otherwise you will be taken on supprise and led out by the Klan and learnt to stretch hemp. Beware. Beware. Beware. Beware.

(Signed)

"PHILLIP ISENBAUM,
"*Grand Cyclops.*
"JOHN BANKSTOWN.
"ESAU DAVES.
"MARCUS THOMAS.
"BLOODY BONES.

" You know who. And all others of the Klan."

Threatening notice from the Klan

him stop the payment of it and send you a new draft. Mr. Ordway has also a life insurance policy on my life for $10,-000 which he will turn over to you. I do this, my dear, because life is uncertain.

I hereby constitute you my sole heir. All my property is yours. If anything happens send for [William] Whipper at once and have him arrange your business for you.

Your affectionate husband,
Robt. B. Elliott

Peggy Lamson, *The Glorious Failure* (New York, 1973)

The Ku Klux Act, passed in 1871, imposed fines and imprisonment on those who "go in disguise for the purpose of depriving any persons of the equal protection of the laws" and gave the President the power to send Federal troops to troubled areas. At the same time a joint committee of the Senate and House launched an exhaustive investigation. Holding hearings in major southern cities, congressmen found massive evidence of a conspiracy to overthrow the Reconstruction governments. The thirteen volumes, almost eight thousand pages, of *Testimony Taken by the Joint Select Committee to Inquire into the Condition of Affairs in the Late Insurrectionary States* (Washington, 1872) abound in eyewitness accounts of Klan violence and terror. Selections from the testimony follow.

Abram Colby, a member of the Georgia legislature:

On the 29th of October 1869, they broke my door open, took me out of bed, took me to the woods and whipped me three hours or more and left me for dead. They said to me, "Do you think you will ever vote another damned radical ticket?" I said, "I will not tell you a lie." I supposed they would kill me anyhow. I said, "If there was an election tomorrow, I would vote the radical ticket." They set in and whipped me a thousand licks more, with sticks and straps that had buckles on the ends of them.

Q—What is the character of those men who were engaged in whipping you?

A—Some are first-class men in our town. One is a lawyer, one a doctor, and some are farmers. They had their pistols and they took me in my night-clothes and carried me from home. They hit me five thousand blows. I told President Grant the same that I tell you now. They told me to take off my shirt. I said, "I never do that for any man." My drawers fell down about my feet and they took hold of them and tripped me up. Then they pulled my shirt up over my head.

They said I had voted for Grant and had carried the Negroes against them. About two days before they whipped me they offered me $5,000 to go with them and said they would pay me $2500 in cash if I would let another man go to the legislature in my place. I told them that I would not do it if they would give me all the county was worth.

The worst thing about the whole matter was this. My mother, wife and daughter were in the room when they came. My little daughter begged them not to carry me away. They drew up a gun and actually frightened her to death. She never got over it until she died. That was the part that grieves me the most.

Q—How long before you recovered from the effects of this treatment?

A—I have never got over it yet. They broke something inside of me. I cannot do any work now, though I always made my living before in the barber-shop, hauling wood, &c.

Q—You spoke about being elected to the next legislature?

A—Yes, sir, but they run me off during the election. They swore they would kill me if I staid. The Saturday night before the election I went to church. When I got home they just peppered the house with shot and bullets.

Q—Did you make a general canvas there last fall?

A—No, sir. I was not allowed to. No man can make a free speech in my county. I do not believe it can be done anywhere in Georgia.

Q—You say no man can do it?

A—I mean no Republican, either white or colored.

Alfred Richardson, another Georgia legislator, traveled to Washington to give his testimony:

This man told me, "They intend to kill you. They say you are making too much money; that they do not allow any nigger to rise up that way; that you can control all the colored votes and they intend to break you up and then they can rule the balance of the niggers."

The same night between 12 and 1 o'clock, these men came. There were about twenty or twenty-five of them, I reckon. I sort of expected them and had my door barred very tight. I had long staples at the side and scantling across the door. One fellow had a new patent ax and he commenced cutting down the door until he cut it spang through. I thought I would stand at the head of the stairsteps and shoot them as they came up. But they came upstairs firing in every direction. I had some small arms in the garret. There was a door up there about large enough for one man to creep in. I thought maybe they would not find me and I could make my escape.

They all went downstairs except one man. He looked in the cuddy-hole where I was and saw me. He shot me three times. I crept from the door of the little room to the stairway. They came upstairs with their pistols in their hands. I shot one of them as he got on the top step. They gathered him up and then they all ran and left me.

Q—Were these men disguised?

A—Some had on the regular old-fashioned doeface. Some had on black cambric with eye-holes. Some wore cambric caps. I have a long white gown in my trunk at my boarding-house. I have got seven of their caps. Some were brought to me and some were dropped in the yard. I have got one of the little horns that they blow when they get scattered and want to blow one another together.

There is not more than three or four weeks but what there is somebody whipped. If they don't whip they ride anyhow and scare people. Sometimes they go by colored people's doors and shoot through the door and ride on without stopping. It frightens them. Several where I live had bought land, two or three acre lots, put houses on them and were getting along very well. Since this thing has been going on, they have commenced selling their lots for little or nothing. They go away to some large town where they lay around and get whatever they can.

I was getting along very well. I owned one lot of seven acres, another of one acre, and another of about a quarter of an acre. I tried to sell them but I could not get anything for them. I moved [to Athens] to keep from being killed and perhaps my wife killed.

Samuel Nuckles, a legislator from South Carolina's upcountry, was also forced to leave his home:

I am a refugee from Union County. I cannot go back there. I have been threatened with the Ku Klux. You see I am a member of the house of representatives. I came here [Columbia] to the session in November. They took a recess for the Christmas holidays. I aimed to go home and went as far as Union village and two of my boys met me and told me not to go home for they threatened to kill me if I did. I have been here ever since. Three of my boys were run off on account of the Ku Klux. They [the Klan] became bitter against me because I went to Washington as one of the committee on account of the whippings and outrages in my county.

On the day of election I was at Gowdey's polling precinct. A gentleman named Bill Byars got mad because the election was conducted so promptly by Henry Owens.

Q—Conducted so what?

A—So promptly, so nicely, you know; having everything carried off so smoothly. Twelve white men would come in and vote, and then twelve colored men. They would keep anyone from pestering the voters as they went in, colored or white. Mr. Byars was standing talking to me and he said, "Nuckles, I'll bet you $500 that in two years from today there'll not be a colored man voting in the town." I said, "How do you know?" He says, "You'll know by waiting." He was only mad because the voting was going so, for after awhile the white men voting gave out and the colored men still kept up by twelves and consequently we beat them that day by two hundred and fifty votes. A very short time after that Mr. Owens was killed.

There are a great many refugees here. They do not want to go back unless something is done. The Republican party is scattered and beaten and run out. They have no leaders up there. That is the report that has been sent to us several times, that if we submit and vote the Democratic ticket we can stay there. But we do not propose to do that.

Q—How old are you?

A—I am about 57 years old. I can read a little and write my name. I first took that up here some few years back. I never was at school.

Q—You were a slave?

A—Yes, sir; a hard-down slave. I was born and bred in Union County and I have been in no place I like better, but it has become so I can't live there, and it seems that I am hardly living here.

Although office holders were the primary targets, every man of influence was liable to attack. Robert Fullerlove, a prosperous farmer, was driven from his home in Choctaw County, Alabama:

Q—How much land do you own there?

A—Four hundred acres, but now I never expect to set my foot on it no more. I have been sleeping out of doors. I have a good house, but is it any use for me to go in it, but not go to bed?

Driven from their homes by Klan, men camp out in
Louisiana swamp (*Boston Public Library*)

Q—Where did you go at night?
A—Under the house and around the cribs and in the corner of the fences; me in one place and my children in another. What is the use of a man trying to live in that condition?
Q—What do you suppose is the cause of this conduct of these white men?
A—They say it is on account of the Radical party, that I was of great influence among the colored people, that I influenced their votes.
Q—How much property have you?
A—I have about twenty head of cattle. I have an ox-team, and seven milk cows. I have corn and fodder and hogs. I am a hard-working man and I love what I have worked and earned, but I can't stay with no satisfaction. It isn't worthwhile. I had a notion of going to Kansas if I could get there.

Elias Hill, a minister and teacher in York County, South Carolina, was so badly crippled that he could not walk. Klansmen dragged him outdoors one night:

The first thing they asked me was, "Who burned our houses?"—gin-houses, dwelling-houses had been burned in the neighborhood. I told them it was not me; I could not burn houses. Then they hit me with their fists and said I ordered it. They went on asking me didn't I tell the black men to ravish all the white women. "No," I answered. They struck me again with their fists and went on. "When did you hold a night-meeting of the Union League and who were the officers?" I told them I had been the president but that there had been no Union League meeting held since last fall. I said, "Upon honor." They said I had no honor and hit me again.

After plundering the house searching for letters they came at me with pistols and asked if I was ready to die. I told them I was not exactly ready, that I would rather live. One caught me by the leg and I made moan when it hurt. One said "G—d d—n it, hush!" He had a horsewhip and he told me to pull up my shirt. I reckon he struck me eight cuts on the hip bone; it was almost the only place he could hit my body, my legs are so short.

One of them brought out a little book and says, "What's this for?" It was a book in which I had an account of the school. I read them some of the names. They asked me, "Will you quit preaching?" I told them I did not know. I said that to save my life. They said I must stop that Republican paper that was coming to me from Charleston. They said I must quit preaching and put a card in the newspaper renouncing Republicanism, but if I did not they would come back next week and kill me.

Then they gathered around and told me to pray for them. They said, "Don't you pray against Ku Klux. Pray that God may bless and save us." I was so chilled with cold lying out of doors and in such pain I could not speak to pray, but I tried to and they said that would do very well.

William Ford, an Alabama sharecropper, was whipped by Klansmen to "convince" him to vote for Horatio Seymour, Democratic candidate for President in 1868:

They asked me who I was going to vote for: Grant or Seymour. I claimed to them, as they had me overpowered, that I would vote for Seymour. I did that to get off. They wanted to know my politics and I answered, "What is politics, sir?"—very ignorant like. They had another man out at the same time and they whipped him tremendous for talking politics.

When the election came off I didn't vote. I was afraid to. I thought if I couldn't vote the Republican ticket I would not vote at all.

As a part of the program to maintain white supremacy, schools and churches were destroyed in all the southern states. Henry Giles was deacon of a church in Nixburg, Alabama:

The first of January, Saturday night, it was burned down. I saw them set fire to it. I had to hide, but I saw them. All of them were disguised. The horses were disguised. Ben Renshaw was shot just before they burned the church. They wanted him to help set fire to it and he didn't want to and they shot him.

They stripped me of everything since I came [to Montgomery]. My wife said they took a cow and a calf and my corn and my meat. She sent me word so. Mr. Maxwell is got my cow, so I understand. He lives about a mile from where I live. My wife had to hide the children out to keep them from perishing.

They even took the church papers out of the trunk I had and all the wine and bottles and tumblers and everything. They took them all.

Q—What was the cause of these people taking offense at your church?

A—They got it into their minds that we were all too strong Republicans. They said we prayed too loud and preached too loud.

Q—What was the church worth?

A—Four or five hundred dollars, if not more.

Q—Was it built exclusively by the colored people?

A—Yes, sir, by our own labor.

Q—What effect has this had upon the colored people? Has it made them afraid to vote?

A—It appears so. They seem to not know what to do.

The hoods and sheets that Klansmen wore were intended to frighten superstitious freedmen as well as to conceal the identity of the attackers. To heighten the ghostly effect, the night-riders often announced themselves as the spirits of Confederate soldiers hailing from hell and due to return in the morning. Newspapers in the North, treating the Klan as a joke, printed caricatures of the disguised horsemen and their terrified victims—caricatures which have persisted in fiction and film almost to the present day. In fact, however, the freedmen who were interviewed had not been taken in by the Klan's masquerade. Witness after witness coolly described the costumes and identified the wearers. After all, as Smith Watley explained, "I have known some of them twenty years":

I said to my wife, "Caroline, what do you reckon Mr. Bowen looked at me so under his hat—so ugly for?" She says, "There's some rascally trick after you by the white folks. You lay out tonight." I says, "You don't want me to sleep with you tonight." I said that just for devilment. That night she said, "You had better go out." I said, "No."

She laid down before I did and in about two hours, three hours, they came. The Ku Klux. She gets up and puts on her clothes and takes me by the hand and pulls me out of bed. I went to the window and saw twelve men in the yard. I says, "I can't whip all those men." She says, "Don't open the door." I says, "I must open it. Don't you hear them?"

He says, "Open in there. I don't walk. All my men flew in from hell." I said, "I had better open the door." She says, "No, don't open it." He says, "We come here. We didn't ride; we didn't walk. Our men flew from hell and are bound to see you tonight." She hung to me and I threw her away and opened the door.

Oliver gathered me on the right arm, and Doctor McClernand on this other arm and Joe Leonard catched me in the breast. They took me out. I counted sixteen men. I knew them all almost.

Q—Had they any disguises on?

A—They had crowns going up from their heads and they had gowns going down like a cloak or sheet, and [masks with] the mouth painted and noses and eyes. The horses had white sheets.

Q—What did they tell you they would do if you ever told about this whipping?

A—They said they would put a thousand balls in my heart, and they put their pistols up against my breast and made me hold up my hand and swear that I would never breathe it. They made all my folks but my wife swear so. They could not get hold of her.

Q—Did they accuse you of being a Radical?

A—They knowed I was a Radical. I had been issuing tickets for many years—ever since we had been voting. I was the regular one for giving out the tickets.

They whipped me Friday night and I took my mule and came on to Montgomery Saturday morning at 9 o'clock.

Q—Have any of these men been arrested for this transaction?

A—No, sir. They had them fetched here but they turned them all loose. I had a warrant and had the last one brung here. I swore to the men but I had no justice nowhere. They made out I didn't know the men that whipped me. I knew the men. I didn't make no mistake because I have known some of them twenty years.

Not all the killings were political. Eliza Lyon's husband was murdered for his savings of six hundred dollars. She was interviewed in Demopolis, Alabama:

They knocked on the door about 11 o'clock at night and asked was Abe Lyon in. They told him to come out, but I jumped up and shut the door and pushed him away. I told him to go out of the other door but it was dark and he was scared. He wheeled around in the room intending to go out, but the men burst the door open and threw a rope right over his head and drew his arms down and picked him up and toted him out.

I screamed for help but no one came near. I stood holloing and four men—white men—came up to me. One held his gun on each side of my head and one in my face and one right here in my chest and they told me if I didn't hush they would blow a hole through me. I took my hand and knocked the gun off a little bit. They didn't shoot me then.

A Klan visit

They carried Abe off up a little hill. They shot him with
a double-barreled gun. Dr. McCall counted thirty-three
holes they shot in him. After they shot him I picked up one
of the children and run out of the gate and off across a field
and stopped in a thicket of woods to see what they were
going to do. They went around and in the house and tore
up everything. Then they made a light and went under
the house and in the hen-house and in the stables. They
shot my dog and then came out and shot off their pistols

and guns. It sounded like there was over a hundred shots at once. I hid myself until it got good daylight and just at sunrise I came out of the woods.

Q—Was any of your property in the house stolen?

A—We had some money. I had a daughter up here and was sending her to school; besides I had three children at home. We had some money in a little square box, I reckon about $600. I wanted some of it to bring up here to school my daughter on. They got it.

Q—Where was this?

A—In DeSotoville, a little village. There were one or two stores there and my husband had put up an elegant blacksmith shop.

Q—Had your husband had any trouble with anybody?

A—None at all. He would not insult a child. He was a very quiet man. He asked them after they picked him up, "Gentlemen, what have I done?" They says, "Never mind what you have done. We just want your damned heart." After they shot him, some gentleman in the crowd says, "Let's cut his head off," and they cut his head loose around to the middle of the side of the neck. I have the penknife that they used. They broke it in his throat.

Q—What was he saving his money for?

A—We wanted to build us a house.

Warren Jones was forced to flee to Atlanta when he tried to collect more than a thousand dollars that his planter-landlord owed him:

The gentleman I was working with, he wanted me to work for nothing. I had made thirty bags of cotton and he promised me half. I went to him after I made the crop and asked for some pay to support my family. He said I should stay and work for nothing. He said if I undertook to leave he would Ku-Klux me. He went to a gentleman in the neighborhood and told him he was going to take my life. That gentleman came to me and said that I had better make my escape. The Ku Klux came to my house but they did not find me. I gathered up what I could in my arms and, with my wife and child, I came away.

Q—How long did you work there?

A—From the 4th of one March until the 20th of the next March.

Q—How much did he give you?

A—Nothing. I had right smart of money when I commenced and I paid for all the labor. He was to give me half and furnish all the stock and the land, but he did not give me anything.

Q—Has the crop of cotton been baled?

A—Yes, sir, and sold. The first seven bags, weighing 502 pounds each, sold for 14¾ cents per pound. The last picking weighed 501 pounds and they sold for 14½ cents a pound.

Q—What are you doing here?

A—I am working at the coal-yard.

Widows lined the benches of the county courthouses where the congressmen were taking testimony. Describing her husband's murder, Charlotte Fowler, a South Carolina freedwoman, recalled their last days together:

I was taken sick and laid on my bed Wednesday and Thursday. He went out working on his farm. He kept coming backward and forward to the house to see how I got and what he could do for me. When he came home he cooked something for me to eat and said, "Old woman, if you don't eat something you will die." Says I, "I can't eat."

Says he, "Then I will eat and feed the little baby." That is the grandchild he meant. I says, "You take that little child and sleep in the bed. I think I have the fever and I don't want you to get it." He said, "No, I don't want to get the fever for I have got too much to do." He pulled off his clothes and got in bed. He called to the grandchild, Tody—she is Sophia—and says, "Tody, when you are ready to come to bed, come, and grandmother will open your frock and you can go to bed."

I was by myself now for the children was all abed. I heard somebody by the door. It was not one person, but two—ram! ram! at the door. He heard it as quick as lightning and said, "Gentlemen, do not break the door down; I will open the door." The little child followed its grandfather to the door. I heard the report of a pistol and this little child ran back to me and says, "Oh, grandma, they have killed my poor grandpappy."

My poor old man! I was a hallooing and screaming. After they shot the old man they came back into the house —"Chup! Chup! Chup! make up a light." I called to the little girl, "Is there any light there?" She says, "No." But the mantel was there, where they put the splinters, and I said, "Light that splinter," and she lit the splinter.

He said, "Hand it here," and she handed it to him and then he says, "Hand me up your arms." Says I, "There isn't any here, sir." Says he, "Hand me up that pistol." I says, "There is none here. The old man had none in slavery and none in all his freedom and everybody in the settlement knows it."

I don't know that anybody had anything against the old man. Everybody liked him but one man and that was Mr. Thompson. Summer before last he had planted some watermelons and he kept losing his watermelons and one day he said he would go and lay and see who took them. Sure enough, he caught two little white boys. One was Mr. Thompson's boy. They had cut up a whole lot of the melons.

A black family

Q—Do you mean that Thompson had anything to do with the killing?

A—I didn't see Mr. Thompson's face for he had a mask on; but he was built so. He lives close to us and I saw him every day and Sunday.

Q—What kind of mask?

A—It was black, and the other part was white and red and he had horns on his head. He came into the house after he killed the old man. Another man came and looked down on the old man and dropped a chip of fire on him and burned his breast. They had shot him in the head and every time he breathed the brains would come out. He didn't die until Friday but he couldn't say a word. He was just bleeding and his brains and blood came out over his eyes.

Q—How old was your husband?

A—I do not know exactly but he was an old man with a head as white as that sheet of paper that that gentleman is writing on. But he was a smart man for his age.

Q—Was your husband as old as seventy-five?

A—I reckon he was.

In the courthouse in Demopolis, Alabama, Betsey Westbrook told of the death of her husband, Robin Westbrook:

They came up behind the house. One of them had his face smutted and another had a knit cap on his face. They first shot about seven barrels through the window. One of them said, "Get a rail and bust the door down." They broke down the outside door. We shut ourselves up in another room in the back of the house and they got another rail and busted open the back door. One of them said, "Raise a light." I was sitting on a little basket on the hearth. They picked it up and pitched it in the fire. It had grease on it and it blazed up. Then they saw where we stood and one of them says, "You are that damned son of a bitch Westbrook." The man had a gun and struck him on the head. Then my husband took the dog-iron and struck three or four of them. They got him jammed up in the corner and one man went around behind him and put two loads of a double-barreled gun in his shoulders. Another man says, "Kill him, God damn him," and took a pistol and shot him down. He didn't live more than half an hour.

My boy was in there while they were killing my husband and he says, "Mammy, what must I do?" I says, "Jump out doors and run." He went to the door and a white man took him by the arm and says, "God damn you, I will fix you too," but he snatched himself loose and got away.

Q—Did you know any of these men?

A—Yes, sir. I certainly knowed three.

Q—What were they mad at your husband about?

A—He just would hold up his head and say he was a strong Radical. He would hang on to that.

Other women reported rapes and whippings. In Columbia, South Carolina, Harriet Simril testified:

They came after my old man and I told them he wasn't there. They searched about in the house a long time. They were spitting in my face and throwing dirt in my eyes. They busted open my cupboard and eat all my pies up and took two pieces of meat. After awhile they took me out of doors and told me all they wanted was my old man to join the Democratic ticket. After they got me out of doors, they dragged me out into the road and ravished me out there.

Q—How many of them?

A—There were three.

Q—One right after the other?

A—Yes, sir, they throwed me down.

Q—Do you know who the men were who ravished you?

A—Yes, sir, there was Ches McCollum, Tom McCollum, and this big Jim Harper. After they had got done with me I had no sense for a long time. I laid there, I don't know how long. The next morning I went to my house and it was in ashes.

Some were whipped to warn them not to "sass white ladies."
Caroline Smith:

The Ku Klux came to my house and took us out and whipped us. They had on pants but they were put on like children's clothes. They had on some kind of false-face. Mr. Rich was the first man who struck me and Mr. Felker was the head man. They caught my husband and beat him and then Mr. Rich said, "Come out of here." They made me get down on my knees. Felker then said, "Take off this," pointing to my dress, "and fasten it around you." They made me fasten it to my waist. He whipped me some and then he made me take my body off which I wore under my dress. He gave me fifty more and then said, "Don't let's hear any big talk from you, and don't sass any white ladies."

Sarah Ann Sturtevant:

They gave me forty licks with a hickory and kicked me in the head and hit me on the back of the head with a pistol. I asked them what they whipped me for and they said they wanted to give me a little shillala for fear I would sauce white women.

Q—Did they whip you over your clothes?

A—No, sir, they stripped them off and fastened them around my waist.

Q—How many of them struck you?

A—There were nine of them and all struck me. They all had hickories but one. The one that hit me the first lick had a whip. Then the others whipped me with a stick.

The founders of the Klan had described it as "an institution of Chivalry, Humanity, Mercy and Patriotism." Between 1868 and 1871, Klansmen killed twenty thousand men, women and children—often their neighbors—and committed tens of thousands of other acts of violence. Reviewing their bloody history, Robert B. Elliott said:

It is the custom of Democratic journals to stigmatize the Negroes of the South as being in a semi-barbarous condition. Pray tell me, who is the barbarian here, the murderer or his victim?

Congressional Globe, 42nd Congress, 1st Session

2. I Must Fight

Black people were by no means quiescent in the face of Klan violence. Growing up in the same frontier tradition as the whites, they, too, owned guns and knew how to use them. From the first days of freedom, the right to bear arms was defended in black newspapers:

Morris Island, South Carolina, December 21, 1865

Editor of *Leader:*

By an order of the War Department the 33rd U. S. Colored Troops is to be mustered out as soon as possible. The major portion of our men have been in the service seven months over their time. This regiment is the pioneer colored regiment of the late war. Although we have faithfully used our guns in the services of the country yet, by special instructions from the War Department, we are denied the privilege accorded to honorably mustered out troops generally, of being allowed to purchase our arms! Is this act of the War Department intended as homage to the Negro Code of South Carolina?

THE REGIMENT

South Carolina *Leader,* December 24, 1865

Savannah, January 29, 1866

Editor *Loyal Georgian:*

Have colored persons a right to own and carry fire arms?

A Colored Citizen

Almost every day we are asked questions similar to the above. We answer *certainly* you have the *same* right to own and carry arms that other citizens have. You are not only free but citizens of the United States and as such entitled to the same privileges granted to other citizens by the Constitution.

The Loyal Georgian, February 3, 1866

At the height of the Klan outbreak, Faith Lichen, a Washingtonian, had a proposal for her brothers and sisters in the South:

A word to the Unionists of the South. You have done all that could be expected of you, and more. Now do something that isn't. Turn on your persecutors. Kill, burn and destroy. I know that you are without weapons, but there is one always by you—the torch. It is fearful, use it, hurl it with all your might into the mansions of the wealthy instigator, not into the huts of the poor tool. Of course I shan't be able to sleep tonight, but no matter. The cries of rebel humanity are no louder than those wrung from loyal men. Making faces at the Peace Society, I am

Faith Lichen

The New National Era, March 30, 1871

The homes and barns of Klansmen were burned in some areas but blacks, for the most part, bent their efforts toward defense rather than retaliation. Armed men stood guard at the homes of political leaders and every village had its folk hero—a man or woman who drove away the midnight marauders. Sir Daniel told congressional investigators about Miles Prior, "as brave a man as I ever saw," who organized the defense of the all-black village of Avery, Alabama:

They were going to burn that little town of Avery. This Miles Prior says, "Let them come." They wanted to burn the schoolhouse. He says, "Fifty men couldn't burn that

Farmer shouldering his shotgun

schoolhouse and let me live." When they got within about two hundred yards, Miles Prior he pulled off his coat and rolled up his sleeves and began to laugh and his wife began to cry, and told him to get away, that they were coming. He said he didn't care; let'em come. They said there were five hundred of them. He said he wasn't afraid; the more that come the more he could kill. There was only four that would stand with him.

Q—How many families were there in that village?

A—About seventy people in the village, big and little, young and old. It was twenty acres of land there that we bought. There was a fence on our line. And he says, "Don't any man fire until they put their foot over the fence." They came right up to the fence and said, "You high man, come over here. We want to see you." Prior was a very tall, stout man and very brave. Prior told them to come over and see him; he wanted to see them. They went back to Stevenson without burning the place. Other nights they would come between midnight and day and just fire on the place and have everything, you know, excited. Sometimes there would be thirty or forty around this man's house, firing into the house.

Q—Do you mean into Prior's house?

A—Yes, sir. It was a weather-boarded house, shanty fashion. They shot into his water bucket and the water would run out. They shot the posts of his chairs. They tried to shoot him through the house. They scalped his leg and he began to holler for the boys to come on, as if he had a big crowd and they all took out through the bushes. It went on that way over a year. Somebody, on a Sunday night, goes and shoots into two [white] citizens' houses in Stevenson and they supposed, you know, Miles Prior being such a brave man was at the head of this thing. Monday morning, Miles Prior went into Stevenson. The authorities got a squad of men to surround him and take him. He ran away down into Crow Creek Valley, in the water. When the water was about up to his breast it appeared to be chilling his heart so he could not swim. He had a pistol and his pistol got wet. They told him to surrender and give up his arms, but he come out and tried to shoot all these men who were standing at the waterside. He busted the caps as he came out. They shot at him and he threw his pistol in the water; he wouldn't give his pistol up. They then took him and put him in prison. They got this Jackson, a railroad man and me and put me in there as a prisoner. They said, "We are going to stop this radical business among you all."

I was very cold. It was right on the ground—one of these stockades. They came about 9 o'clock. They had all the place illuminated with candles. I got down on my knees and began to pray. They said they would hang us. They began to pull at the door and Miles Prior asked me if I would fight.

I said, "No, I have nothing to do but trust Daniel's God." He said, "I am no Christian man. I can't trust Daniel's God. I must fight." I said, "How can you fight? They are all coming in."

He says, "Ten men can't hold me and a regiment can't shoot me." Then he catched right hold of the door. These men were trying to pull it open and Prior catched hold of it and called to us to help him pull. I says, "I have no time to hold the door now. I have to pray." They had a rope fastened to the door and were pulling at it; every man was pulling. He held on to that door against all of them for a quarter of an hour until we could hear the 11 o'clock train coming up from Huntsville. He held on to the door until the train whistled and just after the train whistled he got tired, I reckon, and he suddenly let loose and all those men that were pulling so hard fell backward over one another. As they did that he lunged out of the door and ran over two or three of them and made his escape.

Condition of Affairs (Washington, 1872)

Before the war, southern communities had been proud of their military companies—the Light Dragoons, Washington Artillery, or

Continental Guards which led parades on holidays, held military balls and annual target practices. When federal commanders banned all military organizations in the first postwar years, whites in many cities got around the ruling by joining a volunteer fire company. An editorial in The New Orleans *Tribune*:

One of the first steps to guard against riots is a thorough reorganization of the Firemen's Companies. Among these organizations the spirit of rebellion has taken its last refuge. Not only in New Orleans but in Memphis and Mobile, the fire department has been prominent in the outrages committed against the liberties of the people. As the Firemen's Companies are the only organizations publicly tolerated, it is natural that the rebels use them to maintain an organization among themselves.

General Sheridan's order prohibiting rebel organizations has been evaded by the Confederates joining in a body the existing firemen's companies. Certain companies were reinforced by hundreds—in some cases six hundreds—of new members. Is this large number needed for the Fire Department?

We need LOYAL firemen and this can only be obtained when we shall have a fire department without distinction of color. In that case, as in that of the militia, loyalty will only come when brown and dark skins will be in the rank and file. Why not?

The New Orleans Tribune, May 22, 1867

After Radical Reconstruction got under way, blacks who had been forbidden in slavery days to join any kind of fraternal group were among the first to band together and ask for arms:

Charleston, January 21, 1869

Your Excellency Gov. R. K. Scott:

We the members of the Lincoln Republican Guards, are discuss of celebrating Lincoln's birthday with a parade and target exercise. We ask of your excellency the grant of arms for that day and, sir, if it is granted, we shall use them with all the due caution that is becoming good citizens.

We, the officers of the Republican Guards, Capt. James Green, Francis Teffirere and Alexander Williams

Sir:

This is the same body of men that Gen. Canby grant the use of arms to June 1, 1868, known then as the African Turners. And sir, if it is granted to us now, we shall use them with the same precaution as before. Please, sir, answer this as soon as you can, as we would like to make preparation for the celebration.

Joseph Crane

South Carolina Archives

After the Klan depredations began, most southern states organized state militia units as part of the National Guard. No blacks were enrolled, however, in Georgia, Alabama or Virginia. Two letters from black Georgians:

Macon, September 7, 1873

To the Editors:

The legislature of 1872 passed an act making it obligatory upon the Governor to distribute arms to such companies in existence prior to 1861 as might reorganize; as to other organizations it should be discretionary with him whether he should furnish arms or not. Sheltered under this plain evasion of the Constitution, the Governor has invariably refused arms to colored companies. The Lincoln Guards of this city have made application to the Governor for arms and if refused intend to test the constitutionality of the state law.

The state fair which takes place in this city next month offers a premium of $750 for the best drilled military company in the state. When colored organizations notified the committee of their intention to contest for the premium, they were quietly informed that they would not be permitted to enter the lists.

C.P.C.

The New National Era and Citizen, September 25, 1873

Columbia County, July 15, 1874

To the Editor:

Some months ago a number of young men in our county concluded to organize a military company for enjoyment and pastime. They had only six guns, and these such guns as country people keep for hunting. To supply themselves with something in the shape of arms, they took a pine plank and cut out pieces which they fashioned in the manner of guns and used at their drills.

These young men were ordered to disband by the white people, but knowing they had a perfect right to have such an organization they did not obey. On Friday the 10th, while Fountain Doggett and his three sons were quietly working in their field, six armed white men, one of them the Deputy Sheriff of the county rode up and pretended to have a warrant for their arrest. Not wishing to resist the sheriff, [they] surrendered and were tied together. They had been told they were to be carried to the courthouse for trial, but were carried in a contrary direction. [When] they reached a thickly wooded part of the road, all four of the colored men were brutally shot down.

They hatched up a tale saying these men resisted them and attempted to run, but there is not a shadow of truth in it. They were all lying near together and were shot in front.

The next day these and other parties went through the county and whipped every man they could find who had been connected with the company.

Yours in much tribulation,
COLUMBIA

The New National Era, July 30, 1874

In states where Radical Republicans were in power, the majority of the militia volunteers and many of its officers were black. As second in command of South Carolina's militia, Robert B. Elliott enrolled some fourteen thousand volunteers in an efficient and disciplined organization. The following letter was written to Prince Rivers, then a state assemblyman:

Columbia, July 22, 1869

Sir:

I am directed by His Excellency, R. K. Scott, Commander-in-Chief, to inform you that he has appointed you Captain of a company of special armed forces in the county of Edgefield. You will promptly take proper steps in order to have your company enrolled, drilled and ready for action whenever it may become necessary to act. You will exercise great care in the selection of your men and use great energy in the enforcement of discipline. You will in no case act on the aggressive, but be at all times vigilant and prompt to assume the defensive. Should any of your men commit any violence or be guilty of insubordination, you will immediately cause such offendants to be placed under arrest and report your action to these headquarters.

As soon as your company rolls are completed, you will transmit a copy to these headquarters without delay. In-

Thomas Nast titled this drawing "He Wants a Change Too" (*Peggy Lamson*)

structions will be sent to you from time to time. In for-
warding copy of company rolls you will report whether or
not the men are ready to be mustered in.

Robert B. Elliott, Colonel and Asst. Adjutant General

South Carolina Archives

The South Carolina militia was effective in halting 'Klan activities
in some parts of the state. However, it soon became a part of Governor Scott's personal political machine and a way of funneling
money into the pockets of Scott and his friends. On one occasion
while Scott was in Washington, Chief Constable Hubbard, a white
Northerner, refused Elliott's request for the transfer of horses to the
militia. Elliott protested to the governor, but despite his letter, which
follows, Hubbard sold the horses and split the proceeds with Scott.

Columbia, April 1, 1870

Governor:

In accordance with instructions received from your Excellency, I made a formal demand on Capt. J. B. Hubbard,
Chief of the Constabulary, requesting that he would transfer
to this Dept. all the Horses, Saddles, etc. belonging to the
State and in his possession.

Finding Capt. Hubbard had failed to make the transfer,
I instructed Genl. John B. Dennis to make another demand.
That demand has been as fruitless as the first. I have since
been informed that Capt. Hubbard declined to make the
transfer on the ground that he had not been instructed by
Your Excellency to do so.

I desire to call your Excellency's attention to two points
that are to decide whether I am a menial or an officer of
this State, whether my position is one of responsibility or a
mere nomenclature. If the former, I shall demand from
every individual the amount of respect attaching to it; if

the latter I will not so far forget my manhood as to cling to any such position.

The first point is the common rule which governs all Depts. of State, that in the absence of the chief of a Dept. his duties fall upon the shoulders of the next ranking officer. The next point is the ground upon which Capt. Hubbard declined to make the transfer: that Your Excellency had not seen fit to address a communication to him. It is a rule, as I understand it, that when an officer acting as the head of any Dept. issues an order or makes a requisition it is fair to presume that he acts under proper authority.

Hoping that I may be enlightened by Your Excellency upon the points above set forth,

R. B. Elliott, Col. and Asst. Adjt. Genl. S.C.

South Carolina Archives

During the 1870 election campaign, Elliott protested again when Colonel Mann, commander of a white militia company, used his troops to electioneer:

Columbia, August 8, 1870

Governor:

During the month of June I visited the quarters of the guard in Abbeville. My attention having been called to the fact that the Guard was being used as stumpspeakers and distributors of books, etc. in the interest of certain individuals, I assembled the men and in the presence of Col. Mann, informed them that they could not be allowed to pursue such a course. That they had a perfect right to the enjoyment of their individual opinions and could attend public meetings provided they obtained leave of absence from Col. Mann. Col. Mann then and there took issue with me and declared that no one had the right to so restrict them and as for himself he should pursue just such a course in political matters as he saw fit. The men, emboldened by his attitude, became turbulent and insolent. I told them that if they persisted in such insubordination I would discharge them. I went into the office to give Col. M. some instructions in regard to the making out of payrolls, etc. While there, the three men that have been since discharged came into the office declaring that they did not care a d—n for any nigger. That they were under Col. M. and no one else and so long as he did not find fault with them, they cared not one d—n who else did, etc. Col. M. was present, but did not say one word to stop such proceedings. On the contrary, just as soon as I left he informed the men that he had full power—that I dared not discharge them—that he had more influence with you, etc.—thereby attempting to render me contemptible in the sight of the men.

On my last visit to Abbeville, I found that not only had these men been retained but that I was daily made the object of their ridicule. I determined to assert my prerogative as an officer of this State, entitled to the respect of all in subordination to myself. I therefore discharged them. As soon as the order of discharge was written out, Col. Mann, in an imperious manner demanded the cause of my action, stating that he *presumed* that the right to employ and discharge those composing the guard belonged to him. He seemed then desirous of entering into a heated discussion in the presence of the men, to avoid which, I bade him "good morning" and left.

Robert B. Elliott, Col. and Asst. Adjt. Genl.

South Carolina Archives

Although Elliott favored Scott's re-election and was backed by the governor in his own race for Congress, Scott's subversion of the militia finally became insupportable and Elliott resigned his commission. Other black men followed him into positions of leadership in the militia, but, in all of the southern states, control of the organization remained in the hands of the governors. Although they used the black militia to maintain law and order during minor skirmishes, and to keep themselves in office, they were reluctant to call them up when real trouble threatened. Faced with the possibility of a black-white confrontation which might lead to a war between the races, the white governors disarmed their black troops and turned to the federal government instead. Their refusal to use the only loyal armed force in the South hastened the collapse of Reconstruction.

3. We Submit These Facts for Your Impartial Judgment

The presence of federal marshals and congressional investigators in the South and the arrest of more than five thousand Klansmen broke up the organization, for a time. The Klan's reign of terror had succeeded in ending Reconstruction in North Carolina and Georgia and solidifying Conservative control of Tennessee, Virginia and the border states. Elsewhere, thousands of white men had been driven from the Republican party and thousands of blacks had been kept from voting.

Even after the Democrats took power, mopping-up operations continued in Georgia. In a letter to the Savannah *Journal* Henry M. Turner said:

Mr. Editor:

Soon after Gov. Smith went into the Executive chair, the Negro-haters concluded to change their tactics and the threat went abroad that Negro leaders must go to the penitentiary. I call the attention of the country to one or two cases.

Four years ago Hon. T. G. Campbell, state senator, married a colored man and a woman whom his prosecutors claim to be white, which act he performed before our Supreme Court made that hell-born decision that forbids marriage between white and colored. Last Tuesday Senator Campbell was arrested and incarcerated in jail. The senator is handcuffed as though he was a murderous desperado and hurried off to Atlanta. And what is all this for? Why manacle, shackle and gyve this senator with such unusual ferocity? Is it because he married that couple four years ago? No! It is because they mean to get him out of the senate and defeat his re-election.

SUFFERINGS

OF THE

REV. T. G. CAMPBELL

AND

HIS FAMILY,

IN GEORGIA.

———•◦•———

WASHINGTON:
ENTERPRISE PUBLISHING COMPANY,
1877.

After almost two years in Georgia jails, Tunis G. Campbell wrote an account of his "Sufferings"

The same day they ran off with Mr. Campbell, Hon. James M. Sims and Hon. U. L. Houston were tried upon the pretended plea of rioting in their own church. I do not believe the evidence would have convicted the devil before a jury of angels, yet they were convicted and would have been in prison today but for the fact that they have appealed for a new trial.

H. M. Turner

The New National Era, July 11, 1872

At the same time, Campbell wrote to the chairman of the National Executive Committee of the Republican party:

Atlanta, July 8, 1872

Hon. E. D. Morgan
Dear Sir:
I write to let you know that if Grant is not elected I fear that both colored & white Republicans will be forced to leave the South. Just before every election they commence trying to intimidate by arresting all prominent colored men. As usual they have arrested me again. I was kept in jail three days & then brought up to Atlanta & put in jail here. The intention was to keep me out of my seat in the senate as the legislature will meet this month.

No man will be able to travel anywhere as he will be liable to be taken up at any time upon any pretext, charging him with any crime. I shall be on the stump for Grant & Wilson, but for God's sake *rouse* up the North for there is our hope.

T. G. Campbell, Senator of the 2nd District,
Georgia

William E. Chandler Papers, Library of Congress

"Rouse up the North" was a cry that was also adopted by the Conservatives. The Klan violence had alienated public opinion and brought about government intervention, but perhaps northern sympathies could be swayed by other means. Launching a well-organized propaganda campaign, southern spokesmen charged that the "Africanized" Reconstruction governments were engaged in a riot of corruption and extravagance.

The 1870s was a period not unlike our own when corruption was widespread. While Klansmen were galloping along the byways of the South, Boss Tweed and his henchmen were in the saddle in New York. Before the Tweed Ring was broken up in 1872 it had robbed the city of more than $100,000,000. The Credit Mobilier scandal which came to light a year later implicated congressmen, cabinet officers and the Vice-President in a swindle of major proportions; the "Whiskey Ring," exposed in 1875, involved high officials of the Treasury Department and even President Grant's private secretary.

The South, too, was having its "years of good stealing." Speculators from the North joined with white Southerners in "Railroad Rings," "Printing Rings" and land swindles. They milked state treasuries, bribed legislators and enriched themselves. In 1870, a Louisiana delegation went to Washington:

A delegation of colored Republicans are in this city to lay before the President and the Republicans in Congress the utterly corrupt and profligate management of affairs in Louisiana. They charge the most shameless bribery and flagrant dishonesty. The delegates claim to have ample proof to sustain their charges and the documents will be laid before the President, Secretary Boutwell and others. The delegates ask that the Republican party in Louisiana be aided in this movement for self-purification and they claim that unless it be done there is great danger that the great body of Republicans will, in disgust, allow the next election to go by default or attempt the organization of a movement within the Republican party which, by division, will produce the same result—Democratic success.

The New Era, June 16, 1870

By 1871, black leaders agreed that changes were needed in South Carolina. An editorial from Richard Cain's *Missionary Record*:

Radical members of the South Carolina legislature (*Library of Congress*)

The important developments of the last few months prove conclusively that there is something wrong. The undeniable facts [are] that the Legislature has made appropriations to meet the current expenditures and that the taxes [have] been promptly paid and that yet there is a want of funds to meet legitimate expenses. In every department there is a complaint that there is no money in the treasury. In every one, employees complain that their salaries are not paid.

We know that the colored men of this State will have to bear the odium of all the crimes or misdemeanors of the whites who manipulate the finances. This government of South Carolina is in the hands of white men, placed there by colored men's votes. If there is stealing being done, they do it. If there is robbery of the State of its millions, it is not the Negro who does these things. If there have been overissues of bonds for any purpose, we tell the country that no Negro has had any hand in this matter.

The colored population are as poor today as ever they were, so far as the State bonds has anything to do with their augmented wealth. With the credit of the State gone and the Treasury empty, with the report of frauds in the issue of bonds, is it not the duty of the people to rise up in their might and select another class of men to guide the State? There must be a change. There must be a uniting of all honest men of every class and race in the State for honest government. These public servants proving false to trust must be put out of power and honest men put in their places.

Beaufort *Republican,* November 23, 1871

Black people were the first to feel the effects of the graft and corruption in their state. When South Carolina's treasury was empty, its employees were paid in script which was discounted by the storekeepers who cashed it. In 1872, freedmen complained to Governor Scott:

We pen this note knowing you to be a friend of the colored people. You always did attend to our rights when you was a general and we chose you to be our Governor on that account. We have been working for the County for the past nine months and never received any money. Mr. Sherman told us that he has to charge us 20 cents on every dollar as he had to pay the county commissioners 10 cents and he had to make 10 cents. We don't find fault with the store man needing something but we do find fault with the county commissioners who has been elected by our votes, charging 10 cents on the dollar out of our labor.

This is just what the Democrats promised the Republicans would do to us. We believe there has been some bad men put in office, but we know you to be a friend of ours and we thought we would write you to see if you could do something for us. We would sign our names but we are afraid we would get no work. We are only paid 75¢ a day and think that little enough with the high cost of provisions, without the commissioners cheating us by taking 10¢ on the dollar.

From many Freedmen

South Carolina Archives

A member of the Young Men's Progressive Association of Charleston complained of the depredations of Land Commissioner C. P. Leslie, who bought swamp land for high prices, sold it to the state for even more and pocketed the difference:

Had the white men who misled our people cared anything about them, they could have long since had them in comfortable possessions. They pretended to establish a Land Commission, to supply the freedmen with homes. They had neither limit to the prices of lands nor the number of acres that the State would supply. Instead of buying lands for the poor, hardworking, homeless freedmen, for whom they pretended to care so much and who placed them in office, they divided the money among themselves, putting it in their own pockets, leaving the poor laboring people homeless, barefooted and in rags. These men are not only thieves (having stolen the land appropriation) but robbers, having robbed the freedmen of his chances of obtaining a homestead.

> Kush, *The Political Battle Axe for the Use of the Colored Men* (Charleston, 1872)

As criticism of the Land Commission mounted, Leslie was forced to resign. His duties were transferred to the office of the secretary of state where two black men, Francis L. Cardozo and his successor, Henry E. Hayne, straightened out the tangled records and made land available to settlers at actual value rather than at the inflated prices Leslie had put on it. Cardozo, a master at bringing order out of chaos, spent ten months preparing a complete financial record of the transactions of the Commission. One of his letters to a Commission employee:

May 25, 1872

John Wooley, Esq.
Sir:

Enclosed please find blank Reports which I desire you to fill out for the purpose of closing up your accounts as Agent of the Land Commission.

I have resolved to dispense with the services of Local Agents where possible so as to administer the affairs of the

Land Commission Dept. of my office as economically as possible. Your functions as Agent will cease on receipt of this letter and you will therefore report immediately for the purpose of making a final settlement.

F. L. Cardozo, Secretary of State, S.C.

At the same time, Cardozo stopped the sale of fraudulent state bonds. He wrote to his brother, Thomas:

The Legislature is busily engaged investigating the state of our financial affairs which are in a deplorable and desperate condition. The Governor, State Treasurer and Attorney General constitute the State financial board and there has been great swindling or gross mismanagement of our finances somewhere. As soon as I discovered what seemed to me like swindling or mismanagement, I refused to apply the seal of the State to any more bonds and defied the Treasurer to take me into the supreme court. He hesitates to do so for fear, I suppose, that he will be beaten. The colored men of the State are proud of the stand I have taken and even the Democrats applaud me. The praise of enemies is sometimes suspicious, but when deserved it is gratifying.

The New National Era, January 11, 1872

The Democrats' applause posed a dilemma for Cardozo and other honest Reconstructionists. So many of their colleagues were involved in the swindling that their exposure might defeat the Republicans in the next election. For black people, a Democratic victory was unthinkable. It meant the abrogation of their rights; it could even mean death. When State Treasurer Niles G. Parker was threatened with arrest, his lawyer warned against it. "I am satisfied you have too much discretion to do what you say," he wrote the attorney general. "Mr. Cardozo is the only State official who would not be carried down and made odious to every honest man." Although Parker's speculations were stopped, he was never brought to trial.

The dilemma of the would-be reformers was further compounded by the fact that the corruptionists' pockets were bulging with money for bribes. After Texas' first Reconstruction legislature met, a Texan wrote:

Navasota, Texas, October 20, 1870

Dear Editor:

I am anxious to let you know how we are getting on here. The Republicans are in the majority and we have a noble Governor but our Legislature at its last session failed to meet the expectations of the people. Our leading men in the Legislature proved themselves corrupt and sold themselves for gold. They were all, with a few exceptions, crazy on railroads. I wish you would look at the Central Pacific Railroad bills and see who voted against the Governor's vetoes. If you can get some of our Northern friends to come here and help us to educate the colored people that they will not sell themselves for gold, try to induce them to come, for there is a bright future for everyone who will not sell principle for gold.

James H. Washington

The New National Era, November 3, 1870

In South Carolina, "Honest John" Patterson, a white Pennsylvanian, spent tens of thousands of dollars to win support for the Blue Ridge Railroad. When Governor Scott, a member of the "Railroad Ring," was threatened with impeachment, Patterson approached legislators again. Hastings Gantt, a black assemblyman from Beaufort County, recalled:

At the time the question of impeaching Gov. R. K. Scott was before the house, it was supposed that the matter would be postponed till after the recess and the Beaufort men talked it over and determined to leave the day before the session closed. I was coming out of the State House to go to the train and Col. John J. Patterson met me at the foot of the steps and said we had better not go and leave the impeachment question here on hand. I told him that the understanding was it wouldn't take place till after the recess and that I wasn't willing to stop. He then said if I didn't go home until the recess he would give me $200. But I went home and was not present at the vote on the impeachment question.

South Carolina Archives

Patterson spent fifty thousand dollars to save Scott from impeachment, and forty thousand dollars more to buy himself a seat in the U. S. Senate. During the latter campaign, he set up headquarters on Columbia's main street, a few doors from the capitol. There his henchmen dispensed whiskey, cigars and cash to legislators, and blacks as well as whites accepted all three. Henry Riley, a black assemblyman, was escorted to Patterson's rooms as soon as he arrived in Columbia:

A good many members were there. General Worthington was there. Liquor and cigars were there. The talk was mostly about Patterson's election—Honest John Patterson some called him. That was my first experience of the Legislature. They drank Patterson's health. They said, "Now, all that are in favor of Mr. Patterson's election to the Senate, come and drink." I drank with the others. I had little or no money. Some members told me to see General Worthington. I saw him privately and asked him to lend

Buying a vote

me $25. He handed me the money in cash and said he
would make me a present of it.

*Report of the Joint Investigating Committee on
Public Frauds* (Columbia, 1878)

Nor was this the only time blacks sold their votes. Needy and
inexperienced lawmakers who watched the railroad and bond-ring
lobbyists circulating in the state capitols undoubtedly came to believe that bribetaking was an integral part of the great American

game of politics. Besides, as one black man explained, "I've been sold in my life eleven times. This is the first time I ever got the money."

But it was white men who did the bribing and who received the lion's share of the profits. When northern financiers sought a two-million-dollar appropriation for the Alabama and Chattanooga Railroad, agents for D. N. Stanton, president of the road, paid thirty-five thousand dollars to the white chairman of an Alabama legislative committee and fifty dollars to black legislators. Jere Haralson, a black assemblyman, followed a crowd of lawmakers to Stanton's rooms because he heard "there was money in it":

I was in Montgomery a day or two before Stanton's bill passed the House. I saw a good many members in Stanton's room at the Exchange Hotel. There was a young light-haired man acting for Stanton. He told members present it was an important road. Stanton had about four rooms at the Exchange Hotel and had about all the legislature down there. [His agent] would carry members out of the room, one at a time, down a gangway. He told me he would loan me $50. He handed me the money which I took and went home.

Condition of Affairs (Washington, 1872)

The lobbyists were not all men of the North. When a committee of businessmen asked Governor Warmoth to call a halt to corruption in Louisiana, he replied:

You charge the legislature with passing corruptly many bills looking to the personal aggrandizement of individuals and corporations. Those individuals and corporations are your very best people. For instance, this bank bill that is being lobbied through the legislature now. We have been able to defeat that bill twice and now it is up again to be passed. Who are doing it? Your bank presidents. The best people of the city of New Orleans are crowding the lobbies of the legislature, continually whispering into these men's ears bribes to pass this measure. How are we to defend the State against the interposition of these people, who are potent in their influence in this community?

Condition of Affairs (Washington, 1872)

In South Carolina, Matthew C. Butler and Martin Gary, who were leading the fight against Reconstruction, were members of both the railroad and bond rings. Congressmen who visited the state to investigate the Klan reported:

Even the old aristocratic class, to whom we have been taught to attribute sentiments of chivalric honor, have not scrupled to bribe officials. In the operations of the land commission, the vendors were generally old citizens of the planting class, who held more land than they could utilize, and the frauds committed in the sale of their lands were with their consent and to their advantage.

General M. C. Butler, who was the Democratic candidate for lieutenant governor in 1870, a major general of the rebel army, a large planter, and a leading citizen of high standing, stated under oath before the sub-committee, sitting in South Carolina, that if he had land to sell and could sell it by buying a State senator for $500 he would do so.

Condition of Affairs (Washington, 1872)

After a Democratic member of the legislature said that he saw nothing wrong in bribing an official and compared the transaction with buying a sheep, the congressmen speculated about the reasons for the decline in public morality:

[One] cause seems to be the contempt which the old property-holding class feel for the freedmen and all who cooperate with them politically. This gives to the bribery of such persons, in the eyes of the old native class, the semblance of the purchase of a slave.

Condition of Affairs (Washington, 1872)

Though corruption had become commonplace, some Reconstruction governments were honest and well run. Jonathan C. Gibbs who had an impeccable record as Florida's secretary of state defended his administration:

The present financial condition of Florida is not what the friends of order and progress desire, but it is by no means what it has been represented, either through carelessness or political animosities. The joint committee appointed by Congress to inquire into the condition of the late rebellious states, reports the State as having increased its debt $13,000,000 in four years of carpetbag rule, and its entire debt at $15,000,000. The fact is established beyond the shade of doubt by the last United States Census that the debt of Florida is a little over $2,000,000—$9,000,000 less than the Congressional Committee report of increase. The census shows that Florida ranks as the thirty-fifth state in respect to total indebtedness, and that Delaware and West Virginia alone have less than Florida.

If Cicero were living in our day he would probably burst forth with his indignant but sorrowful protest; "Oh, the times! Oh, the customs!" while we in good round Saxon exclaim, "Lord, how this world is given to lying!"

Jonathan C. Gibbs, "Education in the South" in
the Florida *Senate Journal,* 1874

A letter from Arkansas mocked the Conservatives' charges of misrule:

Little Rock, April 22, 1871

To the Editor:

Although our Southern brethren have descanted eloquently in reference to the corruption and extravagance of the "carpetbag and nigger governments," the half has not yet been told. Before the war our State government was managed with admirable economy. We started to construct a railroad from Little Rock to Memphis and pushed forward with such vim and determination that we completed forty-five miles in twenty years and up till the time of the advent of the carpetbaggers this was the only railroad in the State.

You have no idea how much money they squander on their public free school system. They are so silly and wicked as to take our taxes and squander them in establishing schools for niggers. Just think, Mr. Editor—$400,000 wasted on free schools. Why our State, before the war, got along charmingly and there was not a single free school in it. Here in one year, nearly half a million dollars wasted on schools which we Southern people might have had to spend in horse-racing, playing poker and drinking whiskey.

We tried to fix things so that our men in the legislature could stop the appropriation bill but the plan failed. You would really do us a great favor, Mr. Editor, if you would convince the Northern money men that these carpetbaggers are making such enormous debts that they never can be paid.

PULASKI

The New National Era, May 11, 1871

As Pulaski's reference to "Northern money men" implied, Democratic assaults on Reconstruction were actually adding to the costs of state government. In Mississippi, where fraud was at a minimum and there was only a negligible increase in the state debt, Thomas W. Cardozo explained:

Our State would not be owing a dime but for the warfare the Democrats make on everything we do. [They] do their best to depreciate our bonds within and outside our border. For example, about a year ago this city [Vicksburg] passed an ordinance authorizing an issuance of bonds to the amount of $400,000. A committee went to New York to sell them and were offered 82½ cents [per dollar] for the whole amount. But the day after their arrival the broker who was making arrangements to purchase the bonds received a letter from one of the most virulent Democrats of this city saying that the city would not be able to redeem the bonds and the taxpayers did not intend to pay their taxes to a Radical government. Of course the broker asked for further time and finally the highest we could get for the bonds was 75 cents. The money was needed for the improvement of the city and by this interference the city became the loser of 7½ cents [per dollar] on four hundred thousand dollars!

The New National Era, August 8, 1872

In the face of mounting criticism, black South Carolinians stepped up their efforts to reform. Disillusioned with Governor Scott and other northern-born officials, they backed Franklin J. Moses, a southern aristocrat, as the Republican candidate for governor, and Francis J. Cardozo for state treasurer. With support from the legislature, Cardozo sliced three million dollars from the state debt and effected numerous other economies. The work was uphill, however, for Moses proved to be even more dishonest and extravagant than his predecessor. In 1874, Robert B. Elliott returned from Washington to issue a solemn warning:

Fellow citizens, rights impose duties. We are not now, as once we were, without responsibility because without power, without duties because without rights. Are we so ignorant as to imagine that the world will not hold us to account for our use of these rights? Never was there a people on whom the eyes of the whole world were fixed with more interest than on the people of South Carolina. This proud state has been committed to our keeping. Our former masters have predicted that the Negro would fail; that he would be the victim of the unscrupulous white man and the slave of his own greed and dishonesty. The colored people of South Carolina are now on trial before the whole country.

Today the North doubts whether we can maintain decent government in South Carolina. Today our friends blush for us. It is not our errors and inexperience which threaten to ruin us; it is the disregard of public interests and the total lack of responsibility on the part of some of our public officers.

What we need, what we must have, is an awakening of all of the people to their duty. With one heart, one aim, one determination let us move forward to the reestablishment of an honest, economical and respectable government in South Carolina.

The New York *Times*, February 24, 1874

Speaking in Charleston two weeks later, A. J. Ransier criticized Elliott for giving ammunition to the enemy:

That things are not in a satisfactory condition in this State is too true. That it is possible to get along with lower rates of taxation by a more judicious expenditure of public funds and that we might have selected better men to fill our most important offices cannot be denied, but neither do reckless speeches made by Republicans against their own party help the situation. I am no apologist for thieves. On the contrary I am in favor of a most thorough investigation of the conduct of every public officer in connection with the discharge of whose duties there is anything like well-grounded suspicion. Still I believe that such is the determined opposition to the Republican party that no administration, however, honest, just and economical would satisfy the Democratic masses in South Carolina. It is not for us to deny those charges which may be proven true, while it is for us to deal in the confidence of a caucus and by other judicious means, without giving the Democrats weapons with which to beat out our brains.

The New National Era, March 26, 1874

Elliott's speech had been precipitated by a new Democratic effort to sway public opinion in the North. A Taxpayers' Convention organized by South Carolina's leading white men sent a delegation to Washington. Claiming that state taxes had increased twentyfold since the war, they appealed to the President and Congress for deliverance from "Negro misrule." Although the government could offer them no relief, the northern press responded with an outpouring of sympathy. The Associated Press wired the full text of the Taxpayers' memorial to Congress to newspapers across the country and even editors hitherto friendly to Reconstruction gave it front-page space. After all, high taxes were anathema to everyone—and racism which had been slumbering in the North in the first postwar years was far from dead.

Recognizing the effectiveness of the Taxpayers' propaganda, black spokesmen joined forces to reply. Their answer, drafted by F. L. Cardozo, nailed the lies in the Taxpayers' statement and,

Usually sympathetic to Reconstruction, Nast caricatures black lawmakers after Taxpayers' Convention launched its propaganda campaign (*Boston Public Library*)

with a wealth of facts and figures, documented the reasons for higher taxes. Although it was based on South Carolina's experience, the answer summarized the case for all the Reconstruction governments. The Associated Press refused to send it out over its wires; its circulation was limited to the black press. Similarly ignored by most historians, it is reprinted below with some abridgement:

To the Honorable Senate and House of Representatives of the United States:

Certain citizens of South Carolina, styling themselves "The Taxpayers' Convention," have memorialized your honorable bodies to grant them relief from unjust burdens and oppressions, alleged by them to have been imposed by the Republican State Government. We, the undersigned, members of the State Central Committee of the Union Republican party of South Carolina, beg leave to submit the following counter statement and reply:

The statement that "the annual expenses of the government have advanced from four hundred thousand dollars before the war to two millions and a half at the present time," is entirely incorrect, and the items of expenditures given to illustrate and prove this statement are wholly inaccurate and untrue, and skillfully selected to deceive.

We present a true statement of the appropriation of the fiscal year before the war, beginning October 1, 1859, and ending September 30, 1860, and the fiscal year beginning November 1, 1872, and ending October 31, 1873:

	1859–60	1872–73
Salaries	$81,100	$194,989
Contingents	73,000	47,600
Free schools	75,000	300,000
State Normal School	8,704	25,000
Deaf, dumb and blind	8,000	16,000
Military academies	30,000	. . . .
Military contingencies	100,000	20,000
Roper Hospital	3,000	. . . .
State Lunatic Asylum	. . . .	77,500
State Normal and High School	5,000	. . . .
Jurors and Constables	50,000	. . . .
State Orphan House (colored)	. . . .	20,000
State Penitentiary	. . . .	40,000
Sundries	184,427	444,787
	$618,231	$1,184,876

By the census of 1860, there were in South Carolina at that time 301,214 free population and 402,406 slaves. By the census of 1870 there were 705,606 free population. In 1860, the slave was no charge on the State Government, save when he was hung for some petty misdemeanor, and the State compelled to pay his loss.

It would be, therefore, but just and fair to divide the amount appropriated in 1859–60: $618,231 by the then free population, 301,214, and it will be found that the cost of governing each citizen was $2.05. Then divide the amount appropriated in 1872–73 by the free population now 705,-606, and the cost of governing each citizen is $1.67–$2.05 during the boasted Democratic period and $1.67 under the so-called corrupt Radical rule—a difference of 38 cents *per capita* in favor of the latter. So that if the Democrats had the same number of free citizens to govern in 1859–60 that the Republicans had in 1872–73, it would have cost them $264,616 more than it has cost us.

The State organized upon a free basis necessarily created a larger number of officers, and, therefore, a larger amount of salaries. We are not ashamed of the fact that our appropriation for schools in 1872–73 is four times greater than in 1859–60. Ignorance was the corner-stone of slavery and essential to its perpetuity. Now in every hamlet and village in our state, the schoolmaster is abroad. In 1857 the number of scholars attending the free schools was only 19,356 while in 1873 the number of scholars attending the schools was 85,-753.

There were no appropriations for the State Lunatic Asylum and Penitentiary in 1859–60. The Lunatic Asylum was then supported by the friends of its wealthy inmates, but in 1872–73 the State assumed its support and made liberal appropriation for its unfortunate patients. The erection of the Penitentiary was not begun until after the war and there was therefore no appropriation for it in 1859–60.

The appropriation in 1872–73 for military purposes was but $20,000. We had no occasion to appropriate $130,000 for military academies and contingencies in order to train the young to strike at the nation's life, and to purchase material for the war of secession.

There was no appropriation in 1859–60 for a colored State Orphan Home. The colored orphans that were then uncared for were free, but their parents, when living, were heavily taxed to support white orphans, while their own children, after their death, were neglected.

The statement that "it has been openly avowed by prominent members of the Legislature that taxes should be increased to a point which will compel the sale of the great body of the land and take it away from the former owners" is not correct. It is, however, a fact that the present system of taxation, like that of almost all civilized countries is based chiefly upon real estate. In the days of slavery it was not so. Taxes were levied by the large planters who absolutely controlled the State, upon trades, professions, free colored, a mere nominal *per capita* tax upon slaves and upon the lands assessed at one-tenth their true value. This method of taxing lands enabled the planters to acquire and retain large and uncultivated tracts of land, and thus form that most dangerous of all oligarchies—a landed aristocracy.

It is from this class that secession and the war sprung. Our present method of taxation very naturally and properly prevents the perpetuation of this system.

The statement that "the appropriations made in one year for the printing done amounted to $475,000" is wholly incorrect. These appropriations though made in one year, are for work ordered and performed during a period of three years. It is stated that total appropriations for public printing made by the Legislature for a period of sixty years from 1800 to 1859 is $271,180. This statement is not correct, but even if it were is it a cause for boastfulness that but that amount was expended for printing and the people were kept in ignorance and no public information disseminated amongst them? We think not.

It is stated that "the committees have received large sums as compensation for reporting favorably on private bids." Whatever corruption may exist in the Legislature is to be attributed to the Democrats as well as the Republicans. They never hesitate to offer bribes when they have a bill to pass. Corruption existed long before the advent of the Republican party of this State into power, only it was carried on then with the artistic skill of more experienced operators and not easily seen.

The gentlemen who have assembled, constituting themselves representatives of the so-called taxpayers, are not what they would have the country believe. They are the prominent politicians of the old regime—the former ruling element of the State—who simply desire to regain the power they lost by their folly of secession.

The Republicans admit the existence of evils among them. They have committed errors which they deeply regret. But those errors are being daily corrected. There are enough able and good men among those who have the present charge of the government to right every existing wrong. They are determined to do so. The difficulties under which they have labored have been increased ten-fold by the hostility and opposition of the Democratic party ever since Reconstruction. This is their third effort to regain power. First they expected it through the election of Seymour and Blair; second, through the midnight murders and assassinations of Ku Kluxism; and now, thirdly, by the distortion and misrepresentation of facts, in order to create a public sentiment in their favor and obtain relief from Congress.

Relying upon the justice of our cause we submit these facts to your impartial judgment.

Samuel J. Lee, Chairman, *pro tem*, S. A. Swails,
W. M. Thomas, Joseph Crews, H. H. Ellison,
P. R. Rivers, John R. Cochran, Robert Smalls,
E. W. M. Mackey, John Lee, H. L. Shrewsbury,
George F. McIntyre, Wilson Cook, John H. McDevitt

The New National Era, April 16, 1874

The Reconstructionists continued to rid southern state governments of grafters and thieves, to no avail. What their enemies wanted was not a clean house but a clean sweep of black electoral and legislative power and the restoration of the lily-white rule which had prevailed before the war.

---

4. It Was the Most Violent Time That Ever We Have Seen

By 1873, murders were on the rise again in the South. Sometimes the violence was senseless, inspired solely by race hatred:

Memphis, August 8—Last Monday a Negro named Dan Calhoun who had been digging a well near Brighton station lay down to sleep near his work. While sleeping he was discovered by three white men who, thinking to have some fun, poured the contents of a bottle of turpentine on Calhoun's clothes and set them on fire. Calhoun, awakening and finding himself enveloped in flames, ran shrieking for help and was so badly burned that he died next day. Negroes in the neighborhood in vain attempted to have warrants issued for the arrest of the perpetrators of the crime. The Negroes in armed squads scoured the woods in search of them and becoming enraged, threatened other citizens, but were quieted by Sheriff Locke.

The New National Era and Citizen, August 14, 1873

More often the victims were men who were attempting to assert their rights. Alabama tenant farmers appealed to the governor:

Montgomery, Alabama, August 21, 1874
To His Excellency David F. Lewis, Governor of Alabama
Sir:
The undersigned, colored citizens of Choctaw county, desire to call your attention to the condition of affairs in said

county. A meeting of colored men was called at the house of Edmond Turner, one of the undersigned, about three weeks ago, for the purpose of selecting delegates to represent the Republicans of Choctaw county in the state convention. The white people, learning this, at once assumed an attitude of hostility to us and our families. Caleb Williams, a white farmer, and previous to the war a large slaveowner, rode near the premises of the undersigned and threatened us with death in the event that we took any part in the contest. Colored men have been assaulted, threatened, driven from their homes simply because they had expressed their desire to support Republican candidates. At the present time, not less than ten able-bodied colored men are seeking protection in the swamps of the Tombigbee river, their lives having been threatened, because they participated in the meeting above referred to.

At different times during the past three weeks, divers white men, residents of Mt. Sterling and vicinity, have rode through the neighborhood, disarming all colored men of guns, pistols and ammunition, giving as an excuse that they feared insurrection on our part. Our property has been shamelessly destroyed and it is common for white men on hunting excursions to feed their horses on our growing crops. Jack Turner, one of the undersigned, was notified that he must never "show his face in Choctaw county again."

The present condition of affairs in Choctaw county is almost unparallelled in the history of wrong and oppression. The colored people are in such a state of fear that life itself is almost insupportable. We cannot have our churches, our schools, nor any social intercourse with each other, unless watched and insulted by white men. We are not permitted to own guns to protect our premises from intruders, nor our crops from destruction by beasts and birds.

We are aware that Your Excellency is powerless to render us protection such as we need, but having been faithful sup-

Blacks gather their dead and wounded after White
League attack (*Boston Public Library*)

porters of your administration, we trust that your Excellency
will use your great influence to secure us, at least, in the enjoyment of our rights of life and property.

Edmond Turner

Jackson Turner

Alabama Department of Archives and History

By the end of 1874, Alabama, Arkansas and Texas were in the
Democratic column and the struggle to take over the remaining
Reconstruction governments was in high gear. Members of a newly
formed White League in Louisiana imported guns and cannon from
neighboring states to build a military force. During an early
skirmish, two hundred black men were killed:

The butchery seems to have been prosecuted in the most shocking manner, men with their great knives stabbing and cutting right and left, walking upon the dead and with the stocks of their guns beating out the brains of those that were not yet dead. Who can imagine the depths of the malice that is still in the breasts of these people?

Says one of the assailants at the massacre: "We shan't have no more trouble with the niggers in Grant Parish. When as clean a job is made in every parish in the State we shall begin to have some quiet and niggers will know their place."

The New National Era, May 29, 1873

In September 1874, a White League army fought a pitched battle against the state militia in the streets of New Orleans. They took over the city for five days until federal troops arrived to put down the rebellion. Before the battle of New Orleans, League members distributed a bilingual leaflet calling for a boycott of black workers:

LOUISIANAIS!
POUR SAUVER VOTRE PATRIE IL FAUT RENVOYER LES NEGRES.
(Par la faim 'animal le plus feroce est dompté.)
LOUISIANANS!
TO SAVE YOUR COUNTRY DO NOT EMPLOY THE NEGRO.
(Wild beast can only be tamed by hunger.)

The New National Era, August 20, 1874

During the elections that fall, White Leaguers came to the polls in force. Henry Adams who was then an election supervisor in the parish of Caddo said:

The whites told all the colored men, "If you don't vote our way you had better not go home for we are going to kill every damn nigger that votes the radical ticket today." A great many colored men left the polls. Several white men had large revolvers and told the colored men they had to vote their way or die. So all that voted, voted the Democratic ticket, but seventeen colored men who voted Republican. Of them who had any crops it was taken away from them, and a great many of them was run away.

Senate Report No. 693, 46th Congress, 2nd Session

"How was it," a senator asked, "that where there were five or six colored people to one white man, the white people could bulldoze the Negro and prevent him from voting?" Adams explained:

They raise a little disturbance with some of the colored people. They come to a place where there is a kind of little gathering. One will take a drink—he don't drink enough to get drunk—then comes out and commences to meddle with one of the colored men. Maybe the colored man will say something sort of rash like. If he does, [the white] will haul out a revolver and strike him and maybe, perhaps, shoot him. As soon as [the whites] hear that firing, many come with guns and revolvers, and the first colored man they see, they beat him or shoot him. Then a passel of them will commence firing on them colored men who haven't got anything to fight with. Now, if one of them colored men will show fight, if he hurts one of them, his life ain't no more than a chicken's. He may go home but he won't stay for a passel will come after him that night.

Q—Suppose the colored men should resist these attacks; what would be the result?

A—Well, if the colored people think of showing any resistance, they ain't going to come up boldly and fight.

Q—Who ain't?

A—The white men ain't. If they think the colored men are prepared to fight, they ain't going to attack them. But one kind of peaceable man amongst our people will say, "Don't have a fuss. It shan't come to no riot and we want you all to be quiet." If there is any leader of that kind, they don't defend themselves. But the white men will go around to this softhearted one who don't care for our race and will find out from him about who would have done something. The first thing they know here will come one or two white men in a field on the plantation and they will take them and arrest them. Then they will go to another plantation and another and get them all arrested. And maybe they will come to the jail in a little while and turn them loose. They go and a crowd catches them. They kill them in the woods. You never hear of them after that.

Q—Why do not the colored people arm themselves? Cannot they get arms?

A—They can buy arms if they have the money, till the riot come. If there is a riot started, [the whites] go down by fifties and hundreds in a gang to watch us to see whether the colored men were going to buy arms. At the time a riot is going on, the colored men cannot buy no ammunition.

If the colored men are attacked, they call it a riot, because they are killing the colored men. You never hear of the colored man raising the riot, because he never gets the chance. If he shoots at a white man they kill fifty colored men for the one white man that was shot.

Senate Report No. 693, 46th Congress, 2nd Session

Provoking a riot became a fine art in Mississippi in 1875 when the Conservatives adopted a "Shotgun Plan" with the slogan,

"Shall we call home our troops?" the cartoon asks. Sign carried by white Southerner says "We intend to beat the Negro in the battle of life and defeat means one thing—EXTERMINATION" (*Boston Public Library*)

"Carry the election peaceably if we can, forcibly if we must." With a team of ex-Confederate generals at the helm, thousands of young white men were organized into cavalry and artillery companies. Equipped with the latest in repeating rifles, they drilled in the town squares and rode through the countryside threatening blacks and their white allies. Democratic clubs kept "dead books" in which they ostentatiously wrote the names of Republican leaders.

They shot off cannon at Republican rallies, demanding time for their own speakers and heckling their opponents. And they deliberately provoked riots which escalated into shooting wars.

Coahoma County, a Republican-controlled county across the Mississippi River from Arkansas, was a peaceful farming area with little crime and no violence. In the fall of 1875, its black sheriff, John M. Brown, was running for re-election. When a Republican meeting was scheduled for Friar's Point, the Democrats got busy. Brown said:

I was informed that the Democrats had the names of all the leading Republicans on their dead list and when we met they were to hang or shoot us. I knew of two hundred colored men who were to come in from the country to attend the meeting and I knew that they might, some of them, bring arms. I sent word to them not to come. The white people sent them word that I was going to be hung the next day at 12 o'clock.

That night the white men took charge of Friar's Point. One of these men at the head of the crowd came from Helena [Arkansas] with two hundred guns that were brought down in a skiff. The next morning I saw a great many strange people in town. Our board of supervisors called me to come down as colored men were coming in and they were going to have a fight.

I looked off to the left and saw two hundred coming in with guns, some on horses. There were two hundred and fifty or three hundred white men, all drawn up in a line, with their coats off and armed to the teeth. I said, "I will quiet this thing." They shoved me forward and I went down to the colored men. They said they didn't want any fighting but they thought they had a right to come to a public meeting. I went to General Chalmers [a leading Democrat] and said that I would deputize a hundred colored and a hundred white citizens to keep the peace. He said for me to take the colored men off a little farther away and they would not be shot at. I took them across the bridge and then I went back to General Chalmers to get the white men to go home. As soon as I got within seventy-five yards of them, I saw the white men coming. Pretty soon I heard shotguns going off all around me.

They fired for a while and then I said to the colored men to go put up their guns and that I would see General Chalmers and get the whites to leave. But he went around and urged them on. That night, hearing that re-enforcements were coming, I went off to the next county to telegraph to Governor Ames.

The colored men scattered all over the county, followed by white men. They captured Monroe Lewis and tied a rope around his neck. They had him say his prayers and they discharged two barrels of a shotgun through him. They went to Black's Bayou and found William Alcorn and took him out and killed him. A hundred men came in by Coldwater and had their cooking done by Charles Green. After cooking for them all night he was tired and was lying down. One of the men said that he must try his gun out and shot this old man.

Q—About how many colored people were coming in that day?

A—Not more than two hundred and fifty. I sent to stop them but they were excited and came on.

Q—How many came in from other counties to assist the whites?

A—Four hundred and eight came from Hopson's, one hundred and seventy-five from Cold Water, one hundred from Panola and Tunica counties and some from Arkansas. There must have been one thousand to fifteen hundred from different parts of the state. For some two or three weeks afterwards they were riding through the county.

Q—Were the colored people generally armed?

A—No, sir, they were not. Only a few had old squirrel guns, inferior guns of no account in a fight. There was not a Winchester rifle, nor a Henry rifle nor any other first-class weapon in the hands of the colored men. I had one Henry rifle. I thought I was justified in having that because I was sheriff.

They were fixing for the riot. I was told—white Democrats told me—three months before the riot, that one was coming.

Senate Report No. 693, 46th Congress, 2nd Session

A riot at Clinton also began with a Republican meeting. Eugene B. Welborne, a prosperous black farmer and state representative, told how it started. His statement, and the statements and letters that follow, except where otherwise noted, come from the *Report of the Select Committee to Inquire into the Mississippi Election of 1875*, Senate Report No. 527, 44th Congress, 1st Session.

They had a barbecue and there were speakers invited. It was a kind of joint discussion. Amos R. Johnston [a Democrat] spoke first. After he got through Capt. H. T. Fisher, who was a Republican, was called upon to speak. There were a couple of young fellows standing in front of me— Sivley and Thompson. These gentlemen were a committee sent from Raymond. In the event that the Republican speakers told anything that they thought was not so, they had a right to contradict them. Captain Fisher had spoke two or three minutes when this Sivley says, "Come down out of there, you God damned radical, you. We don't want to hear any more of your lies."

I spoke to Aleck Wilson who was one of our officers there to keep the peace. We had about thirty men that we got the magistrate to deputize. I saw Wilson and said, "I want you to stand here and prevent anything. I see a difficulty brewing." Thompson had a bottle of whisky in his hand. He was drinking, and every now and then they would holler, "Come down! Stop your damned lying there, and come down."

Wilson went up to Mr. Thompson and said, "Mr. Thompson, we listened very quietly to your speaker and you must not go on in that way." He told him he was an officer and that he would have to arrest him if he did not stop. When Wilson said that, they all got right together around Thompson. He said, "Get away from here." Then Wilson attempted to arrest him and Thompson pulled his pistol out and shot him down. When Wilson fell, every [white] man in the line pulled out their pistols and began to fire on the crowd.

On Sunday—that was on Saturday—they just hunted the whole county clean out. Every man they could see they were shooting at him just the same as birds. I mean colored men, of course. A good many they killed and a good many got away. The men came into Jackson, two or three thousand of them. They were running in all day Sunday, coming in as rapidly as they could. We could hear the firing all the time.

In the months before the election, hundreds of black citizens asked Governor Adelbert Ames for protection:

Macon, Mississippi, August 26, 1875

To Hon. Governor Ames:

The county is now in a uproar. The Alabama white people was here on the 25 of August killing up black peoples. Governor, you have stop the Ku Klux one time and, governor, you will have to do it over again for the poor black peoples is laying out into the woods, 'feard to come home. Yesterday there was about 35 or 40 whites came from Louisville with arms for to kill we poor darkies. We poor black

peoples have not got any arms, but governor, I know you
haves it into your power [to] stop the whites from killing
we poor blacks, or you haves it into your power furnish us
arms.

E. C. Walker, Sr.

Vicksburg, Mississippi, September 8, 1875

To Excellency Gov. Ames:

The rebels turbulent; are aiming today to go to Satartia
to murder more poor Negroes. Gov. ain't there no protection? This Confederate military all over the State are better
prepared now for fighting than they was before the war.
They intend to hang you, or get some secret scoundrel to
kill you. We heard that the Vicksburg bandits offered $10,-
000 to any body of men if they would kill you. Gov., they
say we Rads shan't have no meeting, nor hold no election.

WE COLORED CITIZENS

The rebs are riding all through this county now, at night,
taking arms from the colored folk daring to ever leave home.

Bolton, October 13, 1875

Gov. Ames:

I am here in Jackson and cannot leave. The white peoples
is looking for me on every train and have got men on every
road watching for me. They have sworn to take my life because I am president of the club at Bolton. I wish you would,
if please, protect me. I am in a bad fix, with about 6 bales of
cotton in the field and 150 bushel of corn to gather; no one
to tend to it when I am gone. Tell me what to do, if you
please.

Lewis McGee, President of Bolton's Republican Club

The governor responded with an appeal to President Grant for federal troops. Only a year earlier, Grant had sent soldiers to Louisiana, but now the mood of the country had changed. The Conservatives' charges of graft and extravagance had had their effect. In addition, there was a growing interest in investing northern money in southern business. The nation's commitment to the rights of black people was becoming a profitless burden. The President turned down Ames's request, replying through his attorney general, "The whole public are tired out with these annual autumnal outbreaks in the South."

In desperation, Ames then decided to enroll and equip a state militia. Seven companies were formed, five black and two white. The first to be mustered in, composed largely of refugees from Clinton, was captained by state senator Charles Caldwell, with Eugene Welborne as first lieutenant. An ex-slave who made his living as a blacksmith, Caldwell was described by his white contemporaries as "daring and desperate." T. W. Cardozo found him "robust and genial":

He was a member of the Constitutional Convention, took an active part in the reconstruction of the state, was elected senator in 1869. He is brown in complexion with loose hair, wears a mustache which is about as well cultivated as cotton is in Yankee country, but has a peculiarly welcome smile in greeting you.

The New National Era, February 20, 1873

Caldwell's company performed one mission, marching through "enemy" territory with flags flying and drums beating, to deliver arms to a militia company at Edwards' Depot. They returned safely with two hundred new recruits, but theirs was the only action by Mississippi's black militia. Alarmed by Conservative threats and letters like the following, Ames signed a "Peace Agreement" with the Democrats.

Vicksburg, October 13, 1875

Governor Ames:

Dear Sir:

Ever since Sat. the Democrat party has been like roaring lions. They have sworn to not let us colored militia organize in this city and have been going with their guns—going round the halls to see if any of them are gathered together, to break them up and making their threats what they intend to do with the governor; that if he sends Chas. Caldwell to Vicksburg with guns to arm the Negroes, that he will never get there. An extra train leaving here in the morning [with] the leading tigers of this city [is] going to make Governor Ames call in them arms and disband that Negro militia.

[Unsigned]

The "Peace Agreement" required the governor to disband the militia; in return the Democrats promised a fair and peaceful election. The militiamen reluctantly turned in their arms but the riots and assaults multiplied. In every county, black candidates for office were threatened, shot, forced to resign:

Richard Gray was running for treasurer of Noxubee County:

We had a meeting. Dr. Algood spoke and then I spoke. While speaking they commenced shooting off in the air and cursing. I saw the meeting was about to be broken up and we all just quit and went away. There was a big crowd in the street hallooing, jeering and talking about killing Dr. Algood. I walked up in the middle of the street but did not open my mouth to anybody. All at once an old gentleman by the name of Mattison came up. He was an old man, pretty gray. He said I had insulted him, and I said, "Never in my life. We have been friends, I think." He slapped me and just then a young man named Pierce walked right up and fired on me. He shot me and I fell.

I had never had any cross words and this gentleman had always seemed friendly. I had been a barber there for twenty-odd years, never had any fuss with any of them. I do not know why he did it, only I suppose it was a political affair.

George Glenn was candidate for justice of peace in Madison County:

Mr. Tom Tucker came up to me. He says, "I will give you 32½ cents for your chance."

I said, "No, sir, not for $10,000. As the people have placed confidence in me I am going to run until I am beat."

He says, "You will be beat anyhow, because if you get it you are a dead man and if you don't get it you are a dead man."

I says, "All right; I am going to run anyhow."

He said, "A rope will pull your neck after this campaign."

About midnight a friend of mine ran into my room and waked me up and said, "They are after you." I ran out in my drawers and undershirt into a cottonpatch about a mile from the house. They came and fired—we could see them—they fired and fired into the house. As they were going off I heard them say, "We haven't got him now, but we will get him."

Former state senator Robert Gleeds was running for sheriff of Lowndes County:

In the latter part of the canvas the young men had a cannon and pistols, very much like an army. The election was wound up on the 2nd of November and on the night before in our city, three buildings were set on fire and four men killed. Most of the colored people were run out of their houses during the night. It was the worst time we have ever had as far as an election was concerned.

The first fire broke out near my house. I went to work to get my family and as many of my things out as I could. Then a young man came to me and said, "They will kill you when this fire burns low." The next morning a man told me that he did not think it would be safe to go back and I went out in the country and staid until Saturday after the election. Prior to the election we had a meeting at the courthouse. Dr. Lipscomb and Judge Simms, the candidate on the Democratic side were invited to speak and I had a few words to say myself. I asked, "What could we do? Was there any concession we could make that would secure peace and a quiet election?" [Dr. Lipscomb] said the way we could have it was by abstaining from voting altogether. Of course I couldn't concede that for others but I was willing to forego any sacrifice as far as I was individually concerned. I told him we used to ask for life and liberty but now if we could just be spared our lives so we could go peacefully along as men and human beings we would be satisfied.

He said there was no danger to our lives and he criticized me very severely for saying as reported in the Declaration, that we were entitled to life, liberty and the pursuit of happiness.

It was the most violent time that ever we have seen.

Four days before the election, Charles Caldwell wrote to the governor:

"EVERY THING POINTS TO A DEMOCRATIC VICTORY THIS FALL."—SOUTHERN PAPERS.

Black voter holding Republican ticket faces armed election official (*Boston Public Library*)

The intimidation and threatening of colored voters continues uninterrupted and with as much system, determined purpose and combination of effort as if it were a legitimate means of canvassing. The peace agreement is held in utter contempt and only serves as a cover for perpetrating the very wrongs it was intended to prevent. In behalf of the people I represent I appeal to your Excellency for the protection which the laws of the State guarantee to every citizen regardless of party or race.

Without a state militia or federal troops, Ames had no way to enforce the laws. The violence continued. J. L. Edmonds, a school teacher, reported from Clay County:

Where we appointed a meeting [the Democrats] would go there and speak as they pleased. They would take a cannon and load it up with chains and leave it with the mouth pointing toward the crowd of colored people. When they fired they had nothing in it more than powder, but when they were going to speak they would have it turned around and chains hanging around it.

They had a parade at West Point. I was standing on the corner talking and some other colored men came up, and a colored man says, "I do not care how many are riding around, I am a Republican and expect to vote the ticket." Just then a man walked up with a pistol and shot him. Pretty soon another colored man made some expression and he was shot at.

They had flags—red, white and crimson flags. The whole street was covered. You could not hear your ears hardly for the flags waving and flapping over your head. They had one United States [flag] at the courthouse but most of the flags were just the old Confederate flags.

They said they were going to beat at this election. They said that at the meetings, on the stumps and at the schoolhouses around the county. They said they would carry the county or kill every nigger. They would carry it if they had to wade in blood.

W. H. Bell, a lawyer, was an election registrar in Hinds County:

On the day of the election I went to the courthouse. There were, I suppose, about 400 colored men standing around. I noticed all around town armed white men. Some had Winchester rifles slung upon their backs. Everybody had a navy six. Most of the colored men went armed that were able to get them. That is they had a pistol—small-arms. It is a habit of the people there mostly to go armed.

Q—What proportion of them had pistols?

A—There was not, I suppose, more than about three out of every twenty who were able to have pistols. The colored people, after making a crop, are generally not able to have anything left. They are unable to get anything—hardly food.

We went into the courthouse to hold the election. As registrars we had charge of one of the boxes there. In the hall there were several white men who acted as challengers, allowing the voters to come in. They admitted just such men as they pleased and I as registrar could not object to anything. The colored men entered and many of them were rejected.

After about two hours I went out the back door of the courthouse and saw a colored man there that I knew, by the name of Tears, who was an overseer of the poor. He had a Democratic badge on. I said to him, "Mr. Tears, what does this mean that you have a Democratic badge on and a Democratic ticket in your hand?" He said, "Mr. Bell, I am obliged to do it. I am as good a Republican as you are, but I am obliged to vote this ticket."

Well, the night after the election, we were not done making up the returns. We went into the courthouse. I was the only colored man there. About 11 o'clock a young man came in armed with a 16-shooter strung upon his back and a navy six by his side and in his hand a bottle of whiskey. Well, now, I must confess, though not a coward, that I felt some intimidation, so much so that I left the board of registration in charge of the Democratic registrar and never returned.

Eugene Welborne described Clinton on Election Day:

We could hear in the morning, the cannons commencing to shoot in every direction, just a firing. You could see men with their sixteen-shooters buckled on them charging all through the country. They went in squads.

One crowd would come in from Raymond and say, "One hundred and fifty niggers killed in Raymond; one white man slightly wounded." The guns were firing continually. Word came from Jackson, "The white men have whipped the niggers and run them out."

We did not know what in the world to do. Senator Caldwell was there and I said, "Senator, I think we might just as well give up. We can't do anything here. These men are riding all about the county with their sixteen-shooters." He says, "No. We are going to stay right here. I don't care what they say to you, don't you say a word." We voted as rapidly as we could.

Our votes were pretty strong all day and we would have polled our usual vote, even with all the intimidation, if they would have let us. But our Republicans that were appointed by the board of registration were told that it would not be healthy for them to serve and they made the whole thing Democratic. So when a Republican would come in to vote this fellow looked on the book and said, "I cannot find your name here. Stand aside." They turned off 80 Republicans, one after the other, that way.

I saw Senator Caldwell standing at the door. Said I, "What are you going to do about these registration papers?" "I think," says he, "we will go in and see these fellows." So we went in and spoke to one of the officers. When Mr. Caldwell said, "I know that this man's name was on that book," they said it didn't make any difference what he knew, that he was not going to vote.

The Democrats won, of course. In Coahoma County, where thirteen hundred Republicans had voted two years earlier, only two hundred and thirty Republican votes were counted. In Yazoo County, where there had been twenty-five hundred Republican votes, only seven were counted. In some other heavily black areas, the votes for Republican candidates ranged from twelve, to two, to none. For days after the election, frustrated voters asked the governor for a recount:

Macon, Mississippi, November 3, 1875

Governor Ames:

Here is about 25,000 Radicals of we colored population never got to cast a vote and we all wants to have this election over. The Democrats work it so all the Democrats could vote and would not let we Radicals vote. Robert Patty got elected for chancery clerk and we all don't want him.

The Democrats shoots their big guns and we colored people daren't to beat a drum, and if we beat it they comes up and cuts the head out of it. We wish to have peace, but we can't live at this rate. Here is two precincts that have never cast a vote on account of the ballot box not be open. All are anxious for that election to be held over. The Democrats are imposing on us, trying to [defraud] us out of our rights, which rights was revolved to us by the will of God and the assistance of the Republican party. But it seems the Democrats wants to drive us [as] the wind drives the clouds before it.

WE COLORED REPUBLICANS

Macon, Mississippi, November 5, 1875

Dear Sir:

Five thousand colored people in this county dissatisfied with the result of the election. They want to know if the Government is going to protect them in their liberty. If not, will the Government put them on the block and sell them to the highest bidder, and let the proceeds go toward paying off the national debt?

W. M. Connor

In sharp contrast to these was a letter from Hiram R. Revels to President Grant. Revels, who had been removed from the presidency of Alcorn College by Governor Ames, supported the Democrats during the 1875 campaign. The following year, Mississippi's Democratic governor named him president again. His letter, excerpted below, was used by Conservatives to convince the nation that all was well in Mississippi. It is one of the few pieces of correspondence from black men which has been reprinted in histories of Reconstruction.

Holly Springs, Mississippi, November 6, 1875

To His Excellency, U. S. Grant,

President of the United States:

Since Reconstruction, the masses of my people have been enslaved in mind by unprincipled adventurers who were willing to stoop to anything to secure power. My people are naturally Republicans, but as they grow older in freedom so do they in wisdom. A great portion of them have learned that they were being used as mere tools and, as in the late election, they determined, by casting their ballots against these unprincipled adventurers, to overthrow them.

The great mass of the white people today accept as a fact that all men are born free and equal and I believe are ready to guarantee to my people every right and privilege guaranteed to an American citizen. The bitterness and hate created by the late civil strife has, in my opinion, been obliterated in this state, except perhaps in some localities. If the state administration had appointed only honest and competent men to office and sought to restore confidence between the races, bloodshed would have been unknown, peace would have prevailed, Federal interference been unthought of, harmony, friendship and mutual confidence would have taken the place of the bayonet.

H. R. Revels

James W. Garner, *Reconstruction in Mississippi* (Macmillan, 1901)

The Democrats had won, but their victory was not yet total. Though they had captured all of the state cabinet posts, John R. Lynch had been re-elected to Congress and almost a third of the counties were still Republican-controlled. All that fall, the terrorism continued. W. H. Bell who had been practicing law in Clinton was one of many black men who was driven from the state:

I got on the train at 3 o'clock at night with my family. When we got to Canton a big rough white man got on and began to rush up and down the car with a bottle of whisky, asking friends to drink. Several young fellows got on between Clinton and Holly Springs. My wife was sitting near the door and these young fellows were standing in the aisle right near her and this big fellow was running up and down the car insulting everybody in there mostly that was colored.

I whispered to my wife, "I believe these men are going to assassinate me." She said, "I am under that impression myself. Suppose you get off at the next station and pretend that you want to get something and stay off."

I got off at a little place called Michigan City, but they all got down on the platform and watched me. I had given my wife her ticket and told her to wait in Louisville, Kentucky, to go to a colored friend there and I would meet her there. The whistle blew and I ran as if to get on the car. I jumped on the palace sleeping-car behind. I swung on and called the porter and, says I, "There is some men in that car that seem to be wanting to attack me. I want to get off within two miles of the next station." Said he, "When the whistle blows, get off. I'm satisfied that there is going to be trouble." Said I, "Take charge of my wife when she gets to Louisville." I knew him well; he was from Louisville himself.

I got within two miles of Grand Junction—there was a little cabin of colored people—I jumped off the car while it was going at full speed and went up to these colored people's house and staid until about three o'clock the next morning. When the cars came along, I jumped on and went to Louisville and met my wife.

Bell's neighbor, Charles Caldwell, did not escape. On Christmas night, 1875, he walked downtown after dinner. An acquaintance invited him to have a drink. Margaret Ann Caldwell told what happened:

My husband told him no, he didn't want any Christmas. He said, "You must take a drink with me." He took him by the arm and told him to drink for a Christmas treat, and carried him into Chilton's cellar. They jingled the glasses and at the tap of the glasses somebody shot from outside of the gate window, and he fell to the ground. As they struck their glasses, that was the signal to shoot.

When he was first shot, he called for Preacher Nelson. Charles said, "take me out of the cellar," that he wanted to die in the open air and not like a dog closed up. Nelson carried him to the middle of the street. Whether he stood up right there in the street while they riddled him with thirty or forty of their loads I do not know, but they shot him all that many times. All those balls went in him.

He asked them to let him see me. They told him no and he then said, taking both sides of his coat and bringing them up so, "Remember when you kill me you kill a gentleman and a brave man. Never say you killed a coward. I want you to remember it when I am gone."

Some said they killed him because he carried the militia to Edwards. The time the guns were sent there, he was Captain under Governor Ames. They said they killed him for that.

They shot Sam, his brother, when he was coming in from the country. They shot him for fear he would go out of town

"The Target" (*Boston Public Library*)

and bring in people and raise a fuss. The bodies were brought to my house.

At one o'clock the train came from Vicksburg with the "Modocs" [an armed band of whites who took their name from the Modoc Indians]. They all marched up to my house and went into where the dead bodies laid, and they cursed them, those dead bodies, and they danced and threw open the window and sung all their songs, and challenged the dead body to get up and meet them. They carried on like a parcel of wild Indians over those dead bodies. They carried on all that in my presence, danced and sung and done anything they could. I heard them curse and challenge them to get up and fight.

5. We Lost All Hopes

When John R. Lynch went to Washington to take his seat in Congress, he asked President Grant why he had refused Ames's request for federal troops:

The President said he had sent Governor Ames's requisition to the War Department with instructions to have the necessary assistance furnished without delay. He had also given instructions to the Attorney-General to use the marshals and the machinery of the Federal judiciary to insure a peaceable and fair election. But before the orders were put into execution a committee of prominent Republicans from Ohio had called on him. An important election was pending in that State. This committee, the President said, informed him in a most emphatic way that if the requisition of Governor Ames were honored, the Democrats would not only carry Mississippi—a State which would be lost to the Republicans in any event—but that Democratic success in Ohio would be assured. If the requisition were not honored Ohio would be saved to the Republicans.

The President assured me that it was with great reluctance that he yielded—against his own judgment and sense of official duty—to this committee, and directed the withdrawal of the orders which had been given the Secretary of War and the Attorney-General.

"Yes," said the President. "I should not have yielded. But it was duty on one side and party obligation on the other. I hesitated but yielded to party obligation. If a mistake was made, it was one of the head and not of the heart. That my heart was right and my intentions good, no one who knows me will question. But I was satisfied that Mississippi could not have been saved to the party in any event and I wanted to avoid the responsibility of the loss of Ohio, in addition."

John R. Lynch, *The Facts of Reconstruction* (New York, 1913)

President Grant's "mistake of the head and not of the heart" left only South Carolina, Louisiana and Florida with Reconstruction governments. Using the "Mississippi Plan" as a model, the Conservatives moved decisively to capture these states. On July 4, 1876, the nation's eyes were on the Centennial Exposition in Philadelphia. In honor of the one-hundredth anniversary of American independence, the world of the future was on display. Visitors who came to marvel at Alexander Graham Bell's first telephone, models of oil wells and mock-ups of luxurious Pullman cars, were unaware that another "war for independence" had begun in the little town of Hamburg, South Carolina.

Hamburg was an all-black town on the edge of South Carolina's upcountry, the area where the Democrats had their greatest strength. During the 1874 election campaign when whites in neighboring communities had begun to organize Rifle and Sabre Clubs, Hamburg's intendant (a position corresponding to mayor) wrote to the governor:

Town Hall, Town of Hamburg, August 19, 1874
His Excellency, F. J. Moses, Jr., Governor of South Carolina
I respectfully recommend to your immediate and favorable consideration the application of 75 of the Citizens of this Town who have formed themselves into a Company and wish to be received into the National Guards and be armed as such. I have several reasons for urging this matter, but will only allude to one. We are situated on the banks of the Savannah River, a bridge connecting us with the City of Augusta [Georgia]. We call your attention to the papers of last Tuesday and today which show the danger

Statue of "The Freed Slave" by an Austrian sculptor attracted attention at Centennial Exposition in Philadelphia (*Boston Public Library*)

the poor colored and few white Republicans of this town are in when 50 men or more leave their State to come to ours for the purpose of aiding in a riot. In our rear some 6 or 8 miles we hear of two well-organized cavalry companies (whites) fully armed, ready for any purpose. We are entirely unarmed.

Therefore I pray your Excellency to receive the Company of which I am a member, commission the officers and use your authority in immediately arming them. The Citizens have for the last three nights been guarding this Town as the rumors are that those men would pay us a call with their Sharps rifles. Hoping your Excellency will assist us, I am your Obedient Servant,

John Gardner, Intendant of Hamburg

South Carolina Archives

Company A of the 18th Regiment National Guard was duly organized in Hamburg. Although it had only eighty-four members, its existence must have seemed an affront to men like Matthew C. Butler who headed the Sweetwater Sabre Club in nearby Edgefield. On the Fourth of July 1876, when the members of Company A were celebrating the holiday with a parade, Butler and his friends stage-managed a dispute with them. Dock Adams, captain of Company A, later testified:

We were about the center of the street. They turned the corner and came up in a slow trot. I saw that they intended to drive through the company and I halted. I said, "Mr. Getsen, I do not know for what reason you treat me in this manner." He asked me, "What?" I said, "Aiming to drive through my company when you have room enough on the outside to drive in the road." He said, "Well, this is the rut I always travel." Said I, "That may be true, but if you had a company here I would have gone around and showed some respect." "Well," said he, "this is the rut I always travel and I don't intend to get out of it for no d—d niggers." I said, "All right, I will let you through." I gave command to the company to "open order" and let him go through. Some of the men got a little flustrated because they drove through the company, but I ordered them to hush.

A day later, Butler, lawyer for the men in the buggy, swore out a complaint against Adams, charging that the militia company had obstructed the highway. On the day of Adams' trial, white men armed with sixteen-shooters converged on Hamburg.

They were getting drunk very fast and saying they were going to kill every God-damned nigger and especially Dock Adams. General Butler sent word that the only thing that would settle the matter was for the company to surrender the arms and officers to him. I sent word back that the arms belonged to the State and I couldn't give them up to no private citizen. He sent word that he was going to have them in fifteen minutes. I told him, well, then he would have to take them by force. So then he commenced placing his men—men mounted on horses—in front of the drill-room. Down below on the river he had some thirty or forty and about two hundred yards from the drill-room there stood I suppose, eight hundred men, all in arms. He placed them all around the square.

I only had twenty-five members of the company in the drill-room. After he got all the men placed he sent word to me to know if I was going to give the guns up; that the time was out. I sent word back that I didn't desire any fuss; that I was not going to give the guns to anybody. Then, there was a signal-gun fired. These horsemen that I was telling you about fired upon the drill-room. They shot out nearly all the windowpanes; the glass rattled all over the floor. They kept closing up like they were coming up to the drill-room and after awhile I gave orders to fire, for it was the only chance of our lives.

I heard somebody holler down the street to bring two kegs of powder; that they were going to blow that building up. I tore up some lumber and made a ladder and got out the back way of the building. Before I went I sent the men out. When I got to them there wasn't but fifteen men. I think there were over three thousand [white] men. They were coming from Augusta, three or four hundred together. The lower part of Market street had been completely blocked up with them.

The fight lasted until about half past one o'clock before we did get out. None of the men with me got killed. I put them down next to the river where it was very thick with bushes. After I got these men safe—they were out of ammunition then—said I, "You stay here and I will go back and find the [other] men." I went back and went under most every house there, far enough to call under it. Some one or two men answered. The balance were scared, I suppose, and wouldn't answer.

Hiding in a back yard, Adams watched Butler's men ransack his home:

I could look right into my bedroom and sitting room window. I saw them taking down my pictures and breaking up the furniture. They took all my clothes, my mattresses and feather-bed and cut it in pieces, destroying everything I had. They took all my wife's clothes and everything.

By that time they commenced getting very thick in the square. I jumped over a little fence and went up in the postmaster's house. The house fronted one street, this way (illustrating by diagram) and here came another street. Right on this street, there were over a thousand men. They had their headquarters there. Every time a party would bring a colored man that they had captured they would bring him to what they called the "dead-ring." Every time they would come in General Butler would yell, "Good boys! God damn it! turn your hounds and bring the last one in." And they would ask, "Can you find that Dock Adams? We want to get him." Some asked what kind of man I was and some would agree—"man with side-whiskers and a moustache." One man said, "We'll have him before day," and I was standing right there looking at him through the blinds. That was between two and three o'clock. So finally they said, "Well we had better go to work and kill all the niggers we have. We won't be able to find that son of a bitch." They called them out one by one and would carry them off across the railroad, and stand them up there and shoot them. M. C. Butler was telling them what men to kill. They were shot, I guess, about 4 o'clock in the morning. The moon was shining very bright—about as bright as ever you seen it. I remained in the house until you could just discover day. I went out through the back way and got on the South Carolina Railroad and came to Aiken.

Q—When they were killing those colored men, was anything said about politics?

A—Yes, sir. You could hear it all the time: "By God! We will carry South Carolina now. About the time we kill four or five hundred men we will scare the rest." Even before it begun you could hear "We are going to redeem South Carolina today!" You could hear them singing it on the streets, "This is the beginning of the redemption of South Carolina."

Testimony as to the Denial of the Elective Franchise in South Carolina at the Elections of 1875 and 1876, Senate Miscellaneous Document 48, 44th Congress, 2nd Session

---

But "redemption" did not proceed as smoothly in South Carolina as it had in Mississippi. There were enough influential black men in the state to bring the Hamburg massacre to the attention of the nation. While Robert Smalls denounced it in Congress, Robert B. Elliott called a Convention of Colored People in Columbia. The convention drew up an "Address to the People of the United States" which appealed "to the Christian and humane sentiment of the country to extend toward us moral, and if need be, material assistance in our

Samuel J. Tilden, Democratic candidate for President, is depicted as condoning the Hamburg massacre (*Peggy Lamson*)

effort to cultivate 'the victories of peace.' " Fearful of federal intervention, the Democrats foreswore large-scale "riots" in favor of a steady campaign of intimidation. Their official battle plan, which called for Democratic clubs armed with rifles and pistols, said in part:

Every Democrat must feel honor bound to control the vote of at least one Negro, by intimidation, purchase, keeping him away.

We must attend every Radical meeting. Democrats must go in as large number as they can, and well-armed, behave at first with great courtesy, and as soon as their speakers begin tell them that they are liars and are only trying to mislead the ignorant Negroes.

In speeches to Negroes you must remember that they can only be influenced by their fears, superstitions and cupidity.

Treat them so as to show them you are the superior race and that their natural position is that of subordination to the white man.

Never threaten a man individually. If he deserves to be threatened, the necessities of the times require that he should die. A dead Radical is very harmless—a threatened Radical is often troublesome, sometimes dangerous, always vindictive.

Every club must be uniformed in a red shirt and they must be sure and wear it upon all public meetings and particularly on the day of election.

William A. Sheppard, *Red Shirts Remembered* (Atlanta, 1940)

The battle plan was quickly put into action. A petition to Governor Chamberlain who was running for re-election against Wade Hampton, a former Confederate general:

August 22, 1876

We the colored citizens of Laurens County feel under the necessity of appealing to you. We are under intimidation with our lives in jeopardy every day by men in the Democratic Party who are bent upon coercing us to vote for them. We can assure you, sir, that Laurens of 1876 is not Laurens of 1872. No, sir, it is not. For then a black man and the poor white man could dare to say who he would cast his ticket for, without being starved, whipped or shot to death. But now he neither dares to speak nor act without being in extreme danger. Don't think that we are unnecessarily alarmed. The threats are loud and openly proclaimed. More than that they are being put in execution almost daily. No week pass without some of our people are either whipped, chased or shot at by the night riders. The boast here is that you leading men about Carolina, have given up Laurens into their hands. If that be true we see no reason for it as we are

"Of course he wants to vote the Democratic ticket" (*Boston Public Library*)

as determined now as ever to support the Republican ticket. And with a large number of poor whites to join us.

South Carolina Archives

Richard T. Greener, who was still a professor at the University of South Carolina, canvassed in the upcountry with a group of Republican candidates. His account of their tour conveys the electrically charged atmosphere of the campaign:

A meeting was appointed for Newberry. When we arrived, about two or three thousand colored people escorted us to the room of the local committee. We found from fifteen hundred to two thousand Red Shirts galloping up and down. We delayed in getting ready for the meeting and during that time the Red Shirts had taken complete possession of the square in front of the courthouse. As I went to take my place upon the platform I couldn't get up the steps on account of the horses and horsemen. Finally I managed to get up to the platform. We found that in speaking we would only be addressing the mounted clubs. Lawyer Pope said that they ought to crowd back as they were on horseback, and let the colored people come down to the front so that they could hear. Colonel Lipscomb absolutely refused and we started our meeting at the side addressing the colored people that were there.

They cursed us—called us "Damned radical liars" and every other epithet and interrupted us generally. Colonel Lipscomb and D. Wyatt Aiken both reared up on their horses and shook their fists at me and told me that I was a liar.

We went on from Newberry to Abbeville. At different stations men would come into the cars with pistols. One man came in with at least three, two in his bosom and one in his belt. He sat directly on the seat where I was. When we reached Hodge's Station the entire car was taken possession of by these men. They were crowding so that when I attempted to go through the car I couldn't. After the train started we had very little trouble but for about half an hour at the station it was about as near pandemonium as I have seen.

At Abbeville rifle clubs had been coming from different counties so there were nearly two thousand of them in the streets. The people were very much frightened, because at the last meeting when Governor Chamberlain spoke there was considerable violence. However, we went off to the fairgrounds, about a mile out of town, and had a very pleasant meeting, without interruptions.

In the afternoon when we went to take the train, a crowd of young men, clad in red shirts, came up to me. I sat down on the platform and had a pleasant talk with them. They said I ought not to be a damn radical &c but no violence was offered except that we didn't know but something might break out. I was rather on my good behavior, perhaps.

From there to Walhalla which is a German settlement. After the meeting I got into the midst of about one hundred of them and they put a great many impertinent questions. I was separated from my colored friends and they were really frightened for my safety. I went along with my hand in my overcoat pocket on my revolver all the time, yet trying to talk pleasantly. They asked me if I didn't think Mr. Cardozo was a thief and scoundrel and I told them no, I didn't, that I thought he was an honest man and that I could prove it. I went on trying to vindicate the policy of Governor Chamberlain until finally my friends came up.

We reached Laurens and the cavalry, as usual, began to gather from every direction. The colored people came in on mules and horses, charging and rearing in the same manner as the Democrats. That was the only place we had seen that they were so determined. They were pretty courageous. There were two hundred and fifty to three hundred of them.

Q—How many whites were there on horseback?

A—About twenty-five hundred. They had entire possession of the streets.

Q—What information can you give in regard to rifle-clubs?

A—Well, sir, they were very well organized. They were in full force at Abbeville, Anderson and Newberry, points quite distant from each other. They were well drilled and disciplined; they could assemble in three or four counties at once. There was communication between them and they knew when our meetings were to be held. They came galloping, hallooing and shouting. They are good riders and a rough set of men. Probably they looked to me more ferocious than they really were, being accustomed to city life. Sometimes they were blessed with long beards and hair and apparently hadn't been shaved in a long while.

Every leading man, during this campaign, carried a pistol. I never carried one before but I surely wouldn't have been without one in traveling through that upcountry. It wouldn't have been safe. From the time I started until I arrived home I never felt certain whether I was going to get back alive or not.

Testimony as to the Denial of the Elective Franchise in South Carolina at the Election of 1875 and 1876, Senate Miscellaneous Document No. 48, 44th Congress, 2nd Session

There were also episodes of counter-intimidation. In the low country where blacks greatly outnumbered whites, Democratic meetings were broken up and black women armed with clubs patrolled the polling places on Election Day.

John Mustifer, a black Democrat, testified:

Womens had sticks. No mens were to go to the polls unless their wives were right alongside of them. Some had hickory sticks; some had nails—four nails drive in the shape of a cross—and dare their husbands to vote any other than the Republican ticket.

My sister went with my brother-in-law to the polls and swear to God if he voted the Democratic ticket she "would kill him dead in his sleep." I got a son was to have been married in December. On the cause of him voting the Democratic ticket the woman refused to marry him. And many more desire to vote the Democratic ticket and on account of these women and the threats, they voted Republican.

John Bird was also threatened:

They sent in a lot of women after me and they took hold of me and said, "Kill him. He is a Democrat man." The row continued about two hours. A Republican got up and told them to keep quiet or the poll would be thrown out. Said he was from Washington, Columbia or somewhere, that he came there to give them advice not to vote for Hampton, that if they voted for Hampton they would be treated like a dog. But he would advise them not to interfere with Mr. Bird, that he had a right to electioneer for Hampton. They still cried, "Carry Bird away from here. He come to carry South Carolina Democrat."

A man wanted to vote a Democratic ticket. The crowd crowded him, took the ticket and told him, "If you don't vote Republican, we will put fifty lashes on your behind."

We had a Democratic club with fifty names enrolled. They sent word [that] if we came to give us three thousand lashes on our arse and throw us in the river. This was before the election. I have been grinding at the government mill and they refuse to let my children grind their corn saying, "No damn Democrat should grind on it."

House of Representatives Miscellaneous Document No. 11, 45th Congress,
1st Session

In the upcountry, guns rather than clubs kept black voters from the polls and permitted whites to vote over and over again. The following affidavit is one of many attesting to fraud and intimidation in Edgefield and Laurens counties:

Personally appeared before me Wiley J. Williams and Abram Landman, two of the managers of Box 1, Edgefield Court House and D. B. Cottin, clerk for said Box, and made oath that on the morning of the election they appeared to the Court House. That according to the instructions given by the commissioners of election, they intended to hold the election under the arch of the C.H. steps. That H. A. Glover, one of the managers, took the Box and carried it up into the C.H. That at that time the C.H. was crowded with armed white men, and there were arms stacked away. That about 9 o'clock this crowd had all voted yet they remained in the C.H. and on the C.H. steps in such a manner that colored men could not approach. That during the day many of these parties voted 4 or 5 times and when we protested we were told that it was none of our business. That Wm. T. Gary of Augusta, Ga., told these managers that he had several boys here today from Georgia.

That these deponents finding that they could not carry out the election according to law were anxious to abandon the poll but were told that they would not be allowed to leave. That all of these white men were armed and these deponents were compelled to yield to anything they demanded. That about 4 o'clock the steps of the C.H. were taken possession of by Butler, Gary and J. C. Sheppard who delivered speeches to the horsemen who were crowded around. That not more than 35 or 40 colored men voted at this Box during the entire day and that most of these were accompanied to the Box by U.S. Marshal. That when the poll was closed after 6 o'clock the Box was taken possession of by Wm. T. Gary of Augusta, Ga., J. M. Cobb and J. C. Sheppard of Edgefield, who assisted without authority in the counting of the votes. That when the votes were counted in several cases 4 or 5 Democratic votes were folded together.

That in the face of all these facts, these deponents declare that the whole affair was contrary to law and enter their solemn protest against the counting of said votes for or against any of the candidates

Sworn to before me
this 9th day of Nov. 1876
Jesse Jones, C.C.C.P.

Wiley J. Williams
his
Abram × Landman
mark
D. B. Cottin

On November 28, 1876, Republican legislators met in South Carolina's state house while Democrats organized rival legislature in hall nearby (*Peggy Lamson*)

At least a thousand black men were prevented from voting in Edgefield County but so many whites voted repeatedly that the final count showed two thousand votes more than there were voters. Yet, even with these fraudulent votes, Francis L. Cardozo and Henry E. Hayne were re-elected as state treasurer and secretary of state and Robert B. Elliott became South Carolina's new attorney general. When, after two weeks of deliberation, the State Board of Canvassers threw out the disputed returns from Edgefield and Laurens, the Republican victory was decisive. Daniel H. Chamberlain was governor and his supporters had a majority in the General Assembly.

The Democrats, however, refused to accept the decision of the Board of Canvassers. Backed by an army of Red Shirts, they organized their own legislature in a hall near the state house and installed Wade Hampton as governor. With two governors and two legislatures, civil war was averted only by the presence of federal troops. Grant, who had refused to support the Reconstruction government of Mississippi, proclaimed that Chamberlain was governor and ordered the troops to "sustain him in his authority."

The Republican party now needed its constituents in the South. Samuel J. Tilden, Democratic candidate for President, had swept the North and West, winning 184 electoral votes, only one short of victory. However, if the Republican candidate, Rutherford B. Hayes, received the electoral votes of the three Reconstruction states he could still win. The day after the election, the chairman of the Republican National Committee sent telegrams to southern leaders: "Hayes is elected if we have carried South Carolina, Florida and Louisiana. Can you hold your state? Answer immediately."

The Reconstruction states could indeed deliver their electoral votes to Hayes. With the possible exception of Florida, he was entitled to them. But that only touched off four months of wheeling and dealing in Washington. John R. Lynch later explained:

Although the action of the returning boards in South Carolina, Louisiana and Florida gave Mr. Hayes a majority of one vote in the electoral college, the Democrats in the House of Representatives were not willing to acquiesce in the result, claiming that Mr. Tilden had been elected. Hon. Henry Watterson of Kentucky delivered a fiery speech in which he declared that one hundred thousand armed men would march to Washington to see that Mr. Tilden was inaugurated. The situation looked very grave. It seemed as if there would be a dual government, both Hayes and Tilden claiming to be the legally elected president. To prevent this was the problem then before Congress and the American people.

The creation of an electoral commission to decide the disputed points was finally accepted by both parties. When the bill creating this commission came before the House I spoke and voted against it. I had a suspicion that it was the outgrowth of an understanding which would result in the abandonment of Southern Republicans by the national administration.

Mr. Lamar, [Congressman from Mississippi] for instance, did not hesitate to declare that it was more important that the South should have local self-government than that the president should be a Democrat. In other words what Southern Democrats wanted was to be let alone —that the national administration should keep hands off and allow them to manage their own affairs.

I had a suspicion that this concession had been granted upon condition that the Southern Democratic leaders in Congress would consent to the proposed commission and to the ratification of this decision whatever it might be. To such a bargain I did not care to be even an innocent party. That my suspicions were well founded, subsequent events more than demonstrated.

The Autobiography of John Roy Lynch, John Hope Franklin, ed.
(Chicago, 1970)

The black congressmen were excluded from the secret meetings of party officials. Within the next weeks, however, the shape of the bargain became clear. The Democrats in Congress agreed to accept Rutherford B. Hayes as President in return for a hands-off policy in the Reconstruction states. A month after his inauguration, Hayes ordered the withdrawal of federal troops from the South. When the soldiers marched from the state house in Columbia, Chamberlain decided that further struggle was useless. In an "Address to the Republicans of South Carolina" he said:

Today—April 10, 1877—by order of the President whom your votes alone rescued from overwhelming defeat, the Government of the United States abandons you, and by the withdrawal of troops now protecting the State from domestic violence abandons the lawful government of the State to a struggle with insurrectionary forces too powerful to be resisted.

Walter Allen, *Governor Chamberlain's Administration in South Carolina*
(New York, 1888)

A day later, he turned over the Great Seal of the state of South Carolina to Wade Hampton. The new governor moved promptly to oust the Republicans who had been elected to state cabinet posts. In reply to a letter asking them to vacate their offices, Robert B. Elliott wrote to Hampton's secretary:

Office of Attorney-General
Columbia, South Carolina, April 16, 1877

Sir:

On the 7th day of November last we were legally elected to the several offices the functions of which we now respectively exercise. Of this fact we were duly apprized by the State Board of Canvassers who alone were competent by law to determine the result of the election. Upon receipt of the notification, we qualified by executing the necessary bonds and taking the oaths of office and we entered upon the discharge of our duties as officers of the State. We therefore respectfully decline to comply with the request indicated by the Governor.

We are not insensible to the fact that it is physically competent for the Governor to carry his wishes into effect by excluding us from access to our offices and their records. Whilst we shall make no resistance to such a process should he determine to institute it, we trust that the same sense of "responsibility for the proper discharge of the administration" which he pleads as justification for the covert threat of force, will inspire him to pause before taking a step that

Columbia, South Carolina in December 1876 (*Peggy Lamson*)

will obviously trench upon rights guaranteed by that Constitution which he has sworn to obey.

Robert B. Elliott, Attorney-General, S.C.

South Carolina Archives

A fortnight later the state supreme court decided "that the Defendant [Elliott] be ousted from the office of Attorney General of the State of South Carolina." Similar decisions were handed down in the cases of Cardozo and Hayne. When the new state assembly met, Matthew C. Butler, hero of Hamburg, was elected United States Senator from South Carolina.

Hampton had been in office two months when Simon P. Smith, recently graduated from Howard University, returned home to Columbia. He wrote to his benefactor:

Columbia, June 11, 1877

Rev. E. F. Williams
Dear Friend:

I was very happy to see this old place once more after having been absent so long. Of all the cities that ever I have visited, I think Columbia is the most beautiful. Nearly every

Thomas Nast's obituary for Reconstruction (*Boston Public Library*)

street is shaded by large trees; they form almost an arch across the streets. There are trees of all kinds, flowers of every description. This is a Paradise.

But while I give you but a faint description of the beauties of this place, it grieves me to think that the Ruling powers here are those who are endeavoring to crush the life out of the colored people. They have refused to make an appropriation for the State University. Everything about this Institute now is dead. The professors are all leaving because they cannot get support.

I visited the state senate and house and the Democrats were very jubilant; but Republicans were in despondency. I talked with two colored representatives whom I knew and two colored senators. I also had a long conversation with Cardozo. They are all without hope. They all think that the colored man is done in this state. Colored men who had influence here once have no more today than I have. The Rebels are making colored men do common work for $.25 per day. How can he live! Labor is worth nothing and provision higher than anywhere else. I know not what our people will do here now!

Yours, S. P. Smith

American Missionary Association Archives,
Amistad Research Center

And so it went in Louisiana and Florida too.

"In 1877, we lost all hopes," said Henry Adams, the once hopeful Louisianan. "The whole South—every state in the South—had got into the hands of the very men that held us slaves."

INDEX

DOROTHY STERLING was educated at Wellesley and Barnard colleges and began her writing career on the Federal Writers Project. After many years as a researcher at Time, Inc., she began writing books for adults and young readers. Mrs. Sterling is well known for her books on black history and culture, including *Freedom Train: The Story of Harriet Tubman; The Making of an Afro-American: Martin Robison Delany; Captain of the Planter: The Story of Robert Smalls; Tear Down the Walls;* and *Speak Out in Thunder Tones.* In addition to writing, she has edited a series of biographies on noted blacks and served as a consulting editor on black history books for adults. The parents of two grown children, Mrs. Sterling and her husband, Philip, live in South Wellfleet, Massachusetts.